Robert Bruce Kennard

Essays and Reviews

Robert Bruce Kennard

Essays and Reviews

ISBN/EAN: 9783337075286

Printed in Europe, USA, Canada, Australia, Japan

Cover: Foto ©ninafisch / pixelio.de

More available books at **www.hansebooks.com**

DE CARDONNEL AND FARMER WILSON

"ESSAYS & REVIEWS."

THEIR

ORIGIN, HISTORY, GENERAL CHARACTER & SIGNIFICANCE,
PERSECUTION, PROSECUTION, THE JUDGMENT OF
THE ARCHES COURT,—REVIEW OF JUDGMENT.

BY THE
REV. R. B. KENNARD, M.A., Oxon.
RECTOR OF MARNHULL, DORSET.

Vere rem reputanti, Philosophia naturalis, post verbum Dei, certissima superstitionis medicina est; eademque probatissimum fidei alimentum.
BACON, *Nov. Org.* 1 *Aph.* 89.

LONDON:
ROBERT HARDWICKE, 192, PICCADILLY.
1863.

" When signs of the times are beheld, foretelling change, it behoves those who think they perceive them to indicate them to others, not in any spirit of presumption or of haste; and, in no spirit of presumption, to suggest inquiries as to the best method of adjusting old things to new conditions."—MR. WILSON, *Essays and Reviews*, p. 148.

" There can hardly be a case in which the spirit of intolerance shows itself in a more unamiable light, or with more pernicious effects, than when it confounds the advocates with the assailants of Christianity, and not only repels their services in behalf of the common cause, but charges them with treachery and apostacy, because they would wage the contest on a different ground from that in which it has itself been used to take its stand."—BISHOP THIRLWALL, *Charge*, 1857, p. 70.

CONTENTS.

CHAPTER I.

Origin of " Essays and Reviews " in the application of the Inductive Method of Inquiry to the subject matter of Theology ... ... *page* 1

CHAPTER II.

The Immediate Antecedents and Special Provocatives of the Work in the Theological Literature of the Day 16

CHAPTER III.

The General Character and Significance of the Work, tending to confirm the Divine Inspiration and Authority of Holy Scripture 31

CHAPTER IV.

The Persecution—its Origin in the Misapprehension of the Principle of Authority in the Church—its Immediate Occasion in the Excitement of Religious Parties created by the appearance of two Articles in the " Westminster " and " Quarterly " Reviews ... 136

CHAPTER V.

The Prosecution ... ... *page* 174

CHAPTER VI.

The Judgment—Review of Judgment 238

APPENDIX 287

PREFACE.

THE following pages are put forth in the hope that they may help to dispel the cloud of prejudice and misrepresentation through which the volume of "Essays and Reviews" has hitherto been regarded by what is commonly called "the religious world." For this end the writer has endeavoured to point out the true place of that work in the history of religious thought—its origin in the inductive method introduced by Bacon, and its more immediate antecedents and special provocatives in the literature of the present day.

In the outcry first raised against the book, and the prosecution to which two of its authors have been subsequently subjected, the reader will be careful to notice the hand of that Divine Providence which is ever evoking good out of evil—over-ruling the angry passions and perverse designs of ignorant men to the diffusion of His Truth and the setting forth of His manifold Wisdom in the world. Already the immediate consequence of that outcry has been the calling men's attention to, and awakening their interest in, the great problems of human history and Divine Providence discussed in this now celebrated volume; while the first result of the prosecution is a judgment in the Court of Arches, proclaiming the freedom of the clergy in all matters touching the interpretation and criticism of the Scriptures, and thereby inaugurating a new era of Biblical criticism in the history of the Church of England. Henceforth the clergy of our National Church may rest assured that there is nothing in the laws or constitution of that Church, which fetters the free and unbiassed exercise of their reason in the discharge of that duty so solemnly laid on them by their ordination vow, to be "diligent in reading of the Holy Scriptures, and in such studies as help to the knowledge of the same." What, indeed, may be the ultimate result of this newly-proclaimed freedom we will not venture here to anticipate. Suffice it to say that, as we believe in God as a God of Truth and of Love, we believe that nothing but good can flow from the progress of inquiry and the clearer elucidation of Truth. Let us only be walking as children of Light and of God in the pathway of Light and of Love; and then we may "go forth to meet the shadowy future" with good hope and unshaken confidence in Him who foresees the end from the beginning, who came into the world that He might bear witness unto the Truth, and who has given us His Holy Spirit to comfort us and to lead us into all Truth. Let us only, in short, be faithful to the light of Reason and of God within us, and we shall find that our progress, both in knowledge and in love, will be marked by no obscure, uncertain signs; that our march onward will be, indeed, like "the path of the Just," which "is as a shining light that shineth more and more unto the perfect

We have heard a great deal lately of the "danger of free inquiry," but it may reasonably be questioned whether the real dangers, which threaten the peace and prosperity of our Zion, do not arise from another and directly opposite quarter—from that spirit of insolent dogmatism which claims to dispense with inquiry, and, substituting reckless assertion for argument, and denunciation for proof, affects an *authority* which it is forsooth dangerous to question and impious to reject. "The fullest and worst demonstration of this intolerant spirit (observes the Bishop of St. David's) is an eagerness for the making of new heresies, an endeavour to contract the terms of admission into the Church or its ministry, so as to exclude or disquiet all who do not belong to the favoured party. If such attempts should succeed, it is easy to see the nature, though impossible to measure the extent, of the calamity which would ensue. In the meantime, the contests to which they give rise waste the Church's strength, shake the confidence, and chill the affections, of her most intelligent children and attached members, and afford not only matter of exultation and triumph, but real advantage to her adversaries." *

To talk of "the danger of free inquiry" is, indeed, singularly inconsistent with the claims of Protestantism, which consists in nothing so much as in the unqualified assertion of the right and *duty* of free inquiry. It is also opposed to the interests of all true religion, which has everything to gain and nothing to lose from the result of such inquiry. It is no less inconsistent with the actual

---

* Charge of the Bishop of St. David's, 1857, p. 6.

history and progress of Christianity in the world. "It was ushered into the world," we are reminded, "with the injunction, *Go and teach all nations,* and every step of its progress is to be ascribed to instruction. The first churches were planted in cities, and those the most celebrated and enlightened. In remote villages its progress was extremely slow, owing, unquestionably, to that want of mental cultivation which rendered them the last resort of superstition; insomuch that, in the fifth century, the abettors of the ancient idolatry began to be denominated *Pagani,* which properly denotes the inhabitants of the country in distinction from those who reside in towns. At the Reformation, the progress of the reformed faith went hand-in-hand with the advancement of letters; it had everywhere the same friends and the same enemies, and, next to its agreement with the Holy Scriptures, its success is chiefly to be ascribed, under God, to the art of printing, the revival of classical learning, and the illustrious patrons of science attached to its cause. In the representation of that glorious period, usually styled the Millennium, when religion shall universally prevail, it is mentioned, as a conspicuous feature, that *men shall run to and fro, and knowledge shall be increased.* That period will not be distinguished from the preceding by men's minds being more torpid and inactive, but rather by the consecration of every power to the service of the Most High. It will be a period of remarkable illumination, during which *the light of the moon shall be as the light of the sun, and the light of the sun as that of seven days.*"*

* Robert Hall's Works, vol. i. p. 205.

Such is the testimony of a celebrated Nonconformist divine to the benefits arising from the alliance of true Religion with free inquiry, sound learning, and real science of whatever kind. And we, Christians of the Church of England, are more especially bound to bear our witness to the sanctity of that alliance which the Church has herself confirmed and consecrated in the Festival of the Epiphany, bidding us, year by year, to behold in the coming of those "Wise Men from the East to Jerusalem" the symbol and the pledge of the manner in which the wise and learned of this world shall come from the East and from the West, from the North and from the South, to the city of the living God, the heavenly Jerusalem,— there to pay the glad homage of their highest wisdom to Him "who of God is made unto us Wisdom," "in whom are hid all the treasures of Wisdom and Knowledge," who came as "a Light to lighten the Gentiles"—to "teach the way of God in Truth," and who was and is Himself the very Truth. As English Churchmen, then, we should remember, the first condition of a true faith is a belief in the Divinity of all true knowledge; nor need we fear that what God has permitted to be true in fact can be inconsistent with the faith in Himself taught us by His Son.

"He is guilty of high treason against the faith (says Dr. Temple*) who fears the result of any investigation, whether philosophical, or scientific, or historical. And therefore nothing should be more welcome than the extension of knowledge of any and every kind; for every

* Essays and Reviews, p. 47.

increase in our accumulations of knowledge throws fresh light upon the real problems of our day. If geology proves to us that we must not interpret the first chapter of Genesis literally; if historical investigation shall show us that inspiration, however it may protect the doctrine, yet was not empowered to protect the narrative of the inspired writers from occasional inaccuracy; if careful criticism shall prove that there have been occasionally interpolations and forgeries in that Book, as in many others, the results should still be welcome. Even the mistakes of careful and reverent students are more valuable now than truth held in unthinking acquiescence. The substance of the teaching which we derive from the Bible will not really be affected by anything of this sort. While its hold on the minds of believers, and its power to stir the depths of the spirit of man, however much weakened at first, must be immeasurably strengthened in the end, by clearing away any blunders which may have been fastened on it by human interpretation.

"At this time, in the maturity of mankind, as with each man in the maturity of his powers, the great lever which moves the world is knowledge, the great force is intellect. St. Paul has told us 'that though in malice we must be children, in understanding we ought to be men.' And this saying of his has the widest range. Not only in the understanding of religious truth, but in all exercise of the intellectual powers, *we have no right to stop short of any limit but that which nature—that is, the decree of the Creator, has imposed on us.* If we have made mistakes, careful study may teach us better. If we have quarrelled about words, the enlightenment of the understanding is the best means to show us our folly. If we have vainly puzzled our intellects with subjects beyond human cognizance, better knowledge of ourselves will help us to be humbler. Life, indeed, is higher than all else; and no service that man can render to his fellows is to be compared with the heavenly power of a life of holiness. But next to that must be ranked whatever tends to make men think clearly and judge correctly. So valuable, even above all things (excepting only godliness), is clear thought, and the labours of the statesman are far below those of the philosopher in duration, in power, and in beneficial results. Thought is now higher than action, unless action be inspired with the very breath of heaven. For we are now men, governed by principles, if governed at all, and cannot rely any longer on the impulses of youth or the discipline of childhood."

To attempt in these days to check the freedom of inquiry and discussion by criminal prosecutions and pecuniary fines is indeed a pitch of folly little short of insanity. One might as well attempt to sweep back the ocean with a broom. Have we, indeed, in this nineteenth century, so far forgotten the teaching of experience and the lessons of history? More than two hundred years ago it pleased King Charles, acting by the counsel of Archbishop Laud, to declare his Royal will, that "in these both curious and unhappy differences, which have for so many hundred years in different times and places exercised the Church of Christ, all further curious search be laid aside, and these disputes shut up in God's promises, as they be generally set forth to us in the Holy Scriptures."

"No doubt," remarks Archdeacon Hare, "King

Charles had often thought, and it is not impossible may have been reminded by Laud himself, what a wise lesson Canute set to kings, when he showed them how powerless they are to arrest the tide, even for an inch or an instant. Yet they deemed they could arrest a fiercer tide, which had been rolling, as they confess, for many centuries, under the sway of laws no less mighty and irreversible. This proclamation was issued in 1627, with what success the history of the next thirty years proves: *and such will ever be the end of attempts to settle religious controversies by the interposition of authority.*"

When some time since proceedings were threatened in Convocation against the Essayists, Archdeacon Hale deprecated the folly of the attempt, which (he said) would only end in the confirmation, by learned authorities, of the statements most complained of in the Essays. The result of the prosecution, commenced in face of this warning, has fully verified the Archdeacon's prediction; and is there any one among our ecclesiastical agitators so foolish as to suppose that the decision of a law court would have any tendency to reverse the judgment of these "learned authorities" already pronounced in favour of "Essays and Reviews?" The utmost that it could do would be to thrust out of the Ministry a number of Divines who are now amongst its chief ornaments, to repel every young man of intelligence from seeking ordination in our dioceses, and so to reduce the National Church of England to the condition of an illiterate sect or a mere satellite of the Church of Rome.

But we do not believe that any such calamity is in store for our Church. We are confident that in this case we have not only justice and truth but also the plain letter of the law on our side; and we look forward, in this confidence, to the judgment of the Privy Council to prove that the noblest, no less than the meanest, intellects may find their place in the ministry of a Church which we have hitherto been accustomed to regard as at once the broadest and the most comprehensive, the most rational and the most learned, the most tolerant and the most Protestant, the most Evangelical and withal the most truly Catholic, Church in the world.

R. B. K.

MARNHULL RECTORY,
Jan. 6th, 1863.

"ESSAYS AND REVIEWS."

CHAPTER I.

ORIGIN OF "ESSAYS AND REVIEWS," IN THE APPLICATION OF THE INDUCTIVE METHOD OF INQUIRY TO THE SUBJECT-MATTER OF THEOLOGY.

IN order to trace the movement which has given birth to "Essays and Reviews" to its source, we must go back as far as Bacon. The *Novum Organum* of that great philosopher is, in the history of human thought, the spiritual parent of that inductive and critical school in theology which numbers amongst its chief disciples and most distinguished ornaments the authors of this now celebrated volume. As Lord Bacon complains "that they who have presumed to dogmatize on Nature, as on some well-investigated subject, either from self-conceit or arrogance, and in the professorial style, have inflicted the greatest injury on philosophy and learning;" so the Essayists put forth their volume, in the hope that it will be "received as an attempt to illustrate the advantages derivable to the cause of religious and moral truth, from a free handling, in a becoming spirit, of subjects peculiarly liable to suffer by the repetition of conventional language, and from traditional methods of treatment." They belong, in fact, to the Critical, as distinct from the Dogmatic school. The method of the Dogmatic school, like that of those pseudo-philosophers of whom Bacon complains, is to start from certain traditionally received doctrines respecting God and the world and the expression of the Divine thought and will, and to make their whole system of theology conform to these doctrines, as indubitably certain and for ever fixed. The principle of the Critical, Historical, or Inductive school, on the other hand, is to begin with inquiring into the facts presented by the phenomena of Nature and of man; and from these, when discovered, to strive to form some conception, however inadequate, limited, and imperfect, of God, and of His relation to the world and to man. Or, to state the distinction between the two schools more concisely in the words of an excellent writer,—*the Dogmatic school tests the facts by its own assumed doctrines, the Critical school deduces its doctrines from the facts.*

" It is true," observes Mr. Wilson, " that no human being has either ideas innate of Universe, God, Eternity, Infinity; or even innate capacity for forming adequate ideas of any of them. But we have the capacity for attaining ideas of different degrees of distinctness and of adequacy, *as a result of observation*, which, in their turn, become *à-priori* elements, guides, and forms to subsequent investigation and reflection. Hence human knowledge strides on, now on the foot of ideal anticipation, now on that of experience and verification.

" Upon each age, therefore, devolves the duty of criticising those which have preceded it; nor can any one people, or any one generation, assume that all has been made known of God and man and the universe which ever can be known, or that no errors attach to its conceptions which may afterwards be thrown off. Much less can any generation rightly abandon its office of carrying forward the torch of truth, or attribute to its predecessors that they attained in times past the limits of knowledge, and that revelation, in its larger sense, has no further page to be unrolled."

And thus, while it is the characteristic of the Dogmatic school to cling to and idolize the past, the principle of the Critical school is to believe in God as well in the present and the future as in the past. "A fond and superstitious reverence for antiquity, and the authority of men who have been esteemed great in their generation," remarks Bacon, "has retarded men from advancing in true knowledge, and almost enchanted them. But the opinion which men cherish of *antiquity* is altogether idle, and scarcely accords with the meaning of the word itself. For the old age and increasing years of the world should, in reality, be considered as antiquity (Mundi enim senium et grandævitas pro antiquitate vere habenda sunt); and this is rather the character of our own times than of the less-advanced age of the world in those of the ancients. For the latter, with respect to ourselves, are ancient and elder,—with respect to the world, modern and younger. And as we expect a greater knowledge of human affairs and more mature judgment from an old man than from a youth, on account of his experience and the variety and number of things he has seen, heard, and meditated upon; so we have reason to expect much greater things of our own age (if it knew but its strength, and would essay and exert it) than from antiquity; since the world has grown older, and its stock has been increased and accumulated with an infinite number of experiments and observations. It would, indeed, be dishonourable to mankind, if the regions of the material globe,—the earth, the sea, and stars, should be so prodigiously developed and illustrated in our age, and yet the boundaries of the intellectual globe should be confined to the narrow discoveries of the ancients.

"With regard to authority, it is the greatest weakness to attribute infinite credit to particular authors, and to refuse his own prerogative to Time, the author of all authors, and, therefore, of all authority. For Truth is rightly named the daughter of Time, not of Authority. Is it not wonderful, therefore, if the bonds of antiquity and authority have so spell-bound the power of man that he has been unable to become acquainted with things themselves?"—*Nov. Org.* i. Aph. 84.

So far Lord Bacon; and do we not seem to catch, as it were, the echo of the same complaint from Mr. Wilson when he says: "If Reason hitherto gives doubtful and hesitating answers to our interrogatories, it is because we interrogate her, severally, in the caves hewn out by our fathers in the hill-side, during the Stone age; and echoes come back to us for answer, in the syllables of our own questions. If Reason has done so little towards the clearing up of many Christian problems,—less than it may be capable of doing, it is because its jurisdiction has been questioned; its sentence appealed from, whenever it has run counter to the separate and concrete faiths which divide Christendom: it has been invoked as an ally against some systems, but not permitted to detect fallacies in others; bidden to argue from definitions, but not suffered to analyze them; allowed to deduce, but not to examine premises; and to infer from analogies, but not to choose its own range for induction.

"It is commonly laid down that Reason is no proper judge of divine things; and it is true that we cannot, by any faculty, know the Great Being as He is; but we can study His manifestations, observe, collect, compare, infer—and this is to reason. And as Reason is confessedly inadequate to Him, though sufficient for us, its true humility when it finds evidence defective or contradictory, and its own insight weak, is to suspend its judgment.

"We must thus suspend our judgment when we find ourselves unable to interpret even that which is presented to us directly, much more that which is indirectly handed down to us in a record wherein we are not spoken to face to face; but our fathers repeat to us things which they saw, and their thoughts upon them, and the words and thoughts of many others than themselves. Those manifestations of the Divinity were unique; but we have not seen with our own eyes, nor heard with our own ears—whose descriptions and whose interpretations shall we receive, and how receive, how understand? Shall we accept the words of those who are said to have handled with their hands the Word of life—gladly would we—but what is their sense?

"Too often, indeed, have men yearned after a certitude which shall not be given them here; willingly would we reap where we have not sown. But the only true prophecy for man is preparation; his only reasonable assurance is in the adaptation of means to ends. This is a practical faith, the faith that makes a man just, desiring the things which it sees reason to hope for, and working towards them. And the excellence of such a faith is, that it works, because of the character of that which is set before it, not because of a stringency of evidence which would turn hope into reality: much less does it pride itself on accepting traditions as revelations, hypotheses as causes, probabilities as facts!"— *Schemes of Christian Comprehension. Oxford Essays*, 1857.

Again, we find Bacon complaining of the antagonism to natural philosophy which has been manifested in every age by superstition and a blind and immoderate zeal for religion. "For we see that among the Greeks those who first disclosed the natural causes of thunder and storms to the yet untrained ears of man were condemned as guilty of impiety towards the gods. Nor did some of the old fathers of Christianity treat those much better who showed by the most positive proofs (such as no one now disputes) that the earth is spherical, and thence asserted that there were antipodes.

"In short, you may find all access to any species of philosophy, however pure, precluded by the ignorance of certain divines (ex quorundam theologorum imperitiâ). Some, in their simplicity, are apprehensive that a too deep inquiry into nature may penetrate beyond the proper bounds of decorum, transferring and absurdly applying what is said of sacred mysteries in Holy Writ against those who pry into divine secrets, to the mysteries of nature, which are not forbidden by any prohibition. Others, with more cunning, imagine and consider that if the secondary causes be unknown, everything may more easily be referred to the Divine Hand and Word (which they conceive to be of the greatest importance to religion); but this is nothing less than to seek to serve God by falsehood—*Deo per mendacium gratificari.* Others fear, from past example, lest motion and change in philosophy should terminate in an attack upon religion. Lastly, there are others who appear anxious lest there should be something discovered in the investigation of nature to overthrow, or at least shake religion, particularly among the unlearned. The two last apprehensions appear to resemble animal instinct, as if men were diffident, in the bottom of their minds, and secret meditations, of the strength of religion, and the empire of faith over the senses; and therefore afraid that some danger awaited them from an inquiry into nature. But any one who properly considers the subject, will find Natural Philosophy to be, after the Word of God, the surest remedy against superstition, and the most approved support of faith. She is, therefore, rightly bestowed upon Religion as a most faithful attendant; for the one exhibits the will, and the other the power of God. Nor was He wrong who said, '*Ye do err, not knowing the Scriptures nor the power of God*;' thus uniting in one bond the revelation of His will and the contemplation of His power. In the meanwhile, it is not wonderful that the progress of natural philosophy has been restrained, since Religion, which has so much influence on men's minds, has been led and hurried to oppose her through the ignorance of some and the imprudent zeal of others."—*Nov. Org.* i. Aph. 89.

Methinks the Venerable Archdeacon of Taunton and his friends might well ponder these words of wisdom from Lord Bacon. They might serve, with very little modification and adaptation, as an appropriate preface to the next new edition of the "Essays and Reviews," more particularly to the contributions of Professor Powell and of Mr. Goodwin.

But our author is not content with pointing out the cause of the opposition to science, in the ignorance, and bigotry, and misguided zeal of the clergy. He traces it to its source, in the habits and regulations of schools and universities, destined for the abode of scholars and the promotion of learning. "The lectures and discourses," he complains, "are so ordered there, that anything out of the common track can scarcely enter the thoughts and contemplations of the mind. If, however, one or two have perhaps dared to use their liberty, they can only impose the labour on themselves, without deriving any advantage from the association of others; and if they put up with this, they will find their industry and spirit of no slight disadvantage to them in making their fortune; for the pursuits of men in such situations are, as it were, chained down to the writings of particular authors, and if any one dare to dissent from them, he is immediately attacked as a turbulent and revolutionary spirit."

Now, it cannot be denied that great improvement in this respect has been made since Bacon's time in the condition of our schools and universities; yet with the recent instances before us of the exclusion of Professor Müller from the Sanskrit chair at Oxford, and of the refusal of any adequate remuneration to Mr. Jowett for his labours as Professor of Greek, we must still acknowledge that much more remains yet to be done before the old leaven of a bigoted antiquarianism is thoroughly purged out of our ancient universities, and they become, under God, the chief means of exhibiting England to the world as a church and people understanding, receiving, fostering, the progress of new ideas, foreign learning, free inquiry, not as the destruction, but as the fulfilment of religious belief and devotion. A better acquaintance with physical science, and a deeper insight into those laws by which man and the universe are governed, could not fail to put an end to many a long-established apotheosis of error and worshipping of folly. "Yet some of the moderns," remarks Bacon, "have indulged this folly with such consummate levity, *that they have endeavoured to build a system of natural philosophy on the first chapter of Genesis, the Book of Job, and other parts of Scripture;* and this folly," he adds, "is the more to be resisted and restrained, because out of it have sprung not only a fantastical philosophy but an heretical religion. *Itaque salutare admodum est, si mente sobriâ fidei tantum dentur quæ fidei sunt.*"

Should any object that this method of induction, however sound it may be in investigations of Nature, is totally inapplicable to the subject-matter of theology, I answer in the words of Bishop Hampden,* that the same rule of proceeding does, in fact, apply both to theology and science. So far as the investigation of what has been revealed by God is concerned, we must employ the same method as in philosophy. If we would learn what the Holy Spirit would have us learn from the Bible; if we would test what we have received as Divine truth by the Bible, *we must study the Sacred Records as we study*

---

* Preface to Bampton Lectures, 2nd edition, p. 48.

Nature. The method of induction is to be used here as there; and in thus reasoning on Scripture, we only do what God has laid upon us to do in giving us His word. God has put His word, like His works, before men. Both are open to misconstruction and misapplication. Ignorance, and folly, and ingenuity are permitted to raise their systems out of each; and these systems, for a while, prevail more or less. Some live their centuries, others their years or their days; but they have their allotted period, and sound philosophy and sound theology are sure to triumph in the end. So true is it that—

> Our little systems have their day,—
> They have their day, and cease to be;
> They are but broken lights of Thee,
> And Thou, O Lord, art more than they.

"There is," remarks Bishop Butler, " a great resemblance between the light of Nature and of Revelation. And as it is believed that the whole scheme of Scripture is not yet understood; so, if it ever comes to be understood, it must be in the same way as natural knowledge is come at,— *by the continuance and progress of learning and liberty*, and by particular persons attending to, comparing, and pursuing intimations scattered up and down it, which are overlooked and disregarded by the generality of the world. For this is the way in which all improvements are made; by thoughtful men tracing on obscure hints, as it were, dropped us by Nature accidentally, or which seem to come into our minds by chance. Nor is it at all incredible that a book which has been so long in the possession of mankind should contain many truths as yet undiscovered." *

But it may be asked: "Is, then, Divine Truth *to be discovered? Is it not rather to be defended?*" "Yes, assuredly," we reply; "but it is also to be discovered; and one of the main ways of defending it, is by discovering it. Not to the Apostles alone, but to the Church in all ages, was the promise of the Spirit given, *to guide us to the whole Truth.* For, though the Truth is one, and ever the same, it is also infinite, full of infinite riches, capable of infinite expansion, of infinite, ever-varying applications to new forms of life, to new modes of thought, capable of animating and vivifying every condition of human intelligence or feeling. Errors, too, are continually springing up in every age, growing like suckers from the Truth itself, as planted in an earthly soil; and these can only be eradicated by our discovering the Truth, and separating it from them, by showing when, and where, and how, they diverge, and through what perverse strainings of particular truths they have

* Analogy, ii. c. 3.

gained ground. Verily, it would be a kind of death-warrant to a Church to declare that Truth is no longer to be pursued in it. Evils will, indeed, result from an erroneous pursuit, as from every other perverted blessing; but these can only be overcome by our persevering, with God's help, diligently and undauntedly in the pursuit, trusting to the promised aid of His Spirit, and in the assurance that here also the Divine Law will be fulfilled, that they who seek shall find. It was by hoodwinking the intellectual eye, by checking and repressing the pursuit of Truth, that the Church of Rome almost quenched the Spirit within her. We may be blinded, indeed, by gazing rashly at the light; but we are sure to be blinded by living in darkness; and even though we retained our eyesight, we could not see. By wrapping up the Truth in a napkin, we shall not preserve it, or discharge the duty which our being intrusted with it imposes upon us. We must put it out to use; we must make more with it. The more we have, the more we ought to make, and the more we shall make; whereas, from those who have not, from those who think they have only to keep it locked up and defended, will be taken away even that which they seem to have. *When they look into their chest, they will find nothing in it but a mummy.*"

So wrote Archdeacon Hare (Letter to the Dean of Chichester, 1848) in reply to the outcry raised against the appointment of Dr. Hampden. I have transcribed the passage, as singularly applicable to the present very similar attempt to stifle all really free inquiry and fair discussion in the Church, and as indicating, at the same time, a growing conviction, in the minds of our best divines, of the need of a more earnest, single-minded, unbiassed pursuit of Truth; of following her, at all seeming hazards, whithersoever she may lead, after the example of Him who " came into the world that He should bear witness to the Truth." This straightforward course, observes Archbishop Whately,* may not, indeed, obtain "the praise of men." The zealous, thorough-going love of Truth is not very much admired or liked, or indeed understood, except by those who possess it. But Truth, as Bacon says, " only doth judge itself; and howsoever these things are in men's depraved judgments and affections, it teacheth that the inquiry of Truth, which is the love-making or wooing of it,— the knowledge of Truth, which is the presence of it, — and the belief of Truth, which is the enjoying of it, — is the sovereign good of human nature."

* Bacon's Essays, edited by Abp. Whately, p. 14.

CHAPTER II.

THE IMMEDIATE ANTECEDENTS AND SPECIAL PROVOCATIVES OF THE WORK IN THE LITERATURE OF THE DAY.

So far of the origin and spiritual parentage of the book. We now proceed to consider its history and the immediate circumstances of its appearance. It will be remembered that when the volume first began to attract public attention, it was commonly, though inaccurately, spoken of under the title of the " Oxford Essays and Reviews," being in fact regarded generally as a continuation of the twofold annual series of " Oxford " and " Cambridge Essays," contributed by members of the two universities, commencing in 1854. Such, however, was not the case; but the prevailing impression was still not altogether without some foundation in fact. It seems that when, after the appearance of four volumes, the Oxford and Cambridge series came to an end, it was determined by some of the leading members of the Critical school in the Church to continue the publication in a single series, and with a more distinctively theological aim. Several of the most distinguished scholars and divines of both universities were invited to contribute; but the number was ultimately reduced to seven, who have jointly produced a volume which has obtained for them an amount of praise and of blame without example in the history of English theology, and has withal distinguished them as pre-eminently *The Essayists* of the English Church.

For many years past, indeed, the want has been felt of some accredited organ for expressing the views of the more liberal-minded English Churchmen—" of a journal which should treat of theological subjects in a manner resembling the free and scientific tone in which they are handled in France and Germany." It has long been thought, and not without reason, to be a great anomaly that the Critical school should alone be unrepresented in the periodical literature of the day. In 1835, a scheme to supply this want was discussed between Archdeacon Hare and Dr. Arnold. Dr. Whately, the present Archbishop of Dublin, and Dr. Hampden, now Bishop of Hereford, were proposed by Arnold as certain to approve of the scheme, and as possible contributors to a Theological Review, which should have for one of its main objects, " to make some beginning of Biblical Criticism, which," he adds, " as far as relates to the Old Testament, is in England almost non-existent." Excellent, however, as was the idea, it was not then destined to be carried out. Notwithstanding the importance attached by Arnold to such a journal, he found it practically impossible to bear up against the storm of misrepresentation and obloquy with which it was evident that any attempt of the kind would be met by the two great parties into which the Church was then divided. But though postponed for a time, the scheme was never wholly abandoned. Meanwhile, the extreme violence of the Church parties proved their ruin. The clamour raised in 1847 by the extreme of both parties against the appointment of Dr. Hampden to the see of Hereford had the effect of drawing public attention to his Bampton Lectures, a work eminently calculated to open men's eyes to the human origin and purely relative value of much of the so-called orthodox Church Theology. "They indicated," it has been well said, "a change in the relations of dogmatic theology to religion, which has since that time become a recognized and accomplished fact." The attack made shortly afterwards by the Bishop of Exeter on Mr. Gorham, and his (happily unsuccessful) attempt to thrust, with him, the whole Evangelical party out of the Church, resulted in a practical proof of the really liberal and comprehensive character of our Church formularies. Mr. Wilson's Bampton Lectures of 1851 followed on the same side, exposing with masterly hand the process whereby the true spirit of Christianity had been age after age constrained, fettered down, and well-nigh quenched; and setting forth the vast superiority of its moral power as the most vital principle transmitted from Christ through the Spirit, whereby the society of His saints is continually perpetuated and enlarged; and they, past, present, and to come, linked together in one holy communion and fellowship. The writings of Hare, Maurice, and Kingsley all bore in the same direction; and, lastly, the joint commentaries of Dr. Stanley and Mr. Jowett on the Epistles of St. Paul seemed fairly to have prepared men's minds for receiving something better, deeper, and truer than the old mediæval theology, whether recast in a Tractarian or a Calvinistic form, had been able to supply. The time foreseen by Mr. Wilson, in 1851, had already come, when, to use his own words, " the maturer judgment, which later ages are enabled to form upon all the historical facts wherein Christianity, in one sense, consists; the wider knowledge, and the more acute and discriminating criticism which can now be brought to bear upon the words in which its Divine origin is communicated to us; and perhaps, above all, the growing precision with which psychology and moral science analyze the nature on which the Gospel is to operate, necessitate the illustrating of long-acknowledged truths in a new manner; the resolving of ancient forms of expression into their modern equivalents, and the application of the Gospel to human nature as it really is, and not as it has been represented by Manichean doctors."

Meanwhile the old Church parties stood firm, compact, immovable, regarding with undisguised dislike, but with little apprehension, the new movement without them, indifferent to everything save the maintenance of their respective systems, which were fast hardening into a mere lifeless traditionalism. That awakening of the religious life out of the spiritual torpor of the last century, which had produced Evangelicism in the Low Church, and Tractarianism in the High Church party, was subsiding, in the case of the clergy, into an unreasoning scripturalism on the one hand, and a haughty sacerdotalism on the other; while the more thoughtful and intelligent among the laity could find no true resting-place between the Puritanical fanaticism of the one extreme, and the hierarchical semi-Romish dogmatism of the other.* In short, a crisis had evidently come in the history of the

* " One party in the Church superstitiously magnifies the personal ministry and its sacramental office; another, in antagonism to it, shackles all living energy under a bondage to the scriptural letter; a third, outside of the National Church, sets up most loudly a claim of liberty, but really crushes by weight of democracy all freedom in ministers of religion, and turns the Biblical Scriptures into a mere authority for its own traditions."—*Introduction to a Brief Examination of prevalent Opinions on Inspiration.* By the Rev. H. B. Wilson, p. xxx.

English Church, which in the history of Christian Theology has so often recurred, " when the moral consciousness of an age has got beyond its recognized theology, so that the one can no longer satisfy the requirements of the other. The theology of an age naturally embodies itself in books, catechisms, or Church symbols, where, of course, it remains stereotyped and fixed; in the mean time, however, the living consciousness of the Church ever unfolds, as age after age rolls on, and adds new experiences of the scope and power of Christian truth. The inevitable result of this is, that those who take their stand *pertinaciously* upon the formal theology of any given period, remain stationary, as it were, in the religious consciousness of that period, while that of the age itself goes so far beyond them, that their theology is no longer an adequate exponent of the religious life of the times, and can no longer satisfy its just demands. *Since the time of the Reformation, the religious consciousness of Europe, unfolding the principles then started, has been advancing more and more towards the moral conception of Christianity;* and in consequence of this, we find the dogmatic theology of the earlier portions of this era unable to satisfy the moral and spiritual requirements of the present age. The effect of this is seen in the struggle which is manifestly taking place between those professed theologians who insist upon abiding strictly by the ideas, and even the phraseology of the past, and between the minds which represent the advancing spirit of the age, unchecked, as they too often are, by a due reverence for antiquity. Party struggles like these have unhappily the tendency to drive both sides for a time into the extreme position of antagonism, so that the one falls back entirely upon ancient authority, while the other thoughtlessly sets it at defiance."*

"The living faith of the nation," observes Archdeacon Hare, "wanes away when it is debarred from intercourse with all that has life in it; when it is told that, if it ventures to meet its enemies, it will be as grasshoppers before them. If such a fear comes over our faith, what shall we say? except *Let us go back into Egypt, for there, at all events, we shall have something substantial.* This has often been seen in Romish countries. Everything connected with religion, in such a state of things, becomes hollow, nominal, unreal. Instead of a living object of faith, they who celebrate their formal rites in the place where their forefathers worshipped, find out after a while that they are dancing round a dry mummy of Orthodoxy; *or, if they do not find it out themselves, the younger generation are sure*

---

* Morell's Philosophy of Religion, p. 250.

to do so, and will be scared away by the sightless eyes, and the dark shrouded features."

But in such a crisis what were the better-informed and more liberal-minded of the clergy—those of them who could discover the signs of the times, who saw and felt the want of the age—what were they to do? As the disciples and ministers of Him who testifies of Himself, "*To this end was I born, and for this cause came I into the world, that I should bear witness unto the truth,*" they felt that they had a simple duty to discharge, and they discharged it. In answer to the solemn, earnest, perplexed inquiry, *What is Truth?* pressed upon them from so many quarters, they felt themselves bound to reply by proclaiming the Truth, so far as it had been revealed to themselves. They felt that the time had come to speak to the people without disguise —to open to them, free from any veil of German or Latin, the discussions of modern science and of Biblical criticism. They felt that, if the laity are to retain any real respect for their teachers, there must no longer be two ways of treating the great questions of God's Providence, Christ's Redemption, and Man's Destiny—one enjoyed by critics and esoteric bishops as a luxury, and the other forced upon the clergy and the people as a duty; but one way for all, the frank expression of such measure of the Truth as by the Divine blessing each severally may be enabled to attain. They saw clearly that while the progress of science and the diffusion of knowledge were opening new worlds in the earth and in the heavens to the rising generation, the question must ever and anon recur to them with increasing emphasis—" Are these also capable of being brought within the sphere of Christianity, or must we choose between secular and religious knowledge, between our reason and our faith?" Upon the answer to this question, they foresaw, must depend in great measure, humanly speaking, the future of Christianity; for the conviction of the truth of Christianity rests, they knew, far more than may at first sight appear, on the conviction of its universality; and if it could be proved that large provinces of human thought, important elements of human progress, were altogether foreign, if not hostile, to its teaching, then, far more than by any direct attack on its outward evidences, would its hold be loosed over the minds of men;— it might still be held to have been *a* religion; it could hardly be practically held to be *the* religion of man and of God : for then it would cease to be, according to the idea of its Divine Author and Founder, the *world-subjecting principle*—the new " leaven " cast into the old and corrupt mass of human society, destined to pervade with its influence, and to penetrate every part, " until the whole is leavened;" expressly designed to assimilate, to take up into itself and appropriate, whatever belongs to man and his earthly relations, for the kingdom of God.

All the powers of the human mind, all the subtlety of the intellect, all the aspirations of the imagination, may, it is true, be marshalled in opposition to Faith; and if our faith is faithless, they will be. But if our faith is strong and faithful, it will wield them as weapons of light to convince the gainsayer, and to advance the kingdom of God and of Christ, and, therefore, of goodness and of truth, in the world.

It was under this deep and firm conviction that the authors of "Essays and Reviews" undertook to discuss some of the leading questions of the day in the volume before us. "Let us (they said in effect) not be afraid of the advance of human thought; let us advance with it; let us go onward with the foremost, let us outreason the subtlest; let us outsoar the boldest: for we know that all things shall be subdued under the Son of God; all the powers of the intellectual, and of the physical, as well as of the moral world." To say that they were precluded from this course by their ministerial obligations and responsibilities is as false as it is insulting. Rather should we say that with their views, and under their sense of the wants of the age, they could not have done otherwise, without abandoning their proper office as the authorized spiritual guides and leaders of the people, and falling under the condemnation pronounced against those who had betrayed in like manner a similar trust—"*Woe unto you, for ye have taken away the key of knowledge: ye entered not in yourselves, and those that were entering in ye hindered.*"

In the interest of Truth, then, and with a full conviction of the responsibilities of their sacred office, they determined to vindicate for the clergy practically the right of treating openly, in language addressed to the people generally, questions equally interesting and important to all, but which had hitherto (at least in this country) been almost entirely confined to books circulated among scholars. They associated, at the same time, a layman with them in the undertaking, as a further proof that they had no desire to retain, as the peculiar possession of a spiritual aristocracy, the sole right of debating the most momentous questions of the day—questions concerning prophecy, miracles, inspiration, the right understanding of the Scriptures, and their relation to other sources of knowledge; subjects in which all have an interest equal to our own, and on which very numerous classes in this age and country are as capable of arriving at sound conclusions as are we of the clergy.

Objection to such a course on any purely moral or religious grounds there is and can be none; and if it could be shown that there was anything in the obligation imposed by our laws on the clergy which precluded such an alliance between them and their brethren of the laity, it would behove the State to provide at once for the removal of any such odious and baneful distinctions between the people and their accredited teachers. "If," says Mr. Wilson, "there is any unsatisfactoriness in the position of the Critical school among the clergy, it is due to Parliamentary enactments and sanctions which the State has given to ecclesiastical forms. What the State has enacted it is competent to repeal. And if historical monuments, guides to study, and aids to worship, have been so hampered by State recommendations as to become mainly a controversial material and an armoury of invidious imputations, then it concerns the State to sweep away those legal provisions, or modify them, in the interest of its own well-being, and of Christian progress." Nor let it be said that in so doing the State would be presumptuously interfering with the functions of the Church. Objections of this sort are, we know, frequently alleged with great pomp in certain quarters against any State interference with the doctrines and discipline of the Church; but, judged by the standard of Protestant principles, and viewed in the light of reason and of common sense, what do they amount to? The Church, as an abstraction, is, whatsoever it may be, a mere creation of the mind, possessing no living concrete existence capable of forming any judgment, or delivering any sentence at all; and as an actual succession of Christian persons—of poor weak, erring, fallible men, it has no organ, according to Protestant principles, for pronouncing, and could not, without the greatest presumption, affect to pronounce, any judgment which shall be final and binding upon future generations, or which can do more than convey the opinion of a certain number of Christians in a given time and place, subject, therefore, to subsequent revision and correction.

"It has sometimes," observes the author just quoted, "been made matter of reproach against Protestantism that it has leant too much on the secular power; and such an appeal as is now made to the influence of lay opinion may be represented by some as abandoning the true grounds on which the Christian Church is constituted. Of course it is not intended to be reconciled with the supposition of any faculty of perceiving truth being supernaturally communicated through an episcopal or any other ministerial succession. Yet ordained persons, though they have no knowledge supernaturally communicated to them, are not incapacitated from acquiring it, through the same inlets with other men; and in knowledge, as well as in moral co-operation, it is 'by that which every joint supplieth' (clergyman or layman) that the Church can 'grow to be an holy temple.' And perhaps the Churches of the Reformation have not leant more upon the secular power than the Church of the fourth century upon the Roman emperors, or the mediæval Church upon Charlemagne. Constantine certainly took as influential a part in the setting forth of doctrine as the Protestant princes at the diets of Spires and Augsburg, or as Edward VI. and Elizabeth took with us. But the fact is, those princes really represented the preponderance of the minds of their nations, which naturally and necessarily in those times expressed themselves through the sovereign, both in politics and religion. In modern times, at least in such a country as our own, political power is more diffused than formerly, by reason of an acknowledged diffusion of the capacity for exercising it. It would be very inconsistent not to allow a proportionate influence to a better-informed laity on religious and ecclesiastical subjects. Where the knowledge is, there is the power; where the power is, there is the responsibility: and those who succeed to rights, and are fit for an enlarged exercise of them, cannot escape the corresponding duty. Princes, in conjunction with the Reformers, modified the creed of the Church in the sixteenth century; they would have abandoned their rights, deserted their duty, and betrayed the cause of Truth, if they had stood aloof, on the ground that they were not priests. A numerous well-informed laity will be equally treacherous to the noblest of causes, and to their own and their nation's highest interests, if they do not concern themselves with a movement in the nineteenth century, on the ground that they are neither priests nor princes. They have succeeded practically as citizens to an ample share of political power anciently confined to the sovereign alone; they are equally fitted to exercise a larger influence upon the creeds of their Church, and the terms of its communion."

Without entering into further detail of a more strictly personal and private character, the above is submitted to the reader as a brief history of the composition of the volume, and of the immediate provocatives to its publication.

It can scarcely be necessary, but may perhaps be well, to add that the authors of "Essays and Reviews" are responsible for nothing here stated, beyond what is extracted, by way of illustration, from their respective contributions.

CHAPTER III.

THE GENERAL CHARACTER AND SIGNIFICANCE OF THE WORK, TENDING TO CONFIRM THE DIVINE INSPIRATION AND AUTHORITY OF HOLY SCRIPTURE.

HAVING so far explained the history, we now proceed to consider more distinctly and apart the general character and significance of the Book. In order to gain a clear idea of this, the reader must go to the book itself, and there peruse each Essay as a whole, carefully, thoughtfully, and prayerfully for himself. The utmost which I can attempt is to furnish him with an introduction to the Essays themselves, by briefly pointing out the leading objects and distinctive characteristics of each :—

1. The first Essay in the series—On the Education of the World—is by the Rev. Frederick Temple, D.D., Chaplain in Ordinary to the Queen, Head Master of Rugby School, Chaplain to the Earl of Denbigh. It was composed originally as an Advent sermon, and as such was actually preached before the authorities and the students of Oxford. Its subject is the "Fulness of Time," and its object is to point out how the coming of our Lord in the flesh is the great central fact of all human history—the meeting-point of the

ages—the goal to which all former dispensations looked forward, and to which the Christian Church has ever since looked backward, as to the commencement of her highest spiritual life, and growth, and strength,—the source of her all-embracing power and continually-extending influence in the world. From this point of view, accordingly, we have a sketch given us of the history of the world, and of the religious development of the human race, which the writer shows to have borne a striking analogy to the training and growth of the individual through the stages of childhood, youth, and manhood.

"The power," he says, "whereby the present ever gathers into itself the results of the past, transforms the human race into a colossal man, whose life reaches from the creation to the day of judgment. The successive generations of men are days in this man's life. The discoveries and inventions which characterize the different epochs of the world's history are his works; the creeds and doctrines, the opinions and principles of the successive ages, are his thoughts; the states of society at different times are his manners. He grows in knowledge, in self-control, in visible size, just as we do; and his character is in the same way, and for the same reason, precisely similar to ours. . . . . .

"We may, then, rightly speak of a childhood, a youth, and a manhood of the world. . . . . .

The world was once a child under tutors and governors until the time appointed by the Father. Then, when the fit season had arrived, the Example to which all ages should turn was sent to teach men what they ought to be. Then the human race was left to itself to be guided by the teaching of the Spirit within.

"The education of the world, like that of the child, begins with Law. . . . . . To the child obedience is the highest duty, affection the highest stimulus, the mother's word the highest sanction. The conscience is alive, but it is, like the other faculties of that age, irregular, undeveloped, easily deceived. The mother does not leave it uncultivated, nor refuse sometimes to explain her motives for commanding or forbidding; but she never thinks of putting the judgment of the child against her own, nor of considering the child's conscience as having a right to free action. . . . . . Now, precisely analogous to all this is the history of the education of the early world. The earliest commands almost entirely refer to bodily appetites and animal passions. The earliest widespread sins were brutal violence and sensuality. . . . . . Such sins are, it is true, prevalent in the world even now. But the peculiarity of these early forms of licentiousness is their utter disregard of every kind of restraint, and this constitutes their childish character.

"The education of this early race may strictly

be said to begin when it was formed into various masses, out of which the nations of the earth have sprung. *The world, as it were, went to school, and was broken 'up into classes.* The whole lesson of humanity was too much to be learnt by all at once. Different parts of it fell to the task of different parts of the human race, and for a long time, though the education of the world flowed in parallel channels, it did not form a single stream."

He then goes on to show how each of the leading nations of antiquity contributed, under Providence, to the formation and development of the general character of the race.

The training of " the Jewish nation, selected among all as the depository of what may be termed, in a pre-eminent sense, religious truth," he traces through the institution of the Law, the teaching of the Prophets, and the great lesson of the Babylonish captivity.

"The results of this discipline of the Jewish nation may be summed up [he observes] in two points—a settled national belief in the unity and spirituality of God, and an acknowledgment of the paramount importance of chastity as a point in morals.

"The conviction of the unity and spirituality of God was peculiar to the Jews among the pioneers of civilization. . . . . . That this belief was not with them the tenet of the few, but the *habit* of the nation, was the fact which made the Jews the proper instrument for communicating the doctrine to the world. They supplied that spiritual atmosphere in which alone the faith of new converts could attain to vigorous life. They supplied forms of language and expressions fit for immediate and constant use. They supplied devotions to fill the void which departed idolatry left behind. The rapid spread of the Primitive Church, and the depth to which it struck its roots into the decaying society of the Roman empire, are unquestionably due, to a great extent, to the body of Jewish proselytes already established in every important city, and to the existence of the Old Testament as a ready-made text-book of devotion and instruction.

" Side by side with this freedom from idolatry there has grown up in the Jewish mind a chaster morality than was to be found elsewhere in the world. . . . . . In chastity the Hebrews stood alone; and this virtue, which had grown up with them from their earliest days, was still in the vigour of fresh life when they were commissioned to give the Gospel to the nations. The Hebrew morality has passed into the Christian Church, and sins of impurity (which war against the soul) have ever since been looked on as the type of all evil; and our Litany selects them as the example of deadly sin.

" Such was the training of the Hebrews. Other

nations meanwhile had a training parallel to and contemporaneous with them. . . . . . When the seed of the Gospel was first sown, the field which had been prepared to receive it may be divided into four chief divisions: Rome, Greece, Asia, and India.* Each of these contributed something to the growth of the future Church. And the growth of the Church is, in this case, the development of the human race. . . . . . Rome contributed her admirable spirit of order and organization. To her had been given the genius of government. She had been trained to it by centuries of difficult and tumultuous history. Storms which would have rent asunder the framework of any other polity only practised her in the art of controlling popular passions; and when she began to aim consciously at the empire of the world, she had already learnt her lesson. She had learnt it as the Hebrews had learnt theirs, by an enforced obedience to her own system. In no nation of antiquity had civil officers the same unquestioned authority during their term of office, or laws and judicial rules the same reverence. That which religion was to the Jew, including even the formalism which encrusted and fettered it, law was to Rome. And law was the lesson which Rome was intended to teach the world.

"To Greece was entrusted the cultivation of

---

* See Appendix, Note A.

the reason and the taste. Her gift to mankind has been science and art. . . . . . Her highest idea was, not holiness, as with the Hebrews, nor law, as with the Romans, but beauty. Greece, in fact, was not looking at another world, nor even striving to organize the present, but rather aiming at the development of free nature. The highest possible cultivation of the individual, the most finished perfection of the natural faculties, was her dream. . . . . . All our natural and physical science really begins with the Greeks, and indeed would have been impossible had not Greece taught men how to reason. . . . . . To the Greeks we owe all modern literature.

"The discipline of Asia was the never-ending succession of conquering dynasties, following in each other's track like waves—an ever-moving yet never-advancing ocean. . . . . . This perpetual baffling of all earthly progress taught Asia to seek her inspiration in rest. She learned to fix her thoughts upon another world, and was disciplined to check by her silent protest the over-earthly, over-practical tendency of the western nations. She was ever the one to refuse to measure Heaven by the standard of the earth. Her teeming imagination filled the Church with thoughts 'undreamt of in our philosophy.'

"Thus the Hebrews may be said to have disciplined the human conscience, Rome the human will, Greece the reason and taste, Asia the spiritual imagination. Other races that have since been admitted into Christendom also did their parts. And others may yet have something to contribute; for though the time for discipline is childhood, yet there is no precise time beyond which all discipline ceases. Even the grey-haired man has yet some small capacity for learning, like a child; and even in the maturity of the world, the early modes of teaching may yet find a place. But the childhood of the world was over when our Lord appeared on earth. The tutors and governors had done their work. It was time that the second teacher of the human race should begin his labour. The second teacher is Example. . . . . .

"The second stage, therefore, in the education of man, was the presence of our Lord upon earth. Those few years of His Divine presence seem, as it were, to balance all the systems, and creeds, and worships which preceded, all the Church's life which has followed since. Saints had gone before, and saints have been given since; great men and good men had lived among the heathen; there were never at any time examples wanting to teach either the chosen people or any other. But the one Example of all examples came in 'the fulness of time,' just when the world was fitted to feel the power of His presence. . . . . . He came in the 'fulness of time,' for which all history had been preparing, to which all history since has been looking back. Hence the first and largest place in the New Testament is assigned to His life four times told. This life we emphatically call the Gospel. If there is little herein to be technically called doctrine, yet there is the fountain of all inspiration. There is no Christian who would not rather part with all the rest of the Bible than with these four Books. There is no part of God's Word which the religious man more instinctively remembers. The Sermon on the Mount, the Parables and the Miracles, the Last Supper, the Mount of Olives, the Garden of Gethsemane, the Cross on Calvary —these are the companions alike of infancy and of old age, simple enough to be read with awe and wonder by the one, profound enough to open new depths of wisdom to the fullest experience of the other.

"Our Lord was the example of mankind, and there can be no other example in the same sense. But the whole period, from the closing of the Old Testament to the close of the New, was the period of the world's youth—the age of examples; and our Lord's presence was not the only influence of that kind which has acted upon the human race. Three companions were appointed by Providence to give their society to this creature whom God was educating,—Greece, Rome, and the Early Church. To these three mankind has ever since looked back, and will ever hereafter look back, with the same affection, the same lingering regret, with which age looks back to early manhood. In these three mankind remembers the brilliant social companion, whose wit and fancy sharpened the intellect, and refined the imagination; the bold and clever leader with whom to dare was to do, and whose very name was a signal of success; and the earnest, heavenly-minded friend, whose saintly aspect was a revelation in itself."

Last of all comes the time—as in the individual so also in the race—when the susceptibility of youth to the impression of society wears off, and the age of reflection begins. "From the storehouse of his youthful experience the man begins to draw the principles of his life. The spirit or conscience comes to full strength, and assumes the throne intended for him in the soul. As an accredited judge, invested with full powers, he sits in the tribunal of our inner kingdom, decides upon the past, and legislates upon the future, without appeal, except to himself. He decides not by what is beautiful, or noble, or soul-inspiring, but by what is right. Gradually he frames his code of laws, revising, adding, abrogating, as a wider and deeper experience gives him clearer light. . . . . .

"Such is the last stage in the education of a human soul, and similar (as far as it has yet gone) has been the last stage in the education of the human race. Since the days of the Apostles no further revelation has been granted, nor has any other system of religion sprung up spontaneously within the limits which the Church has covered. Henceforth the Church, in the fullest sense, is left to work out, by her natural faculties, the principles of her own action.

"From the very first the Church commenced the task by determining her leading doctrines and the principles of her conduct. These were evolved, as principles usually are, partly by reflection on past experience, and by formularizing the thoughts embodied in the records of the Church of the Apostles, partly by perpetual collision with every variety of opinion. This career of dogmatism in the Church was, in many ways, similar to the hasty generalizations of early manhood. The principle on which the controversies of those days were conducted is that of giving an answer to every imaginable question. . . . . . In fact, the Church of the Fathers claimed to do what not even the Apostles had claimed—namely, not only to teach the truth, but to clothe it in logical statements, and that not merely as opposed to then prevailing heresies (which was justifiable), but for all succeeding time. Yet this was, after all, only an exaggeration of the proper function of the time. Those logical statements were necessary; and it belongs to a later epoch to see 'the law within the law' which absorbs such statements into something higher than themselves.

"Before this process can be said to have worked itself out, it was interrupted by a new phenomenon, demanding essentially different management. A flood of new and undisciplined races poured into Europe, on the one hand supplying the Church with the vigour of fresh life to replace the effete materials of the old Roman empire; and, on the other, carrying her back to the childish stage, and necessitating a return to the dominion of outer law. The Church instinctively had recourse to the only means that would suit the case—namely, a revival of Judaism. The Papacy of the Middle Ages, and the Papal hierarchy, with all its numberless ceremonies and appliances of external religion, with its attention fixed upon deeds, and not on thoughts, or feelings, or purposes; with its precise apportionment of punishments and purgatory, was, in fact, neither more nor less than the old schoolmaster come back to bring some new scholars to Christ. . . . . . .

"When the work was done, men began to discover that the law was no longer necessary. The time was come when it was fit to trust to the conscience as the supreme guide, and the yoke of the mediæval discipline was shaken off by a controversy which, in many respects, was a repetition of that between St. Paul and the Judaizers. But, as is always the case after a temporary return to the state of discipline, Christendom did not go back to the position or the duty from which she had been drawn by the influx of the barbarian races. The human mind had not stood still through the ages of bondage, though its motion had been hidden. The Church's whole energy was taken up in the first six centuries of her existence in the creation of a theology. Since that time it had been occupied in renewing by self-discipline the self-control which the sudden absorption of the barbarians had destroyed. At the Reformation it might have seemed at first as if the study of theology were about to return; but, in reality, an entirely new lesson commenced—the lesson of toleration. Toleration is the opposite of dogmatism. It implies in reality a confession that there are insoluble problems, upon which even revelation throws but little light. Its tendency is to modify the early dogmatism by substituting the spirit for the letter, and practical religion for precise definitions of truth. This lesson is certainly not yet fully learnt. . . . . . But on the whole the steady progress of toleration is unmistakable. The mature mind of our race is beginning to modify and soften the hardness and severity of the principles which its early manhood had elevated into immutable statements of truth. Men are beginning to take a wider soar than they did.* Physical science, researches into history, a more thorough knowledge of the world they inhabit, have enlarged our philosophy beyond the limits which bounded that of the Church of the Fathers. And all these have an influence, whether we will or no, on our determinations of religious truth. There are found to be more things in heaven and earth than were dreamt of in the patristic theology. God's creation is a new book to be read by the

---

* "I trust that the world, in which you will have to play your future parts, will have grown wise enough to feel it essential, while we exhibit a conscientious and unswerving adherence to our own sense of right, at the same time to think that it is no point of duty to make ourselves offensive or disagreeable to those who hold a different set of opinions. Every year—every day—convinces me more and more not only of the entire wrongfulness, but also of the utter unreasonableness of intolerance—intolerance in any matter, especially in matters of religion. When we, indeed, look a little backward and around us, and consider that it has pleased the Almighty to permit the various creeds and churches of Christendom to be supported and adorned by such men as Luther, Bossuet, Fénélon, Jeremy Taylor, John Wesley, Bishop Hall, Dr. Chalmers, and Dr. Channing,—men with the fire of Divine eloquence on their lips and the teaching of Divine piety in their hearts,—surely there can be none of us who must not think how likely it is that in many points we must be wrong, how impossible it is that on all points we can be right."—*Lord Carlisle, Address to the students at the annual meeting of the Queen's University*, Oct. 16, 1862. (*Times' report*, Oct. 18, 1862.)

side of His revelation, and to be interpreted as coming from Him. We can acknowledge the great value of the forms in which the first ages of the Church defined the truth, and yet refuse to be bound by them; we can use them, yet endeavour to go beyond them, just as they also went beyond the legacy which was left us by the Apostles.

"In learning this new lesson, Christendom needed a firm spot on which she might stand, and has found it in the Bible. Had the Bible been drawn up in precise statements of faith, or detailed precepts of conduct, we should have had no alternative but either permanent subjection to an outer law, or loss of the highest instrument of self-education. But the Bible, from its very form, is exactly adapted to our present want. It is a history; even the doctrinal parts of it are cast in an historical form, and are best studied by considering them as records of the time at which they were written, and as conveying to us the highest and greatest religious life of that time. Hence, we use the Bible—some consciously, some unconsciously — not to override, but to evoke the voice of conscience. When conscience and the Bible appear to differ, the pious Christian immediately concludes that he has not understood the Bible;" agreeably to the canon of Bishop Butler, "*that if in Revelation there be found any passages, the seeming meaning* *of which is contrary to natural religion, we may most certainly conclude such seeming meaning not to be the real one."**

The above brief abstract of the principal points treated of in this Essay is submitted to the general reader not as a substitute for, but as an introduction to, the perusal of the Essay itself. The advanced scholar may not, it is true, find in it any great contribution to his previous knowledge, and may perchance hesitate to admit in all its details the analogy somewhat, perhaps, too elaborate and precise drawn between the individual and the race. The main argument, however, remains, I conceive, quite unassailable, and is admirably adapted to increase our reverence for, and confirm our faith in, that revelation whose most distinctive characteristic is, that it came, "at sundry times and in divers manners," as was best suited to the changing circumstances and varying dispositions of those to whom it was originally addressed.† The general theological position, it has been justly observed,‡ can only be shaken by impugning the sacred text on which the sermon was founded: "*The Advent took place in the form and at the time most fitted for the production of the effect intended.*" This is the substance of the whole argument. The only fault which can be found with it, is that it

---

* Analogy, part ii. chap. 1. † See Appendix, Note B.
‡ Edin. Review, April 1861.

is as old as St. Paul. It can be disputed only by maintaining that the great event which it vindicated, occurred in a wrong shape and on a wrong occasion—not in the fulness but in the immaturity of time.

2. The second Essay, "Bunsen's Biblical Researches," is by the Rev. Rowland Williams, D.D., Vicar of Broad Chalke, Wilts; late Vice-Principal and Professor of Hebrew, St. David's College, Lampeter; author of "Christianity and Hinduism," "Rational Godliness," &c. Our author's object in this Essay is to put the reader in possession of some of the most important results of modern Biblical criticism. For this purpose he has selected for his text the Biblical researches of the late Baron Bunsen.

"Bunsen's enduring glory (he observes), is neither to have paltered with his conscience nor shrunk from the difficulties of the problem; but to have brought a vast erudition, in the light of a Christian conscience, to unroll tangled records, tracing frankly the Spirit of God elsewhere, but honouring chiefly the traditions of his Hebrew sanctuary. No living author's works could furnish so pregnant a text for a discourse on Biblical criticism."

As this Essay has been made the subject of a criminal prosecution for heresy, it will demand our most careful consideration. A production, which could have provoked a Bishop of our

Protestant Church to a course so unusual, and apparently so utterly inconsistent with those principles of free inquiry which constitute the foundation of our common Protestantism, and on which alone the position of the Church of England as a Protestant establishment can possibly be maintained — must needs awaken no little curiosity as to what are "these dangerous and pernicious* opinions," which the most tolerant of Churches is unable to tolerate, or the most forbearing of Bishops to endure. And as in this instance Dr. Williams is to a great extent the reporter and exponent of the researches and opinions of another, we are naturally eager to inquire who and what is this "last Monster from the Deep,"—this arch-heretic the mere echo of whose voice has so disturbed the calm of the episcopal mind, and startling in their quiet parsonages so many thousands of the clergy, has sent them rushing madly through the country, eager to protest, to remonstrate, to sign addresses, to do anything—against "the dreadful doctrines of this awful book"? This "heretic," this

---

* "*Pernicious*," observes Archdeacon Hare, "might seem a strange epithet as applied to the mere statement of a fact. If the statement is incorrect, let it be corrected; if not, how can it be pernicious? The epithet, however, has a meaning; for history is pernicious, truth is pernicious, to all narrow, arbitrary, exclusive systems in religion, as in every other province of human thought or action."—*Letter to the Editor of the English Review*, p. 28.

"sceptic and something worse," this "deist," this "infidel," this all but "atheist in disguise," is no other than the late deeply lamented Baron Bunsen, the founder of the Bishopric of Jerusalem, and for nearly fifteen years the representative in this country of the Court of Prussia,— a man beloved beyond the common, and revered by all who knew him as one of the brightest ornaments and greatest champions of Protestant Christianity in the world. In a letter to the Rev. W. K. Hamilton, the present Bishop of Salisbury, Dr. Arnold thus expresses "the all but idolatry with which he regarded him." "I cannot find [he writes] what I most crave to see, and what still seems to me no impossible dream, inquiry and belief going together, and the adherence to truth growing with increased affection, as follies are more and more cast away. But I have lately seen such a specimen of this, and of all other things that are good, and wise, and holy, as I suppose can scarcely be matched again in the world. Bunsen has been with us for six days, with his wife and Henry. It was delightful to find that my impression of his extraordinary excellence had not deceived me; that the reality even surpassed my recollection of what he was eleven years ago." And again, "I could not express my sense of what Bunsen is without seeming to be exaggerating; but I think if you could hear and see him, even for one half-hour, you would understand my feeling towards him. He is a man in whom God's graces and gifts are more united than in any other person whom I ever saw. I have seen men as holy, as amiable, as able, but I never knew one who was all three in so extraordinary a degree, and combined with a knowledge of things manifold, sacred and profane, so rich, so accurate, so profound, that I never knew it equalled or approached by any man." And so again he writes to Archdeacon Hare, " In Italy you met Bunsen, and can now sympathize with the all but idolatry with which I regard him. So beautifully good, so wise, so noble-minded! I do not believe that any man can have a deeper interest in Rome than I have, yet I envy you nothing so much in your last winter's stay there, as your continued intercourse with Bunsen."

Of his later life and last moments we have a touching picture from Mons. E. De Pressensé in the *Revue Chrétienne* of December 15, 1860: " All adherents to the cause of full liberty of conscience must deeply mourn the loss of one of its most illustrious defenders. Not alone by this title, but by many others of equal importance to us, do we lament the death of Baron Bunsen. All those who have had the privilege of knowing him, and of receiving the warm expressions of his expansive friendship—all who have seen that noble countenance lighted up in old age with the fire of inward youth, regret him as a personal friend before regretting him as one of the most distinguished representatives of European Protestantism. Never was any man's heart less chilled by science than that of Baron Bunsen. . . . . . Indeed, to feel the pulsations of his truly Christian heart, it only required to be in contact with him, and to see sparkle in his features, and to hear vibrate in his voice, that noble love of truth, and that loyalty to truth which was free from all dogmas of School or Church. His only desire was, as he often said, to throw a bridge between contemporaneous thought, so disturbed by doubts, and Christianity. He cared little whether the bridge lasted or was destroyed, so that the passage to the other side was but effected. He passed through the great theological crisis of the times, and many of his ideas were affected by it; but at the bottom of his heart, and in the essence of his piety, he remained ever the same. He continued to be the man of fervent, mystic piety, who collected with such delight the most beautiful hymns of the Church of his country, and who never wearied of hearing them. His conversation, so rich, so animated, and so elevating, was completely embued with that Christian salt, the strong savour of which cannot be imitated. I shall never forget the last interview I had with him last year, when I saw him in Paris, so full of moral youth under his crown of hoary hairs. . . . .

But alas! we shall see him—we shall hear him no more! or rather let us acknowledge with gladness that we have lost nothing, that all we possessed in him we still possess. How doubt it, when we have read the account of his death which we have from a reliable source?

"It is then that what is in the depths of the soul rises to the surface and its secret thoughts are revealed, for that which enables a man to die well is, after all, that by which he lives. The death-bed of Baron Bunsen was in every way admirable. We are happy in being authorized to record the recollection of it.

"All the tender and noble sentiments with which his heart was filled, were poured out in a last effusion. One feels that he was raised to that luminous height where the mind soars above our poor human systems, which know so little. The Christian father in his gentle dignity, the ardent friend of the German fatherland, the devoted partisan of liberty in the whole world, especially the Christian world, the Christian whose faith is being changed into life; each spoke by turns through his mouth, in the midst of cruel sufferings. Baron Bunsen desired his existence to be prolonged in order to accomplish the labours he had commenced. One night he understood this not to be the will of God, and rising from his arm-chair, he exclaimed, 'O God, I commit my spirit into Thy hands!' He then summoned all his family, and said to them, 'A great change has taken place in my thoughts, not with regard to my immortal soul; not with regard to Christ my only Saviour; but with regard to my body. I feel that I am dying.' After having blessed his children, and expressed his grateful affection for the faithful partner of his life in the most touching terms, saying that he had loved in her that which was eternal, *In dir liebte ich das Ewige*, 'May God,' he exclaimed, 'bless my friends! May my country be blessed! Italy and her liberty! May Prussia be blessed, Germany, England, the whole world! I desire every blessing for the Prince and Princess of Prussia! Gratitude to Niebuhr!' It was Niebuhr who introduced Bunsen to the career he so worthily filled.

"After having thanked his servant for his care with the truest affection, he continued, with a heavenly expression on his countenance, 'Notwithstanding all my weaknesses and shortcomings, I have desired, I have sought for that which is noble here below! But my best experience is that of having known Jesus Christ. I leave this world without hating any one. No, no hatred—hatred is an accursed thing. Oh! how good it is to look upon life from this elevation. One then perceives what an obscure existence we have led upon earth. Upward! upward! It becomes not darker, but always brighter,

brighter. I am now in the kingdom of God. Till now it was only in anticipation. Oh, my God, how beautiful are Thy tabernacles!'"

And so he "died the death of the righteous," November 28th, 1860, at his residence at Bonn, in the seventieth year of his age. His funeral obsequies were performed December 1st, between the hours of three and half-past five. At half-past two, the various companies of the students of the University assembled in the square before the residence of the late Baron, having previously sent a deputation to express their desire to testify their respect for the departed by bearing his body to the grave. The coffin, which was of oak in the form of a sarcophagus, was covered with wreaths of evergreen, intermingled with garlands and flowers, most of them sent by friends. Near the head was a bunch of flowers and a small wreath, which her Royal Highness the Princess of Prussia had sent the preceding week, as a mark of sympathy and remembrance. The Lutheran clergyman having arrived entered the library, in the centre of which stood the coffin. A favourite hymn of the late Baron was then played on the organ; the funeral procession was formed, and proceeded through the town to the cemetery, accompanied by the religious notes of those national hymns he had so loved. The pastors who had given him the Holy Communion a few days before, pronounced at the open grave the words of eternal life, and those assembled retired, saying one to another that Germany had lost a great citizen, science one of its most eminent representatives, and the Church a fervent Christian, who died confessing his faith in Christ. This faith remains as the effectual consolation of all those who knew and loved Baron Bunsen, for they repeat what he said with so much energy—" There is a resurrection."

From this record of the Christian life and death of Baron Bunsen we turn to the review of his Biblical Researches by Dr. Williams. Here we are first introduced to his great work upon Egypt. The interest of this, observes Dr. Williams, centres chiefly " in the fruitful comparison of the oldest traditions of our race, and in the giant shapes of ancient empires, which flit like dim shadows, evoked by a master's hand."

As regards the Pentateuch, " Baron Bunsen finds himself compelled to adopt the alternative of gradual growth. He makes the Pentateuch Mosaic, as indicating the mind and embodying the developed system of Moses, rather than as written by the great lawgiver's hand. Numerous fragments of genealogy, of chronicle, and of spiritual song go up to a high antiquity, but are embedded in a crust of later narrative, the allusions of which betray at least a time when kings were established in Israel."

From his " Egypt " we pass to his " *Gott in*

der Geschichte" (*i.e.*, the Divine Government in History), in which he expounds more directly the strictly religious element of the Bible. "Moses [he thinks] would gladly have founded a free religious society, in which the primitive tables written by the Divine finger on man's heart should have been the law; but the rudeness or hardness of the people's heart compelled him to a sacerdotal system and formal tablets of stone. In favour of this view, it may be remarked, that the tone of some passages in Exodus appears less sacerdotal than that of later books in the Pentateuch. But, be this as it may, the truly Mosaic [according to our author] is not Judaic, but the essentially human; and it is not the Semitic form, often divergent from our modes of conception, but the eternal truths of a righteous God, and of the spiritual sacrifices with which He is pleased, that we ought to recognize as most characteristic of the Bible; and these truths the same Spirit which spoke of old speaks, through all variety of phrase, to ourselves." *

In his treatment of the prophets, " great [observes Dr. Williams] is Baron Bunsen's merit, in accepting frankly the belief of scholars, and yet not despairing of Hebrew prophecy as a witness to the kingdom of God. The way of doing so left open to him, was to show, pervading the Prophets those deep truths which lie at the

---

* See Appendix, Note C.

heart of Christianity, and to trace the growth of such ideas, the belief in a righteous God, and the nearness of man to God, the power of prayer, and the victory of self-sacrificing patience, ever expanding in men's hearts, until the fulness of time came, and the ideal of the Divine thought was fulfilled in the Son of Man. Such, accordingly, is the course our author pursues."

"In distinguishing the man Daniel from our book of Daniel, and in bringing the latter as low as the reign of Epiphanes, our author [says Dr. Williams] only follows the admitted necessities of the case. . . . . . But what seems peculiar to Baron Bunsen is the interpretation of the four empires' symbols with reference to the original Daniel's abode in Nineveh; so that the winged-lion traditionally meant the Assyrian empire; the bear was the Babylonian symbol; the leopard that of the Medes and Persians; while the fourth beast represented, as is not uncommonly held, the sway of Alexander. A like reference is traced to the mention of Hiddekel, or the Tigris, in ch. x.; for, if the scene had been Babylon under Darius, the river must have been the Euphrates. The truth seems, that, starting like many a patriot bard of our own, from a name traditionally sacred, the writer used it with no deceptive intention, as a dramatic form which dignified his encouragement of his countrymen in their great struggle against Antiochus. The original place of the book amongst the later Hagiographa of the Jewish canon, and the absence of any mention of it by the son of Sirach, strikingly confirms the view of its origin; and, if some obscurity rests upon details, the general conclusion, that the book contains no predictions, except by analogy and type, can hardly be gainsaid. But it may not the less, with some of the latest Psalms, have nerved the men of Israel, when they turned to flight the armies of the aliens; and it suggests, in the godless invader, no slight forecast of Caligula again invading the Temple with like abomination, as well as of whatever exalts itself against faith and conscience to the end of the world. It is time [adds Dr. Williams], for divines to recognise these things, since, with their opportunities of study, the current error is as discreditable to them, as for the well-meaning crowd, who are taught to identify it with their creed, it is a matter of grave compassion."

Dr. Williams then proceeds to sum up the result of the Baron's prophetical disquisitions, which is, he says, " to vindicate the work of the Eternal Spirit; that abiding influence which, as our Church teaches us in the Ordination Service,* underlies all others, and in which converge

---

* Come, Holy Ghost, eternal God,
  Proceeding from above,
  Both from the Father and the Son,
  The God of peace and love;

all images of old times and means of grace now; temple, Scripture, finger, and hand of God; and again, preaching, sacraments, waters which comfort, and flame which burns.

"On turning to the 'Hippolytus,'" continues Dr. Williams, "we find a congeries of subjects, but yet a whole, pregnant and suggestive beyond any book of our time. To lay deep the foundations of faith in the necessities of the human mind, and to establish its confirmation by history, distinguishing the local from the universal, and translating the idioms of priesthoods or races into the broad speech of humanity, are amongst parts of the

> Visit our minds, into our hearts
>   Thy heavenly grace inspire;
> That truth and godliness we may
>   Pursue with full desire.
>
> Thou art the very Comforter
>   In grief and all distress;
> The heav'nly gift of God Most High
>   No tongue can it express;
>
> The *fountain and the living spring*
>   Of joy celestial;
> The *fire so bright*, the love so sweet,
>   The unction spiritual.
>
> Thou in Thy gifts art manifold,
>   By them Christ's Church doth stand,
> In faithful hearts Thou writ'st thy law,
>   The *finger* of God's *hand*.
>   *Service for the* "*Ordering of Priests.*"

great argument. Of those wonderful aphorisms which are further developed in the second volume of "*Gott in der Geschichte,*" suffice it here, that their author stands at the farthest pole from those who find no divine footsteps in the Gentile world. He believes in Christ, because he first believes in God and in mankind. In this he harmonizes with the Church Fathers before Augustine, and with all our deepest evangelical school. In handling the New Testament, he remains faithful to the habit of exalting spiritual ideas, and the leading characters by whose personal impulse they have been stamped in the world. Other foundation for healthful mind or durable society he suffers no man to lay, save that of Jesus, the Christ of God. In Him he finds brought to perfection that religious idea which is the thought of the Eternal, without conformity to which our souls cannot be saved."

"This recognition of Christ as the moral Saviour of mankind may seem to some Baron Bunsen's most obvious claim to the name of Christian. For, though he embraces with more than orthodox warmth New Testament terms, he explains them in such a way that he may be charged with using evangelical language in a philosophical sense. But in reply he would ask, what proof is there that the reasonable sense of St. Paul's words was not the one which the Apostle intended?

" Our author, then, believes St. Paul, because he understands him reasonably."

" Sacrifice, with the Psalmist, meant not the goat's or heifer's blood-shedding, but the contrite heart expressed by it. So, with St. Paul, it meant the presenting of our souls and bodies as an oblation of the reason, or worship of the mind. The ancient liturgies contain prayers that God would make our sacrifices 'rational,' that is, spiritual. Religion was thus moralized by a sense of the righteousness of God; and morality transfigured into religion, by a sense of His holiness. Vestiges of this earliest creed yet remain in our Communion Service.* As in life, so in sacra-

---

* " Here we offer and present unto Thee, O Lord, ourselves, our souls and bodies, to be a reasonable, holy, and lively sacrifice unto Thee, humbly beseeching Thee that all we who are partakers of this holy communion may be fulfilled with Thy grace and heavenly benediction."—— " This is our sacrifice, daily and continually to be offered; our Christian sacrifice, which no other priest but we, each for ourselves, can offer, our spiritual sacrifice—not of brute creatures which know not God, nor of things slain and laid upon God's altar, when their life is ebbed away,—but a reasonable sacrifice of our reasonable minds, of our fancy, of our imaginations, of our judgment, of our reasoning, of all the faculties which God has given us to know truth, and to know Him; and a holy sacrifice of a penitent heart washed in Christ's blood, of a believing heart, of a resigned heart, a self-denying, an obedient, and a loving heart; and yet again a lively sacrifice, a sacrifice of powers, and feelings, and hopes, not dead, nor doomed to die, but living, and to live for evermore, through the power of Christ's Spirit, and the virtue of Christ's offering."—*Arnold's Sermons*, vol. v., p. 277.

ment, the first Christians offered themselves in the spirit of Christ; therefore, in His name. But when the priest took the place of the congregation, when the sacramental signs were treated as the natural body, and the bodily sufferings of Christ enhanced above the self-sacrifice of his will even to the death of the cross, the centre of Christian faith became inverted, though its form remained. Men forgot that the writer to the Hebrews exalts the blood of *an everlasting*, that is, of a spiritual covenant; for what is fleshly vanishes away. The angels who hover with phials, catching the drops from the cross, are pardonable in art, but make a step in theology towards transubstantiation. Salvation from evil through the Saviour's spirit, was shifted into a notion of purchase from God through the price of his bodily pangs. The deep drama of heart and mind became externalized into a commercial transfer, and that effected by a form of ritual. So with the more speculative Fathers, the doctrine of the Trinity was a profound metaphysical problem, wedded to what seemed consequences of the incarnation. But in ruder hands, it became a materialism almost idolatrous, or an arithmetical enigma. Even now, different accepters of the same doctrinal terms hold many shades of conception between a philosophical view which recommends itself as easiest to believe, and one felt to be so irrational, that it calls in the aid of terror. 'Quasi non unitas, irrationaliter collecta, hæresin faciat; et Trinitas rationaliter expensa, veritatem constituat,' said Tertullian."

Finally, Dr. Williams thus sums up his estimate of the character of Baron Bunsen and his writings. "If Protestant Europe is to escape those shadows of the twelfth century, which with ominous recurrence are closing around us, to Baron Bunsen will belong a foremost place among the champions of light and right. Any points disputable or partially erroneous, which may be discovered in his many works, are as dust in the balance compared to the mass of solid learning, and the elevating influence of a noble and Christian spirit. Those who have assailed his doubtful points are equally opposed to his strong ones. Our own testimony is, where we have been best able to follow him, we have generally found most reason to agree with him. But our little survey has not traversed his vast field, nor our plummet sounded his depth."

The above extracts will, I think, be sufficient to suggest a fair idea of the author's style, as well as of the general character and spirit of the Essay, which is not a mere review of Bunsen's Biblical Researches, but a masterly exposition and reproduction in English of the most characteristic points in the late Baron's theology.

3. The third Essay—"On the Study of the Evidences of Christianity"—is by the late Rev.

Baden Powell, M.A., F.R.S., Savilian Professor of Geometry in the University of Oxford, Author of "The Unity of Worlds and of Nature;" "Christianity without Judaism;" "The Burnett Prize; The Study of the Evidences of Natural Theology."*

Like Baron Bunsen, the learned and accomplished author of this Essay has been taken to his rest—withdrawn from the evil to come—since the publication of the volume. Professor Powell no longer lives to answer for himself, and this alone, we might surely have supposed, would have sufficed to protect his memory, at least in the case of near relations † and former friends, from the base imputations and unworthy calumnies which have been heaped, without remorse, on his good name. If the command—*Thou shalt not bear false witness against thy neighbour*—is binding even upon archiepiscopal lips with respect to the living, the maxim—*De mortuis nihil nisi bonum*—ought surely to have restrained those lips from uttering anything to the disparagement of a friend and a brother who was dead. Dr. Whately is, doubtless, a shrewd man, but, with all his talents, he appears to labour under a singular inaptitude to comprehend the systems and to grasp the ideas of others. A

---

* Oxford Essays, 1857, &c.
† He married Dr. Whately's sister.

remarkable instance of this is exhibited in his reflections on Aristotle and the old logicians in his "Elements of Logic;"* and, to judge from his treatment of "Essays and Reviews," and more especially from his censures upon his deceased relative, his Grace's powers of discrimination and critical acumen do not appear to have improved in later years. It would seem also that, like most men labouring under a similar incapacity to comprehend the ideas of others, he clings with a proportionately greater tenacity to his own. Thus, in reference to Dr. Arnold's well-known, and, to most minds, quite satisfactory explanation of our Lord's answer to Pilate—"My kingdom is not of this world"—he does not hesitate to say, "If I could believe Jesus to have been guilty of such *subterfuges*,† I not only

---

* See Ed. Rev., April, 1833, Art. IX.

† "The *subterfuges*" of which the Archbishop complains amount to this—that "unless we are prepared so to expound one place of Scripture that it be repugnant to another," we cannot understand the declaration of our Lord to Pilate, "My kingdom is not of this world," in any sense inconsistent with the assurance of prophecy, that the triumph of Christianity, and the perfect consummation of earthly things will be, that "the kingdoms of this world are become the kingdoms of our Lord and of His Christ." Indeed, our Lord has Himself provided against so manifest a perversion of His words, by distinctly explaining the sense in which His Kingdom is not of this world. "If my Kingdom were of this world," He proceeds to say,—in such sense as you, from my claim to be a king, suppose it to be—a simply earthly sovereignty, "then

could not acknowledge Him as sent from God, but should reject Him with *the deepest moral indignation.*" *

Like Bunsen, too, the late professor had always been a firm and consistent advocate of those principles of free inquiry, independent research, and universal toleration, on which the Church of England, as a Protestant establishment, is founded, however much they may be misrepresented and obscured by a variety of very opposite parties within it. He was, indeed, for many years distinguished as a resolute defender of those principles at Oxford when their defence required far greater courage than is happily the case at present.

His Essay is the hardest, as it is the most purely scientific, in the volume. In order to be understood at all, it must be studied in connec-

---

would my servants fight . . . . ; but now is my Kingdom not from hence." Our Lord, in fact, addresses his answer to the inward thoughts of the Roman governor. That which the Romans so much dreaded was a revolt of Judea; they heard that there was a King of the Jews, and they naturally thought that he would attempt to recover the ancient kingdom of his nation; and to this the answer of Christ is clear and satisfactory—that His kingdom was not an earthly kingdom; that he advanced no claim as the rightful heir of David's throne, to repel Cæsar as a foreign tyrant and usurper. All, in short, that our Lord disclaims, is any title, derived from his spiritual kingdom, to wield the temporal sword in opposition to the powers that be.

* Kingdom of Christ, Essay i. § 11, p. 47.

tion with his other works, and more particularly with his previous Essay on the Evidence of Natural Religion (Oxford Essays, 1857), of which it is, in fact, the natural sequel and supplement. On reference to that Essay, the reader will see that it is a review of the Evidences of Natural Religion, suggested by the awarding of the *Burnett Prizes*. Towards the close of the last century, Mr. Burnett, a merchant of Aberdeen, bequeathed a considerable property for the foundation of two prizes, a larger and a smaller, to be awarded to the best and second best essays or treatises on the subject of Natural Theology, at intervals of forty years. The first of these occasions was in the year 1814, when Dr. Sumner, the late Archbishop of Canterbury, obtained the second prize for his "Records of Creation;" the first being awarded to Dr. Brown, of Aberdeen. The year 1854 thus became the next epoch; on which occasion the trustees appointed as judges, Mr. Isaac Taylor, Mr. Henry Rogers, and Professor Powell. Not less than 208 essays were sent in, and after an arduous work of examination into their relative merits, the judges were at length reduced to a state of almost hopeless perplexity, by the near approach to equality in the apparent superior claims of some eight or ten of the compositions. At length, however, after repeated re-examinations, a perceptible turn of the balance was allowed to decide the question; and thus the two splendid prizes of £1,800 and £600 respectively, were awarded to the two treatises of the Rev. R. A. Thompson, entitled "Christian Theism;" and of the Rev. Dr. Tulloch, entitled "Theism."

Such an object of competition, remarks the Professor, could hardly fail to call forth existing talent so as to allow us to consider these productions as affording a fair average estimate of the actual state of knowledge and attainments in reference to such subjects. Accordingly, regarding the Burnett award as a kind of epoch at which it may be seasonable to review the state of the question in comparison with the past, and in anticipation of the future, he takes occasion from the discussions thus opened to bring before his readers some general reflections on the entire state of the question of the evidences of natural theology, as it stands at the present day, and with reference to the spirit in which it is now viewed both by advocates and opponents.

The result of this review he thus sums up:— "If we would view the case in a perfectly dispassionate and philosophic manner, it will be readily seen that the whole really turns on the precise nature and extent of the inference strictly deducible from the facts of universal natural law and order. . . . . . A train of thought is excited in our minds by the examination of a set of objects placed before us, in which we trace order, connexion, dependence, according to certain determinate laws and relations, which it may cost us much thought and labour to make out. *That connexion exists just as truly in the set of objects as in our thoughts, and even more so.* It matters not what the objects are, nor whence derived. They may be a set of words, a set of parts in a machine, a set of lines or tints in a design, or just as well a set of planes and angles in a crystal, of organized parts in a plant or animal, or of distances and motions in a system of stars or planets. Thought, reason, intelligence, mind, are terms expressive of operations judged of solely by their *results*, but of whose nature we see and know nothing. Order, law, arrangement, are essentially such results and indications of reason or mind; we cannot separate them even in imagination; and we cannot use the one set of terms without regarding them as implying what would be expressed by the other.

"*The order of physical causes is a dependence of ideas in reason*, a series of relations existing in nature, and independent of our conceptions of it. Our faculties merely disclose it, or, at least, some small portions of it, to us. The relation of causes or reasons in nature remains the same, whether we perceive them or not. They existed the same through all time before man was in being; they are embodied in natural order, of which our science is but the reflection; the reason pervading nature is the original of which our reasoning is the copy. We find in nature a sequence of phenomena, laws, and causes, which we did not invent, but which agrees with a sequence of reasoning, which we do invent. The sequence in nature is at least as much and as truly 'reason' as that in our minds; and more properly so as it is *original* and universal, while ours is but a partial glimpse of it caught *at second-hand*. It is a *higher* reason than ours, as it is only *imperfectly* apprehended by ours, and is being continually more and more disclosed to us. It is universal, as co-extensive with nature, to whose extent we can imagine no limit."

"*It is, then,*" he concludes, "*the peculiar function of the* PHYSICAL *argument to correct, to regulate, to confirm the internal impressions by the appeal to external fact.* The *subjective* ideas are thus rendered *objective* also; the vague and undefined emotions are reduced to a definite standard.

"An idol, or anthropomorphic deity, is the creature of imagination and ignorance; a Supreme Mind in nature is the conviction of improved knowledge and scientific research. The anthropomorphic image is only the reflection, of which man's corrupt or imperfect nature is the original. But Supreme Intelligence manifested in the material universe is the original, of which man's highest science is but the reflection.

"The convictions at which we arrive from the physical argument, however limited, yet, such as they are, are the preliminaries to higher instruction, while their confessed imperfections show the necessity for such further enlightenment. Man needs a higher view—a worthy object of adoration, trust, and love."

"A more philosophical natural theology may indeed clear away many false and superstitious misconceptions; but it is the peculiar office and value of such a revelation as that of Christianity, that it fulfils the demands of human nature, and at the same time tends to supersede and to absorb all anthropomorphic idolatry, by the substitution of its peculiar teaching of the manifestation of God in Christ, and in and through Him points to a pure and spiritual object of worship, equally adapted to the wants and desires of the humblest, and satisfactory to the aspirations of the highest stage of human enlightenment."*

This conception of nature as the expression of eternal Reason, constituting a divine κοσμος—a universe all whose parts are subordinated to one another, and to the whole by the constant unfailing operation of certain fixed immutable laws

---

* Oxford Essays, 1857, pp. 183, 203.

—this grand conception, I say, of immutable universal order once fully realized, will help us to approach the Essay before us from the author's point of view. We shall see that here, as in his former contribution, he passes in review the arguments advanced by others, and estimates their value by the light of modern science, and the principles of a sound inductive philosophy. His object generally is to show that the same standard must be applied to the alleged evidences of Christianity as to other kinds of testimony, and that Christianity has nothing to fear from the result.

Any appeal to *argument*, he observes, must imply perfect freedom of conviction; whereas, " with many who take up these questions, they are almost avowedly placed on the ground of practical expediency rather than of abstract truth. Good and earnest men become alarmed for the *dangerous* consequences they think likely to result from certain speculations on these subjects, and thence, in arguing against them, are led to assume a tone of superiority, as the guardians of virtue and censors of right, rather than as unprejudiced inquirers in the matters-of-fact on which, nevertheless, they professedly make the matter to rest. And thus a disposition has been encouraged to regard any such question as one of *right or wrong*, rather than one of *truth or error.;* to treat all objections as profane, and to discard exceptions unanswered as shocking and immoral."

"The present discussion," he warns his readers, "is not intended to be of a controversial kind, it is purely contemplative and theoretical; it is rather directed to a calm and unprejudiced survey of the various opinions and arguments adduced, whatever may be their ulterior tendency, on these important questions; and to the attempt to state, analyse, and estimate them just as they may seem really conducive to the high object professedly in view."

He then proceeds calmly and dispassionately to review the various discussions raised in "the evidences of religion," remarking how much their scope and character have varied in different ages, following both the view adopted of revelation itself, the nature of the objections which for the time seemed most prominent, or most necessary to be combated, and stamped with the peculiar intellectual character and reasoning tone of the age to which they belonged.

This brings him to the question of miracles in general, and the miracles recorded in the New Testament in particular.

"On such questions," he observes, "we can only hope to form just and legitimate conclusions from an extended and unprejudiced study of the laws and phenomena of the natural world. The entire range of the inductive philosophy is at once based upon, and in every instance tends to confirm, by immense accumulation of evidence, the grand truth of the universal order and constancy of natural causes, as a primary law of belief—so strongly entertained and fixed in the mind of every truly inductive inquirer, that he cannot even conceive the possibility of its failure. . . . . . The boundaries of nature exist only where our present knowledge places them; the discoveries of to-morrow will alter and enlarge them. The inevitable progress of research must, within a longer or shorter period, unravel all that seems most marvellous, and what is at present least understood will become as familiarly known to the science of the future as those points which a few centuries ago were involved in equal obscurity, but are now thoroughly understood."

From this point of view the Professor finds it impossible to admit the popular idea of "miracle," as something at variance with nature and law. Such an idea may accord, indeed, well enough with a rude anthropomorphic conception of the Almighty as sitting enthroned in some distant heaven, withdrawn from the universe, and governing it, as it were, from without; asserting from time to time his sovereign authority by reversing the ordinary laws and overcoming the opposing forces of Nature; but it is quite inconsistent with, and unworthy of, the Christian consciousness of Deity as the self-sustaining, all-pervading, infinite

Spirit of the universe, "*not far from any one of us; for in Him,*" as St. Paul says, "*we live and move and have our being.*" "Extended as the infinite space which is His dwelling, penetrating as the magnetic fluid, which is, as it were, one of His inner garments, and to us the most expressive symbol of His omnipresence,—by Him all masses cohere, all celestial globes revolve, all green things grow, all living things feel, all human beings both feel and think, both will and act; nor may we bound His operations by things visible, or by things which can be known by us. As no event or thing can be withdrawn from Him, or be without Him, in past, present, or future, none can be supernatural to Him, or transcend the universe, which is the natural and necessary expression of His thought, according to a Divine nature and a rational necessity."* It was the consciousness of this which led Bishop Butler, even in his day, to predict "that men's notions of what is *natural* will be enlarged, in proportion to their greater knowledge of the works of God, and the dispensations of His Providence. Nor is there [he adds] any absurdity in supposing that there may be beings in the universe, whose capacities and knowledge and views may be so extensive, as that the whole Christian dispensation may appear to them natural—as

* Introduction to a Brief Examination of Prevalent Opinions on Inspiration, p. lix., by the Rev. H. B. Wilson.

natural as the visible known course of things appears to us;"* so that what we are sometimes tempted to regard as interferences may turn out to be fulfilments of general laws not yet perfectly apprehended by us.

"The question, then, of miracles," observes Professor Powell, "stands quite apart from any consideration of *testimony;* the question would remain the same, if we had the evidences of our own senses to an alleged miracle, that is, to an extraordinary or inexplicable fact. It is not the *mere fact*" (he reminds us), "but the *cause* or *explanation* of it, which is the point at issue."

He does not, the reader will be careful to observe, "deny miracles;" but feeling the increasing difficulty which scientific and historical criticism places in the way of the old unreasoning reception of them as mere wonders, he seeks to explain and account for them consistently with the requirements of science, and the demands of an enlightened Christian faith.

"Even in a reasoning point of view," he remarks, in concluding, "those who insist most on the positive external proofs, allow that *moral* evidence is distinguished from demonstrative, not only in that it admits of *degrees*, but more especially in that the *same* moral argument is of *different force* to *different minds*. And the advocate

---

* Anal. part i. chap. 1.

of Christian evidence triumphs in the acknowledgment that the strength of Christianity lies in the *variety* of its evidences, suited to all varieties of apprehension; and that, amid all the diversities of conception, those who cannot appreciate some one class of proofs will always find some other satisfactory, is itself the crowning evidence.

" With a firm belief in constant supernatural interposition, the contemporaries of the Apostles were as much blinded to the reception of the Gospel, as, with an opposite persuasion, others have been at a later period. Those who had access to living Divine instruction were not superior to the prepossessions and ignorance of their times. There never existed an 'infallible age' of exemption from doubt or prejudice. And if to later times records, written in the characters of a long-passed epoch, are left to be deciphered by the advancing light of learning and science, the spirit of faith discovers continually increasing attestation of the Divine authority of the truths they include.

"The *reason* of the hope that is in us is not restricted to *external* signs, nor to any one kind of evidence, but consists of such assurance as may be most satisfactory to each earnest inquirer's own mind. And the true acceptance of the entire revealed manifestation of Christianity will be most worthily and satisfactorily based on that assurance of faith by which the Apostle affirms 'we stand' (2 Cor. i. 24), and which, in accordance with his emphatic declaration, must rest, 'not in the wisdom of man, but in the power of God' (1 Cor. ii. 5)."

4. We come now to the fourth Essay—Séances Historiques de Genève: the National Church; by the Rev. H. Bristow Wilson, B.D., Vicar of Great Staughton, Hunts, late Fellow and Senior Tutor of St. John's College, Oxford, author of "Communion of Saints" (Bampton Lectures for 1851); "Letter to the Earl of Derby on University Reform;" "Schemes of Christian Comprehension" (Oxford Essays, 1857), &c.

Of Mr. Wilson it would indeed be impossible to speak too highly. During his long residence at Oxford he was distinguished as the stanch advocate and consistent defender of Protestant principles — of Protestantism as opposed not merely to Romanism, but to every other form of spiritual tyranny and dogmatism in the Church.* He was elected Fellow of St. John's

---

* "The essence or principle of Protestantism does not consist in any of the systems of doctrine set up at the Reformation period in opposition to the Roman doctrines, however true they may be, or however much of truth they may have in them; but *in the vindication of the natural and Christian freedom of churches and individuals against the assumption of Rome to impose doctrine.* Protestants, indeed, abandon Protestantism when they contentedly rest in the particular applications which the Reformers made of their Protestant principles. *When those concrete results have been enthroned as*

in 1821, and Tutor in 1833—an office for which his accurate scholarship and high scientific attainments eminently qualified him; and which he discharged with exemplary zeal and diligence for seventeen years, adapting his lectures to the capacities of his pupils, and constantly holding up before them, by example, by precept, and by direct teaching, the highest standard of moral and intellectual perfection. Appointed Anglo-Saxon Professor in 1839, and Public Examiner in 1836, and again in 1850, he discharged those high trusts, and especially the latter, with a tact, a discrimination, and a courtesy of manner, at once creditable to himself and honourable to the university. The sermons which he preached before the university, as select preacher in 1835 and 1842, were distinguished by their tone of deep thought and earnest practical piety: they were heard with marked interest and profound attention by all, and led to his appointment as Bampton Lecturer in 1850, on which occasion he delivered his now celebrated course of lectures on the Communion of Saints. The high character and reputation enjoyed by Mr. Wilson, as one of our profoundest living divines, filled, as was natural, the Church of St. Mary's with a vast

---

if they had an authority equivalent to that of the mediæval ecclesiasticism, Protestantism, in the true sense of the word, may be said to have died out."—Three Sermons, by the Rev. H. B. Wilson, Preface, p. xxxii.

academical audience, which increased in numbers and in enthusiasm as he proceeded, lecture after lecture, to set forth in clearer light the superiority of the moral over every other principle as a bond of Christian communion and fellowship. Few indeed who heard him then will forget the impression produced by the words of the preacher—" None can doubt of the efficacy of a principle which, in its highest manifestation, crowns with charity the faith which can remove mountains, and the personal command which can give the body to be burned. Here, indeed, is the Holy of Holies of the spiritual worship of our sanctuary; penetralia to be visited in their inmost recesses by how few! What some of the earlier believers expected to consist in the revelation of a *gnosis*, what some have sought in a mystic union between the divine Spirit and the human, others in a metaphysical dogmatism, others in occult sacramental effects, others in secret inpouring of sensible assurance, others in dry forms or complicated significances, was to be found *in the imitation of Christ*. Here are living waters, free to all who have the courage to draw; here is a tree of knowledge, the fruit of which is sought by few, because not forbidden; the roll of this book must be eaten in faith, but, unlike the scroll of the Prophet, it shall be bitter in the mouth and sweet in the belly." *

* Bampton Lectures, p. 203.

And again, when, after a peroration full of the truest eloquence, he reminded them, in conclusion, how "the unity of moral disposition, and of moral purpose, which has in fact made all sincere followers of Christ one, in all times and in all churches, has, and does, and will traverse their differences, not as a generalization from them, without superseding, or tending directly to supersede, their several creeds and special constitutions, unless it be where they are essentially exclusive and damnatory. But this unity must itself be founded on some faith common to all Christians, some faith capable of being received, without difference, by all men.

"For in making the identity of their disposition and purpose, rather than their dogmatic faith, than their historical faith, than their feelings, than the supernatural influences in which they believe, than their worship, or than their formal virtue, the true Catholic characteristic,— this moral purpose, wherever permanent, must imply an habitual will; wherever there is habitual will, there is fixed faith and conviction; fixed faith and conviction of some good within reach. It is a fixed faith in the supremacy and victory of good over evil. This faith has never been wanting to the true Christian, nor, in degree, to the true believer, from the earliest time. This victory was represented in primeval imagery, in the seed of the woman who should bruise the serpent's head; sung by the Psalmist, 'The young lion and the dragon thou shalt tread under thy feet;' consummated on the cross by Him who was manifested that He might destroy the works of the devil; shown in apocalyptic visions to be the issue of the Redeemer's kingdom—Michael, Ruler of Angels, casting the dragon into the bottomless pit."*

Since the delivery of these lectures Mr. Wilson has been living, an example of every social, moral, pastoral, and domestic virtue, in the quiet vicarage of Great Staughton, to which he was presented by the Fellows of St. John's, and instituted by the present Bishop of Ely in 1850. There he has transferred to his parishioners the pastoral care and attention formerly devoted to his pupils, maturing meanwhile and developing in the retirement of private life those great thoughts and wise suggestions which he has given to the world in his contributions to the Oxford Essays of 1857, and the Essays and Reviews of 1860.

In short, Mr. Wilson is one of those few really great men who in every varying circumstance and relation of life are seen to be as good and self-denying and large-hearted as they are wise and brave and noble-minded, who shine like lights in the world, who are the very salt of the earth; —a man, who, if he could be delegated as the

* Bampton Lectures, p. 278.

representative of his species to the inhabitants of some far-distant world, would suggest to them a grand idea of the human race, as of beings affluent with moral and intellectual treasure, raised and distinguished above the rest of creation as the favourites and the heirs of heaven.* That such a man, after a life devoted to promoting the highest interests of his Church and country, should be arraigned as a criminal before a court of law, and compelled to defend himself against a charge of heresy, preferred at the instance of some nameless dogmatist, is an insult to genius, a mockery of justice, an offence against religion, a disgrace to humanity, such as the world has never witnessed since the great philosopher of Athens was arraigned in like manner before his countrymen, and condemned on a similar charge by the sophistry and intrigues of the infamous Meletus.

But it is time to turn from the Essayist to the

* That is, always supposing that the presence of so great a moral and intellectual superiority would not awaken among them any feelings of hostility or alarm. Otherwise, in the words of M. Richard, " C'est précisément la science dont il ferait preuve qui serait inévitablement pour lui la cause des plus cruelles infortunes. Traité bientôt de révolutionnaire empesté, de réformateur dangereux, d'ennemi acharné de la religion et de l'Etat, le pauvre homme ne pourrait éviter d'être pendu au plus prochaine réverbère. Ainsi vont les choses dans toutes les planètes attardées sur la route de l'avenir, et la nôtre n'est pas la seule, hélas! qui lapide ses prophètes et cloue au gibet ceux qui lui parlent au nom de Dieu."—*Les Lois de Dieu et l'Esprit Moderne*, p. 111.

Essay, which is indeed a lucid exposition and able defence of the fundamental principle of our Constitution in Church and State. It was suggested by a controversy which arose within the last few years in the Church of Geneva. In the course of a series of lectures designed to revive evangelical principles in that Church, it fell to the lot of Count Léon de Gasparin to illustrate the reign of Constantine. He laid it down in the strongest manner, that the individual principle supplies the true basis of the Church, and that by inaugurating the union between Church and State, Constantine introduced into Christianity the false and pagan principle of Multitudinism. Mons. Bungéner followed in two lectures upon the age of Ambrose and Theodosius. He felt it necessary, for his own satisfaction, and that of others, to express his dissent from these opinions. He maintained that the multitudinist principle was not unlawful, nor essentially pagan; that it was recognized and consecrated in the example of the Jewish theocracy; that the greatest victories of Christianity have been won by it; that it showed itself under apostolic sanction as early as the day of Pentecost; that it was, in fact, the principle of the Genevese Church itself, and the only one on which any really national Church could be founded. Mr. Wilson makes the same claim, and maintains the same principle, for the Church of England.

The Apostolic churches, he remarks, were multitudinist, as embracing all who in those days professed and called themselves Christians, and they early tended to become national churches; from the first they took collective names from the localities where they were situated. "And it was natural and proper they should, except upon the Calvinistic theory of conversion. There is some show of reasonable independence, some appearance of applying the Protestant principle of private judgment, in maintaining the Christian unlawfulness of the union of Church and State, corruption of national establishments, and like propositions. But it will be found that when they are maintained by serious and religious people, they are parts of a Calvinistic system, and are held in connection with peculiar theories of grace, immediate conversion and arbitrary call. It is as merely a Calvinistic and Congregational commonplace to speak of the unholy union of Church and State accomplished by Constantine, as it is a Romish commonplace to denounce the unholy schism accomplished by Henry VIII. But in fact both those sovereigns only carried out, chiefly for their own purposes, that which was already in preparation by the course of events. Even Henry would not have broken with the Pope if he had not seen the public mind to be in some degree ripe for it, nor would Constantine have taken the first steps towards an establishment of Christianity, unless the empire had already been growing Christian.

"Unhappily, however, together with his inauguration of Multitudinism, Constantine also inaugurated a principle essentially at variance with it,—*the principle of doctrinal limitation.* It is very customary to attribute the necessity of stricter definitions of the Christian creed from time to time to the rise of successive heresies. More correctly, there succeeded to the fluid state of Christian opinion in the first century after Christ a gradual hardening and systematizing of conflicting views; and the opportunity of reverting to the freedom of the Apostolic and immediately succeeding periods, was finally lost for many ages by the sanction given by Constantine to the decisions of Nicæa. We cannot now be very good judges whether it would have been possible, together with the establishment of Christianity as the imperial religion, to enforce forbearance between the great antagonisms which were then in dispute, and to have insisted on the maxim, that neither had a right to limit the common Christianity to the exclusion of the other. At all events, a principle at variance with a true Multitudinism was then recognized. All parties, it must be acknowledged, were equally exclusive. And exclusion and definition have since been the rule for almost all churches, more or less, even when others of their principles might seem to promise a greater freedom."

To repel this spirit of exclusiveness, especially

from the Church of England, is the main object of Mr. Wilson's Essay. Its dominant idea, if I may so speak, is that in a nation such as ours the Church and the State ought to be co-extensive. This he affirms to be the true principle of the Church of England. *The substitution of dogmatic standards for moral ends* he regards as the great impediment to the practical application and perfect realization of that principle.

"As a matter of fact" (he says) "we find that nearly one-half of our population are at present more or less alienated from the communion of the National Church, and do not therefore supply candidates for its ministry. Instead of securing the excellences and highest attainments from the whole of the people, it secures them, by means of the national reserve, only from one-half; the rest are either not drawn up into the Christian ministry at all, or undertake it in connection with schismatical bodies, *with as much detriment to the national unity as to the ecclesiastical.*"

"For the sake, then, of the reaction upon its own merely secular interests, the nation is entitled to provide from time to time that the church teaching and forms of one age do not traditionally harden, so as to become exclusive barriers in a subsequent one, and so the moral growth of those who are committed to the hands of the Church be checked, and its influences confined to a comparatively few." And so accordingly he argues, that, on the highest grounds of public policy, "it concerns the State to rectify, as far as possible, the mistakes committed in former times by itself, or by the Church under its sanction; and, without aiming at an universal comprehension, which would be Utopian, to suffer the perpetuation of no unnecessary barriers excluding from the communion or the ministry of the National Church."

Then comes the question—the great question of the day—pressed upon us by so vast a difference of opinion in the presence of the same Church formularies—" How can those who differ from each other intellectually in such variety of degrees as our more educated and our less educated classes, be comprised under the same formularies of one National Church—be supposed to follow them, assent to them, appropriate them, in one spirit?" —"If such formularies," remarks Mr. Wilson, " embodied only an ethical result — exhibited simply in a practical form the Christian ideal of perfection—addressed to the individual and to society, the speculative difficulty would not arise. But as they present a fair and substantial representation of the Biblical records, incorporating their letter, and pre-supposing their historical element, precisely the same problem is presented to us intellectually, as English Churchmen or as Biblical Christians.

" It does not seem to be contradicted that

when Church formularies adopt the words of Scripture, they must have the same meaning, and be subject to the same questions, in the formularies as in the Scripture.* And we may go somewhat further and say, that the historical parts of the Bible, when referred to or pre-supposed in the formularies, have the same *value* in them which they have in their original seat; and this value may consist, rather in their significance, in the ideas which they awaken, than in the scenes themselves which they depict. And as Churchmen, or as Christians, we may vary as to their value in particulars—that is, as to the extent of the verbal accuracy of a history, or of its spiritual significance, without breaking with our communion, or denying our sacred name. These varieties

* "Confessions may exist side by side with Scripture, but in different relations to it. They may be expressly founded on Scripture, and claim to be at the same time interpretative and declaratory of its sense; or they may profess to be convenient summaries of it, and refer to it as their own interpreter; or they may in a circular manner both declare its sense and refer to it as their own interpreter and authority. But all Protestant confessions are, in fact, founded thereon—it may even be said that the claim to an infallible authority in the Church of Rome rests upon the earliest Christian records. And as no chain can be stronger than its weakest link, categorical statements or articles, and the most authoritative declarations, can only be received speculatively, subject to at least the same deductions from absolute certainty, metaphysical certainty, as the portions of Scripture itself are, on which they are based."— *Schemes of Christian Comprehension, Oxford Essays*, 1857, p. 114.

will be determined partly by the peculiarities of men's mental constitution, partly by the nature of their education, circumstances, and special studies. And neither should the idealist condemn the literalist, nor the literalist assume the right of excommunicating the idealist. They are really fed with the same truths; the literalist unconsciously, the idealist with reflection. Neither can justly say of the other that he undervalues the Sacred Writings, or that he holds them as inspired less properly than himself.* . . . . .

" Moreover, the same principle is capable of application to some of those inferences which have been the source, according to different theologies, of much controversial acrimony and of wide ecclesiastical separations; such as those which have been drawn from the institution of the sacraments. Some, for instance, cannot conceive a presence of Jesus Christ in His institution of the Lord's Supper, unless it be a corporeal one; nor a spiritual influence upon the moral nature of man to be connected with baptism, unless it be supernatural, quasi-mechanical, effecting a psychical change then and there. But within these concrete conceptions there lie hid the truer ideas of the virtual presence of the Lord Jesus everywhere that He is preached, remembered, and represented, and of the continual force

---

* See Appendix, Note D.

of His Spirit in His words, and especially in the ordinance which indicates the separation of the Christian from the world.

"The same may be said of the concrete conceptions of an hierarchy described by its material form and descent; also of millenarian expectations of a personal reign of the saints with Jesus upon earth, and of the many embodiments in which from age to age has reappeared the vision of a New Jerusalem shining with mundane glory here below. These gross conceptions, as they seem to some, may be necessary to others, as approximations to true ideas. So, looking for redemption in Israel was a looking for a very different redemption, with most of the Jewish people, from that which Jesus really came to operate, yet it was the only expectation which they could form, and was the shadow to them of a great reality.

> 'Lo, the poor Indian, whose untutor'd mind
> Sees God in clouds, or hears Him in the wind.'

Even to the Hebrew Psalmist, He comes flying upon the wings of the wind; and only to the higher Prophet is He not in the wind, nor in the earthquake, nor in the fire, but in 'the still small voice.' Not the same thoughts—very far from the same thoughts—pass through the mind of the more and the less instructed on contemplating the same face of the natural world. In like manner are the thoughts of men various, in form at least, if not in substance, when they read the same Scripture phrases. Histories to some become parables to others, and facts to those are emblems to these. The 'rock' and the 'cloud' and the 'sea' convey to the Christian admonitions of spiritual verities; and so do the ordinances of the Church and various parts of its forms of worship."

Mr. Wilson proposes, then, the formularies remaining intact, that each should receive, and, if required, subscribe, in token of his receiving them as agreeable to Scripture on which they profess to be founded, and, therefore, in *their Scriptural sense*, as each shall be able to determine that sense according to his best light and ability, agreeably to the canon of Bishop Pearson—"*That whatsoever is delivered in the Creed, we therefore believe, because it is contained in the Scripture, and consequently must so believe it, as it is contained there.*" It is true that a door is thus thrown open to many hitherto excluded and repelled by the apparent dogmatism of the Church; and that they may be thereby induced to receive parts of our formularies *in a variety of senses, and even in senses not contemplated by their authors.* But this surely is no objection; it is rather a necessity imposed by the circumstances of our population and our better acquaintance with Scripture and other sources of knowledge in connection with it. Indeed, as in his Bampton Lectures Mr. Wilson very justly observes, we should recognize it as a remarkable characteristic, and " wonderful felicity of the Church to which we belong, that her dogmatic declarations, being suspended upon Scripture—not being interpretations of Scripture—are not final, according to the sense of Scripture, in any one year or century, but are provisional until men shall agree in the sense of Scripture."

Such is Mr. Wilson's proposed solution of the difficulty, and the view of our Church formularies which seems to him to open a prospect of escape from the intellectual and spiritual bondage, which the retention through all ages of ancient forms of creed and liturgy has of itself a tendency to perpetuate.*

And further, it is evident that this principle, whereby, as we have seen, a mutual toleration of wide differences of opinion becomes possible under the same formularies of one National Church, may be extended so as to open a way for intercommunion between different National Churches, without disturbing the forms of their respective confessions, whenever those confessions shall be generally understood to claim for themselves no infallible authority, but simply to embody the teaching of Holy Writ—not as

* Bampton Lectures, pp. 23, 74.

limiting and determining the sense of that teaching absolutely, but as setting forth and summing up its most remarkable and characteristic points relatively to a particular communion. For thus the several churches will each be left free to receive and interpret their neighbour's creed in such sense as may appear to them most agreeable to the Scripture on which it is founded, and which, on its own hypothesis, it cannot contradict. And, from this mutual toleration, those only, it is clear, be they churches or individuals, can be excluded who exclude themselves—who exclude themselves by thinking to exclude others, and seeking to impose on all, in one uniform sense as indubitably sure and certain, their own particular dogmas and conceits, *more Romano—Hæc igitur omnia indubitanter recipio atque profiteor, simulque contraria omnia damno, rejicio, et anathematizo.*[*]

In the name of our common Protestantism, and in behalf of our common Christianity, let all good men unite to cast this spirit out of the Church.

5. The fifth Essay, "On the Mosaic Cosmogony," is by C. W. Goodwin, Esq., M.A., of the Temple.

[*] See Schemes of Christian Comprehension, Oxford Essays, 1857.

When Mr. Goodwin's name first appeared in connection with this volume, he was mistaken for his brother, the present Dean of Ely, and was denounced accordingly as a miscreant and a traitor by those who seem to think that truth was made for the laity and falsehood for the clergy—that truth is tolerable anywhere except in the mouths of the ministers of the God of Truth—that falsehood, driven from every other quarter of the educated world, may find an honoured refuge behind the consecrated bulwarks of the sanctuary. Since the discovery of this mistake Mr. Goodwin has been dismissed "as comparatively blameless," even by his bitterest assailants, while by others his Essay has been pronounced to be a highly creditable and scholar-like production, and welcomed as a worthy contribution to the cause of science. In it Mr. Goodwin seeks to vindicate the mutual independence of Genesis and Geology, and to show the utter futility of all attempts to bring the one into harmony with the other.

"The difficulties and disputes," he remarks, "which attended the first revival of science, have recurred in the present century in consequence of the growth of geology. It is in truth only the old question over again—precisely the same point of theology which is involved—although the difficulties which present themselves are fresh. The school-books of the present day, while they teach the child that the earth moves, yet assure him that it is a little less than six thousand years old, and that it was made in six days. On the other hand, geologists of all religious creeds are agreed that the earth has existed for an immense series of years, to be counted by millions rather than by thousands; and that indubitably more than six days elapsed from its first creation to the appearance of man upon its surface. By this broad discrepancy between old and new doctrines is the modern mind startled, as were the men of the sixteenth century when told that the earth moved.

"When this new cause of controversy first arose, some writers, more hasty than discreet, attacked the conclusions of geologists, and declared them scientifically false. This phase may now be considered past, and although school-books probably continue to teach much as they did, no well-instructed person now doubts the great antiquity of the earth any more than its motion. This being so, modern theologians have directed their attention to the possibility of reconciling the Mosaic narrative with those geological facts which are admitted to be beyond dispute. Several modes of doing this have been proposed which have been deemed more or less satisfactory.

"In truth, however, if we refer to the plans of conciliation proposed, we find them at variance with each other, and mutually destructive. The conciliators are not agreed among themselves, and each holds the view of the other to be untenable and unsafe. The ground is perpetually being shifted, as the advance of geological science may require. The plain meaning of the Hebrew record is unscrupulously tampered with, and in general the pith of the whole process lies in divesting the text of all meaning whatever. We are told that, Scripture not being designed to teach us natural philosophy, it is in vain to attempt to make out a cosmogony from its statements. If the first chapter of Genesis convey to us no information concerning the origin of the world, its statements cannot, indeed, be contradicted by modern discovery. But it is absurd to call this harmony. Statements such as that above quoted are, we conceive, little calculated to be serviceable to the interests of theology, still less to religion and morality. Believing, as we do, that if the value of the Bible as a book of religious instruction is to be maintained, it must be not by striving to prove it scientifically exact, at the expense of every sound principle of interpretation, and in defiance of common sense, but by the frank recognition of the erroneous views of nature which it contains,—we have put pen to paper to analyze some of the popular conciliation theories. The inquiry cannot be deemed a superfluous one, not one which in the interests of theology had better be left alone. Physical science goes on unconcernedly pursuing its own paths. Theology, the science whose object is the dealing of God with man as a moral being, maintains but a shivering existence, shouldered and jostled by the sturdy growths of modern thought, and bemoaning itself for the hostility it encounters. Why should this be, unless because theologians persist in clinging to theories of God's procedure towards man, which have long been seen to be untenable? If, relinquishing theories, they would be content to inquire from the history of man what this procedure has actually been, the so-called difficulties of theology would, for the most part, vanish of themselves."

Mr. Goodwin then proceeds to give a very interesting account of the history of our planet, from which he passes to the account of the creation contained in Genesis, and the various attempts made by theologians to bring that record into harmony with the discoveries of science. The total failure of these attempts he considers to have resulted from the character of the task proposed, which is, he says, in effect, "to evade the plain meaning of language, and to introduce obscurity into one of the simplest stories ever told, for the sake of making it accord with the complex system of the universe which modern science has unfolded." The whole difficulty, he observes, lies in our having previously assumed what a revelation ought to be. "If God made use of imperfectly informed men to lay the foundations of that higher knowledge for which the human race was destined, is it wonderful that they should have committed themselves to assertions not in accordance with facts, although they may have believed them to be true? On what grounds has the popular notion of Divine revelation been built up? Is it not plain that the plan of Providence for the education of man is a *progressive* one; and as imperfect men have been used as the agents for teaching mankind, is it not to be expected that their teachings should be partial and, to some extent, erroneous?"

"Men have, in fact, proceeded in the matter of theology, as they did with physical science before inductive philosophy sent them to the feet of Nature, and bid them learn in patience and obedience the lessons which she had to teach. Dogma and groundless assumption occupy the place of modest inquiry after truth, while, at the same time, the upholders of these theories claim credit for humility and submissiveness. This is exactly inverting the fact: the humble scholar of truth is not he who, taking his stand upon the traditions of rabbins, Christian fathers, or schoolmen, insists upon bending facts to his unyielding standard; but he who is willing to accept such teaching as it has pleased Divine Providence to afford, without murmuring that it has not been furnished more copiously or clearly."

In short, as Bishop Colenso very justly remarks, "we have no reason to expect scientific knowledge of any kind, beyond that of the people of his age, in a Scripture writer. It is not in this way, by securing an historian, or prophet, or evangelist, or apostle, from all errors of detail in matters either of science or of fact, that the power of the Divine Spirit is exhibited in Scripture. The 'spirit and the life,' which breathes throughout the Holy Book—that which speaks to the heart and touches the main-spring of being in a man—that which teaches him what is pure, and true, and loving, and gives him living bread to feed upon in the secrets of his own spiritual consciousness—this is the work of God's Spirit, these are the 'words which the Holy Ghost teacheth;' not a mere historical narrative, or a table of genealogies, or a statement of scientific facts—cosmological, geological, astronomical, or any other—*in all which matters the books of the Holy Scriptures must be tested by the ordinary rules which critical sagacity would apply to any other human compositions.*"*

" It is," observes Dr. Whewell, " in the highest degree unwise in the friends of religion, whether

---

* Commentary on the Romans, p. 122.

individuals or communities, unnecessarily to embark their credit in expositions of Scripture or matters which appertain to natural science. By delivering physical doctrines as the teaching of revelation, religion may lose much, but cannot gain anything. This maxim of practical wisdom has often been urged by Christian writers. Thus, St. Augustine says (lib. I. de Genesi, cap. xviii.), 'In obscure matters and things far removed from our senses, if we read anything, even in the divine Scriptures, which may produce divers opinions without damaging the faith which we cherish, let us not rush headlong by positive assertion to either the one opinion or the other, lest, when a more thorough discussion has shown the opinion which we had adopted to be false, our faith may fall with it, and we should be found contending, not for the doctrine of the sacred Scriptures, but for our own—endeavouring to make our doctrine to be that of the Scriptures, instead of taking the doctrine of the Scriptures to be ours.' And in nearly the same spirit, at the time of the Copernican controversy, it was though proper to append to the work of Copernicus a postil, to say that the work was written to account for the phenomena, and that people must not run on blindly and condemn either of the opposite opinions. Even when the Inquisition, in 1616, thought itself compelled to pronounce a decision on this subject, the verdict was delivered in very moderate language, — that 'the doctrine of the earth's motion appeared to be contrary to Scripture;' and yet, moderate as the expression is, it has been blamed by judicious members of the Roman Church as deciding a point such as religious authorities ought not to pretend to decide, and has brought upon that Church no ordinary weight of condemnation. Kepler pointed out in his lively manner the imprudence of employing the force of religious authorities on such subjects: *Acies dolabræ in ferrum illisa, postea nec in lignum valet amplius.*—' If you *will* try to chop iron, the axe becomes unable to cut wood.'" *

6. Next follows an "Essay on the Tendencies of Religious Thought in England, 1688—1750, by the Rev. Mark Pattison, B.D., Rector of Lincoln College, Oxford." No readers of the articles in the *Quarterly* during the last two years can fail to have been struck with the learned sketches of the great scholars of the seventeenth century — Casaubon, Scaliger, and Huet. Of these Mr. Pattison is the author. His recent election to the rectorship of Lincoln, in face of the popular clamour against the Essayists, is highly creditable to the college, and has been

---

* Indications of the Creator, pp. 140—142.

hailed with delight by all who love Oxford and rejoice to see her taking the lead in every movement destined to promote the cause of true religion and sound learning in the Church and in the world.

The present Essay is the natural sequel to those which we have read with so much interest in the *Quarterly*. In it Mr. Pattison presents us with a rapid sketch of the leading English divines during the first half of the last century, and seeks to determine the exact theological value of their writings—what they have done and what left undone, and the influence they still continue to exercise on the religious belief of the country.

"Both the Church and the world of to-day," he says, "are what they are as the result of the whole of their antecedents. The history of a party may be written on the theory of periodical occultation; but he who wishes to trace the descent of religious thought, and the practical working of religious ideas, must follow them through all the phases they have actually assumed. . . . . . There is a law of continuity in the progress of theology which, whatever we may wish, is never broken off.

"The growth and gradual diffusion through all religious thinking of *the supremacy of reason* was the distinctive characteristic of the eighteenth century.

"A person who surveys the course of English theology during the eighteenth century will have no difficulty in recognizing that throughout all discussions, underneath all controversies, and common to all parties, lies the assumption of *the supremacy of reason in matters of religion*...... The Churchman differed from the Socinian, and the Socinian from the Deist, as to the number of articles in his creed; but all alike consented to test their belief by the rational evidence for it. The title of Locke's treatise, 'The Reasonableness of Christianity,' may be said to have been the solitary thesis of Christian theology in England for great part of a century.

"If we are to put chronological limits to this system of religious opinion in England, we might, for the sake of a convenient landmark, say that it came in with the Revolution of 1688, and began to decline in vigour with the reaction against the Reform movement, about 1830. Locke's 'Reasonableness of Christianity' would thus open, and the commencement of the 'Tracts for the Times' mark the fall of Rationalism."

"The whole rationalistic age must again be subdivided into two periods,—the theology of which, though belonging to the common type, has distinct specific characters. These periods are of nearly equal length, and we may conveniently take the middle year of the century, 1750, as one terminus of division. Though both periods were engaged upon the proof of Christianity, the distinction between them is, that the first period was chiefly devoted to the internal, the second to the external attestations. In the first period the main endeavour was to show that there was nothing in the contents of the revelation which was not agreeable to reason. In the second, from 1750 onwards, the controversy was narrowed to what are usually called the "Evidences," or the historical proof of the genuineness and authenticity of the Christian records. From this distinction of topic arises an important difference of value between the theological produce of the two periods."

"Both methods alike, as methods of argumentative proof, place the mind in an unfavourable attitude for the consideration of religious truth. It is like removing ourselves, for the purpose of examining an object, to the farthest point from which the object is visible. Neither the external nor the internal evidences are properly theology at all. Theology is: first and primarily, the contemplative, speculative habit, by means of which the mind places itself already in another world than this; a habit begun here, to be raised to perfect vision hereafter. Secondly, and in an inferior degree, it is ethical and regulative of our conduct as men, in those relations which are temporal and transitory. Argumentative proof that such knowledge is possible can never be substituted for the knowledge without detriment to the mental habit. What is true of an individual, is true of an age. When an age is found occupied in proving its creed, this is but a token that the age has ceased to have a proper belief in it. Nevertheless, there is a difference in this respect between the sources from which proof may be fetched. When it is busied in establishing the 'genuineness and authenticity' of the books of Scripture, neglecting its religious lessons, and drawing out instead the 'undesigned coincidences,' Rationalism is seen in its dullest and least spiritual form. When, on the other hand, the contents of the Revelation are being freely examined, and reason, as it is called, but really the philosophy in vogue, is being applied to determine whether the voice be the voice of God or not, the reasoner is indeed approaching his subject from a false point of view, but he is still engaged with the eternal verities. The reason has prescribed itself an impossible task when it has undertaken to prove, instead of evolve them; to argue, instead of appropriate them. But, any how, it is handling them; and by the contact is raised, in some measure, to the 'height of that great argument.'"

Mr. Pattison then proceeds to pass rapidly in review the leading divines of the period. His general estimate of the theological value and effect of their writings is instructive, as showing what can, and what cannot be effected by means of the logical understanding in theology. "If," he says, "the religious history of the eighteenth century proves anything, it is this :—that good sense, the best good sense, when it sets to work with the materials of human nature and Scripture to construct a religion, will find its way to an ethical code, irreproachable in its contents, and based on a just estimate and wise observation of the facts of life, ratified by Divine sanctions in the shape of hope and fear, of future rewards and penalties of obedience and disobedience. This the eighteenth century did, and did well. It has enforced the truths of natural morality with a solidity of argument and variety of proof which they have not received since the Stoical epoch, if then. But there its ability ended. When it came to the supernatural part of Christianity its embarrassment began. It was forced to keep it as much in the background as possible, or to bolster it up by lame and inadequate reasonings. The philosophy of common sense had done its own work; it attempted more, only to show, by its failure, *that some higher organon was needed for the establishment of supernatural truth.* The career of the evidential school, its success and failure, — its success in vindicating the ethical part of Christianity and the regulative aspect of revealed truth, its failure in establishing the supernatural and speculative part — have enriched the history of doctrine with a complete refutation of that method as an instrument of theological investigation.

"This judgment, however, must not be left unbalanced by a consideration on the other side. It will hardly be supposed that the drift of what has been said, is that common sense is out of place in religion, or in any other matter. The defect of the eighteenth century theology was not in having too much good sense, but in having nothing besides. In the present day, when a godless orthodoxy threatens, as in the fifteenth century, to extinguish religious thought altogether, and nothing is allowed in the Church of England but the formulæ of past thinkings, which have long lost all sense of any kind, it may seem out of reason to be bringing forward a misapplication of common sense in a bygone age. There are times and circumstances when religious ideas will be greatly benefited by being submitted to the rough and ready tests by which busy men try what comes in their way, by being made to stand their trial, and be freely canvassed, *coram populo*. As poetry is not for the critics, so religion is not for the theologians. When it is stiffened into phrases, and these phrases are declared to be objects of reverence but not of intelligence, it is in the way to become a useless incumbrance, the rubbish of the past, blocking the road. Theology then retires into the position it occupies in the Church of Rome at present, an unmeaning frostwork of dogma, out of all relation to the actual history of man."

But if such be indeed the history of any system of belief hitherto proposed, a serious question arises. Where, in this conflict of opinion, must we look for our ultimate appeal, our test of truth and basis of belief?

" In the Catholic theory," observes Mr. Pattison, "the feebleness of Reason is met half-way and made good by the authority of the Church. When the Protestants threw off this authority, they did not assign to Reason what they took from the Church, but to Scripture. Calvin did not shrink from saying that Scripture 'shone sufficiently by its own light.' As long as this could be kept to, the Protestant theory of belief was whole and sound. At least it was as sound as the Catholic. In both, Reason, aided by spiritual illumination, performs the subordinate function of recognizing the supreme authority of the Church, and of the Bible, respectively. Time, learned controversy, and abatement of zeal, drove the Protestants generally from the hardy but irrational assertion of Calvin. Every foot of ground that Scripture lost was gained by one or other of the three substitutes: Church authority, the Spirit, or Reason. Church authority was essayed by the Laudian divines, but was soon found untenable, for on that footing it was found impossible to justify the Reformation and the breach with Rome. The Spirit then came into favour along with Independency. But it was still more quickly discovered that on such a basis only discord and disunion could be reared. There remained to be tried Common Reason, carefully distinguished from recondite learning, and not based on metaphysical assumptions. To apply this instrument to the contents of revelation was the occupation of the early half of the eighteenth century; with what success has been seen. In the latter part of the century the same Common Reason was applied to the external evidences. But here the method fails in a first requisite—universality; for even the shallowest array of historical proof requires some book-learning to apprehend. Further than this, the Lardner and Paley schools could not complete their proof satisfactorily, inasmuch as the materials for the investigation of the first and second centuries of the Christian era were not at hand. *Such appears to be the past history of the Theory of Belief in the Church of England.*"

And if the above review of the history of our theology is to a certain extent unsatisfactory and negative in its result, the reader should remember that such partial satisfaction of our highest longings is one most important condition of our appointed trial here. We should reflect, too, that however these successive appeals to Catholic tradition, to the letter of Scripture, to Common Reason, to a mystic illumination, have hitherto failed to obtain any perfectly satisfactory answer to the human spirit in its quest after truth, they still form an integral and most important portion of the history of human thought, and may yet serve to show us, in the unfolding of that history, a glimpse of hope for the future sufficient to compensate for all the failures and shortcomings of the past. The principle of traditionalism, rightly understood and explained,—the appeal to the Catholic thought and feeling of the past,—may serve to bring us face to face with our fathers in the faith, and reveal to us in their spiritual conflicts a rich treasure of Christian life and experience. And so, again, the letter of Scripture, interpreted by the light of history and of science, may be transformed from the letter that killeth into the Spirit that giveth life. And, lastly, the Common Reason or logical understanding may yet help us to realize that Spirit and appropriate that life, moulding them into form and evolving out of them a complete system of Christian doctrine and practice.

" In pointing out," observes Mr. Morell, "the persistency of the struggle to adjust the claims of *Reason* and of *Authority*, and in referring to this as the central point of the great controversies of Christianity in the centuries which are past, we are simply keeping within the precincts of *historical fact.* And, be it remembered, historical fact is not to be trifled with; nor is it our place to lament over it, as though, just because it does not satisfy *our* ideas of what the course of religious truth ought to have been, that course is all a sad picture of time lost and talents squandered. History is diviner than we are apt to think it; the wanderings of the human spirit after truth are not all delusion and loss; extremes, however. terrible, have instruction in them, which could never otherwise be realized; and antagonisms of opinion have displayed or called forth a mental *tension,* with which the world could ill dispense. It has been the providential mission of one party to maintain the validity of Divine *Authority* in religion; it has been the mission of another to advocate the claims of *Reason,* and the light that is within us; it has oft-times been the aim of a third to reconcile the claims of the two, and bring the Christian world into harmony and peace. By few, comparatively, has it been seen, that we should purchase the ascendancy either of Authority or of Reason at a dear rate; yea, that it were an unfruitful repose to consummate a perfect reconciliation of the two before the fulness of the time has come; but that, in their very antagonism, we have the secret spring of real progress; and that to the continual separation effected by the Reason, we are marching onwards to an ever higher, broader, and more catholic unity, in the clear comprehension of all that is truly implied in *Divine Authority*. . . . . . .

"We affirm it, therefore, as an expectation which, if there be any truth in the significancy of the past, must *inevitably* be realized: that the scattered and disjointed elements of Protestantism, those pulverised fragments of our religious life, which have been isolated by the asserted supremacy of the individual judgment, and the all-sufficiency of logical processes, must, ere long, seek for a new and a higher unity in the intuitional consciousness. We regard it as a moral certainty, that with the development of a new philosophy a new *method* will be introduced into theological inquiry, and the antagonisms between Reason and Authority will find, at least, a *temporary* resting-place in a more perfect critique of the essential elements of Reason, and the essential nature of a Divine Inspiration.

"Under these influences we look for a broader and purer development of the religious life. The worship of images which the iconoclasts of the middle ages failed to extinguish, and which it was left for Protestantism to destroy, has long passed away from the minds of the enlightened; but the worship of propositions has been too often substituted in its place. In the next great historical era of the Christian life, we shall get beyond the worship of dogmas, and find that the Church has been unrighteously placing those productions of human reason on a level with the Divine *life* in its immediate emanation from the Most High.

"We are not ignorant or thoughtless enough to look even then for a cessation from all antagonism in the Christian Church. All we look for is a continuous progress towards *light* and towards *love*. Were antagonism entirely to cease, the life of Christianity would be paralyzed; but still that antagonism may become more pure, more intelligent, and, if we may so say, more peaceful. Antagonism once led the vanquished to the Inquisition, the faggot, the stake. It now confines its penalties to social contempt and well-rounded abuse. We, or our immediate posterity, may yet live to see religious antagonism performing its office, without carrying with it either a penalty or a sting. *Were the significancy of the past but rightly understood, it must materially help forwards that great and much longed-for result.*" *

7. The seventh and last Essay, "On the Interpretation of Scripture," is by the Rev. Benjamin Jowett, M.A., Fellow and Tutor of Balliol, and Regius Professor of Greek in the University of Oxford.

* Morell's Philosophy of Religion, chap. xi.

In the literary and theological world Professor Jowett is chiefly known as the author of a book on the Epistles of St. Paul, which has reached a second edition, and is, probably, the only English exegetical treatise of the day that enjoys a Continental reputation. In the University of Oxford he stands confessedly master of the situation in the eyes of the rising generation of English students and theologians, over whom he exercises an influence comparable only to that once wielded by Mr. Newman. Nor is it merely his genius and learning which have won for him this high place amongst the Oxford professors; it is rather, we are assured, the daily and hourly devotion of his time and thoughts to the improvement of those with whom, whether as professor or tutor, he is brought into contact. With the scanty stipend of £40 a year, which is the whole sum hitherto granted to his chair by the Crown or the University, he bestows more labour on his pupils than any other member of the professorial body, however ample their income, however meritorious their efforts.

His present Essay is well worthy of the high reputation of its author. Fully to be understood it should be studied in connection with the Commèntaries on St. Paul, to which it furnishes a very useful and appropriate supplement. It is intended to clear away some of the misconceptions which have prevented Biblical students from deriving the full advantages to be reaped from the sacred records, and to point out what those advantages are.

In the interpretation of Scripture, as of any other book, our first object, he contends, should be to ascertain the meaning of the writer—to discover what in the passage before us the author really meant or intended to say. The whole Essay is, in fact, little more than the expansion, illustration, and application of this one idea, this simple principle, the neglect of which has tended so much to confuse the interpreter and perplex the reader of the Bible.

"The book itself remains, as at the first, unchanged amid the changing interpretations of it. The office of the interpreter is not to add another, but to recover the original one. The simple words of that book he tries to preserve pure from the refinements or distinctions of later times. He has no theory of interpretation; a few rules guarding against common errors are enough for him. He wants to be able to open his eyes and see or imagine things as they really are."

But what, in fact, has been the history of the interpretation of Scripture? "More than any other subject of human knowledge, Biblical criticism has hung to the past; it has hitherto been found truer to the traditions of the Church than to the words of Christ. It has made, however, two great steps onward—at the time of the Reformation and in our own day. The diffusion of a critical spirit in history and literature is affecting the criticism of the Bible in our own day in a manner not unlike the burst of intellectual life in the fifteenth or sixteenth centuries. Educated persons are beginning to ask, not what Scripture may be made to mean, but what it does. And it is no exaggeration to say, that he who in the present state of knowledge will confine himself to the plain meaning of words and the study of their context, may know more of the original spirit and intention of the authors of the New Testament, than all the controversial writers of former ages put together."

"Much of the uncertainty which prevails in the interpretation of Scripture arises out of party efforts to wrest its meaning to different sides. There are, however, deeper reasons which have hindered the natural meaning of the text from immediately and universally prevailing. One of these is the unsettlement of many questions which have an important but indirect bearing on the subject. Some of these questions veil themselves in ambiguous terms, and no one likes to draw them out of their hiding-place into the light of day."

Among these questions one of the most important is the question of inspiration. "Almost all Christians agree on the word which use and tradition have consecrated to express the reverence which they truly feel for the Old and New Testaments. But here the agreement of opinion ends: the meaning of inspiration has been variously explained, or more often passed over in silence from a fear of stirring the difficulties that would arise about it. It is one of those theological terms which may be regarded as 'great peacemakers,' but which are also sources of distrust and misunderstanding. . . . . . The subject will clear itself, if we bear in mind two considerations:—First, that the nature of inspiration can only be known from the examination of Scripture. There is no other source to which we can turn for information; and we have no right to assume some imaginary doctrine of inspiration, like the infallibility of the Church of Rome. To the question, 'What is inspiration?' the first answer therefore is, 'That idea of Scripture which we gather from the knowledge of it.' It is no mere *a priori* notion, but one to which the book is itself a witness. It is a fact which we infer from the study of Scripture—not of one portion only, but of the whole. Obviously, then, it embraces writings of very different kinds—the Book of Esther, for example, or the Song of Solomon, as well as the Gospel of St. John. It is reconcilable with the mixed good and evil of the characters of the Old Testament—which, nevertheless, does not exclude them from the favour of God—with the attribution to the Divine Being of actions at variance with that higher revelation, which He has given of Himself in the Gospel; it is not inconsistent with imperfect or opposite aspects of the truth, as in the Book of Job or Ecclesiastes; with variations of fact in the Gospels or the Books of Kings; or Chronicles; with inaccuracies of language in the Epistle of St. Paul. For these are all found in Scripture: neither is there any reason why they should not be, except a general impression that Scripture ought to have been written in a way different from what it has. A principle of progressive revelation admits them all; and this is already contained in the words of our Saviour, 'Moses, because of the hardness of your hearts, &c.'; or even in the Old Testament, 'Henceforth there shall be no more this proverb in the house of Israel.' For what is progressive is necessarily imperfect in its earlier stages, and even erring to those who come after, whether it be the maxims of a half-civilized world which are compared with those of a civilized one, or the Law with the Gospel. Scripture itself points the way to answer the moral objections to Scripture. Lesser difficulties remain, but only such as would be found commonly in writings of the same age and country.

"The other consideration is one which has been neglected by writers on this subject. It is this — that any true doctrine of inspiration must conform to all well-ascertained facts of history or of science. The same fact cannot be true and untrue, any more than the same words can have two opposite meanings. The same fact cannot be true in religion when seen by the light of faith, and untrue in science when looked at through the medium of evidence or experiment. It is ridiculous to suppose that the sun goes round the earth in the same sense in which the earth goes round the sun; or that the world appears to have existed, but has not existed during the vast epochs of which geology speaks to us. But, if so, there is no need of elaborate reconcilements of revelation and science; they reconcile themselves the moment any scientific truth is distinctly ascertained. As the idea of nature enlarges, the idea of revelation also enlarges; it was a temporary misunderstanding which severed them. And as the knowledge of nature which is possessed by the few is communicated, in its leading features at least, to the many, they will receive with it a higher conception of the ways of God to man. It may hereafter appear as natural to the majority of mankind to see the providence of God in the order of the world, as it once was to appeal to interruptions of it.

"Commentators are often more occupied with the proof of miracles than with the declaration of life and immortality; with the fulfilment of the details of prophecy than with its life and power; with the reconcilement of the discrepancies in the narrative of the infancy, pointed out by Schleiermacher, than with the importance of the great event of the appearance of the Saviour. 'To this end was I born, and for this cause came I into the world, that I should bear witness unto the truth.'"

"When interpreted like any other book, by the same rules of evidence and the same canons of criticism, the Bible will still remain unlike any other book; its beauty will be freshly seen, as of a picture which is restored after many ages to its original state; it will create a new interest and make for itself a new kind of authority by the life which is in it. It will be a spirit and not a letter; as it was in the beginning, having an influence like that of the spoken word, or the book newly found. The purer the light in the human heart, the more it will have an expression of itself in the mind of Christ; the greater the knowledge of the development of man, the truer will be the insight gained into the 'increasing purpose' of revelation. In which, also, the individual soul has a practical part, finding a sympathy with its own imperfect feelings in the broken utterance of the Psalmist or the Prophet as well as in the fulness of Christ. The harmony between Scripture and the life of man in all its stages may be far greater than appears at present. No one can form any notion from what we see around us, of the power which Christianity might have, if it were at one with the conscience of man, and not at variance with his intellectual convictions. There, a world weary of the heat and dust of controversy—of speculations about God and man—weary, too, of the rapidity of its own motion, would return home and find rest.

"Of what has been said, then, this is the sum:—*That Scripture, like other books, has one meaning, which is to be gathered from itself without reference to the adaptations of Fathers or Divines; and without regard to* a priori *notions about its nature and origin. It is to be interpreted like other books, with attention to the character of its authors, and the prevailing state of civilization and knowledge, with allowance for peculiarities of style and language, and modes of thought and figures of speech. Yet not without a sense that as we read there grows upon us the witness of God in the world, anticipating in a rude and primitive age the truth that was to be, shining more and more unto the perfect day in the life of Christ, which again is reflected from different points of view in the teaching of His Apostles.*"

Our author then proceeds to distinguish more particularly the interpretation from the application of Scripture, and to point out within what limits and subject to what cautions the latter is admissible.

"The religion of Christ," he observes, "was first taught by an *application* of the words of the Psalms and the Prophets. Our Lord Himself sanctions this application. The new truth which was introduced into the Old Testament, rather than the old truth which was found there, was the salvation and the conversion of the world. There are many quotations from the Psalms and the Prophets in the Epistles, in which the meaning is quickened or spiritualized, but hardly any, probably none, which is based on the original sense or context. That is not so singular a phenomenon as may at first sight be imagined. It may appear strange to us that Scripture should be interpreted in Scripture in a manner not altogether in agreement with modern criticism; but would it not be more strange that it should be interpreted otherwise than in agreement with the ideas of the age or country in which it was written? The observation that there is such an agreement leads to two conclusions which have a bearing on our present subject. First, it is a reason for not insisting on the applications which the New Testament makes of passages in the Old, as their original meaning. Secondly, it gives authority and precedent for the use of similar applications in our own day.

"But, on the other hand, though interwoven with literature, though common to all ages of the Church, though sanctioned by our Lord and His

Apostles, it is easy to see that such an employment of Scripture is liable to error and perversion. For it may not only receive a new meaning; it may be applied in a spirit alien to itself. It may become the symbol of fanaticism, the cloak of malice, the disguise of policy. . . . . . If we are permitted to apply Scripture under the pretence of interpreting it, the language of Scripture becomes only a mode of expressing the public feeling and opinion of our own day. Any passing phase of politics, or art, or spurious philanthropy, may have a kind of Scriptural authority. The words that are used are the words of the Prophet or Evangelist, but we stand behind and adapt them to our purpose. Hence it is necessary to consider the limits and manner of a just adaptation; how much may be allowed for the sake of ornament; how far the Scripture in all its details may be regarded as an allegory of human life—where the true analogy begins—how far the interpretation of Scripture will serve as a corrective to its practical abuse.

"The first step towards a more truthful use of Scripture in practice is the separation of *adaptation* from interpretation. . . . . . The least expression of Scripture is weighty; it affects the minds of the hearers in a way that no other language can. Whatever responsibility attaches to idle words, attaches in still greater degree to the idle or fallacious use of Scripture terms. And there is surely a want of proper reverence for Scripture, when we confound the weakest and feeblest applications of its words with their true meaning—when we avail ourselves of their natural power to point them against an enemy—when we divert the eternal words of charity and truth into a defence of some passing opinion. For not only in the days of the Pharisees, but in our own, the letter has been taking the place of the spirit; the least matters of the greatest, and the primary meaning has been lost in the secondary use.

"Other simple cautions may be added. The applications of Scripture should be harmonized, and, as it were, interpenetrated with the spirit of the Gospel, the whole of which should be in every part; though the words may receive a new sense, the new sense ought to be in agreement with the general truth. . . . . . They should be subjected to an over-ruling principle, which is the heart and conscience of the Christian teacher, who, indeed, 'stands behind them,' not to make them the vehicles of his own opinions, but as the expressions of justice and truth and love.

"And here the critical interpretation of Scripture comes in and exercises a corrective influence on its popular use. We have already admitted that criticism is not for the multitude; it is not what the Scripture terms the Gospel preached for the poor. Yet, indirectly passing from the few to the many, it has borne a great part in the reformation of religion. It has cleared the eye of the mind to understand the original meaning.

"The portion of Scripture which, more than any other, is immediately and universally applicable to our own times is, doubtless, that which is contained in the words of Christ Himself. . . . . . The parables of our Lord are a portion of the New Testament which we may apply in the most easy and literal manner. The persons in them are the persons among whom we live and move; there are times and occasions at which the truths symbolized by them come home to the hearts of all who have ever been impressed by religion. We have been prodigal sons returning to our Father; servants to whom talents have been entrusted; labourers in the vineyard inclined to murmur at our lot when compared with that of others, yet receiving every man his due; well-satisfied Pharisees; repentant Publicans; we have received the seed, and the cares of the world have choked it; we hope, also, at times that we have found the pearl of great price after sweeping the house; we are ready, like the Good Samaritan, to show kindness to all mankind. Of these circumstances of life, or phases of mind, which are typified by the parables, most Christians have experience. We may go on to apply many of them further to the condition of nations and churches. Such a treasury has

Christ provided us of things new and old, which refer to all times and all mankind—may we not say in His own words, 'because He is the Son of Man'?

"There is no language of Scripture which penetrates the individual soul, and embraces all the world in the arms of its love, in the same manner as that of Christ Himself. Yet the Epistles contain lessons which are not found in the Gospels, or, at least, not expressed with the same degree of clearness. For the Epistles are nearer to actual life—they relate to the circumstances of the first believers, to their struggles with the world without, to their temptations and divisions from within—their subject is not only the doctrine of the Christian religion, but the business of the early Church. And although their circumstances are not our circumstances—we are not afflicted or persecuted or driven out of the world, but in possession of the blessings, and security, and property of an established religion—yet there is a Christian spirit which infuses itself into all circumstances, of which they are a pure and living source.

"But the Old Testament has also its peculiar lessons which are not conveyed with equal point or force in the New. The beginnings of human history are themselves a lesson, having a freshness as of the early dawn. There are forms of evil against which the Prophets and the prophetical spirit of the Law carry on a warfare, in terms almost too bold for the way of life of modern times. There, more plainly than in any other portion of Scripture, is expressed the antagonism of outward and inward, of ceremonial and moral, of mercy and sacrifice. There all the masks of hypocrisy are rudely torn asunder, in which an unthinking world allows itself to be disguised. There the relations of rich and poor in the sight of God, and their duties toward one another, are most clearly enunciated. There the religion of suffering first appears — 'adversity, the blessing' of the Old Testament, as well as of the New. There the sorrows and aspirations of the soul find their deepest expression, and also their consolation. The feeble person has an image of himself in the 'bruised reed;' the suffering servant of God passes into the 'beloved one, in whom my soul delighteth.' Even the latest and most desolate phases of the human mind are reflected in Job and Ecclesiastes; yet not without the solemn assertion that 'to fear God and keep His commandments' is the beginning and end of all things."

The sincere Christian, then, need feel no apprehension as to the effect of the critical interpretation of Scripture on theology and on life. The first condition of a true faith is, we should remember, a sincere belief in the divinity of all true knowledge, nor ought we to allow any appearances to the contrary to persuade us that truth and goodness, inseparably united under God's sovereignty, can ever really be at variance with each other. "It is hardly too much to say that the one is but a narrower form of the other: truth is to the world what holiness of life is to the individual—to man collectively the source of justice and peace and good.

"There are many ways in which the connection between truth and goodness may be traced in the interpretation of Scripture. Is it a mere chimera that the different sections of Christendom may meet on the common ground of the New Testament? Or that the individual may be urged by the vacancy and unprofitableness of old traditions to make the Gospel his own—a life of Christ in the soul, instead of a theory of Christ which is in a book or written down? Or that in missions to the heathen Scripture may become the expression of universal truths rather than of the tenets of particular men or churches? That would remove many obstacles to the reception of Christianity. Or that the study of Scripture may have a more important place in a liberal education than hitherto? Or that the 'rational service' of interpreting Scripture may dry up the crude and dreamy vapours of religious excitement? Or, that in preaching, new sources of spiritual health may flow from a more natural use of Scripture? Or that the lessons of

Scripture may have a nearer way to the hearts of the poor when disengaged from theological formulas? . . . . .

"There is an aspect of truth which may always be put forward so as to find a way to the hearts of men. If there is danger and shrinking from one point of view, from another there is freedom and sense of relief. The wider contemplation of the religious world may enable us to adjust our place in it. The acknowledgment of churches as political and national institutions is the basis of a sound government of them. Criticism itself is not only negative; if it creates some difficulties it does away with others. It may put us at variance with a party or section of Christians in our own neighbourhood. But, on the other hand, it enables us to look at all men as they are in the sight of God, not as they appear to human eye, separated and often interdicted from each other by lines of religious demarcation; it divides us from the parts to unite us to the whole. That is a great help to religious communion. It does away with the supposed opposition of reason and faith. It throws us back on the conviction that religion is a personal thing, in which certainty is to be slowly won and not assumed as the result of evidence or testimony. It places us, in some respects (though it be deemed a paradox to say so), more nearly in the position of the first Christians to whom the New Testament was not yet given, in whom the Gospel was a living word, not yet embodied in forms or supported by ancient institutions.

"Nor is the suspicion or difficulty which attends critical inquiries any reason for doubting their value. The Scripture nowhere leads us to suppose that the circumstance of all men speaking well of us is any ground for supposing that we are acceptable in the sight of God; and there is no reason why the condemnation of others should be witnessed to by our own conscience. Perhaps it may be true that, owing to the jealousy or fear of some, the reticence of others, the terrorism of a few, we may not always find it easy to regard these subjects with calmness and judgment. But, on the other hand, these accidental circumstances have nothing to do with the question at issue; they cannot have the slightest influence on the meaning of words, or on the truth of facts. No one can carry out the principle that public opinion or church authority is the guide to truth, when he goes beyond the limits of his own Church or country. That is a consideration which may well make him pause before he accepts of such a guide in the journey to another world. All the arguments for repressing inquiries into Scripture in Protestant countries hold equally in Italy and Spain for repressing inquiries into matters of fact and doctrine, and so for denying the Scriptures to the common people.

"Lastly, let us be assured that there is some nobler idea of truth than is supplied by the opinion of mankind in general, or the voice of parties in a Church. Every one, whether a student of theology or not, has need to make war against his prejudices no less than against his passions; and, in the religious teacher, the first is even more necessary than the last. For, while the vices of mankind are in a great degree isolated, and are at any rate reprobated by public opinion, their prejudices have a sort of communion or kindred with the world without. They are a collective evil, and have their being in the interests, classes, states of society, and other influences, amid which we live. He who takes the prevailing opinions of Christians, and decks them out in their gayest colours—who reflects the better mind of the world to itself—is likely to be its favourite teacher. In that ministry of the Gospel, even when assuming forms repulsive to persons of education, no doubt the good is far greater than the error or harm. But there is also a deeper work, which is not dependent on the opinions of men, in which many elements combine, some alien to religion, or accidentally at variance with it. That work can hardly expect to win much popular favour, so far as it runs counter to the feeling of religious parties; but he who bears a part in it may feel a confidence which no popular caresses or religious sympathy could inspire, that he has, by a Divine help, been enabled to plant his foot somewhere beyond the waves of time. He may depart hence before the natural term, worn out with intellectual toil, regarded with suspicion by many of his contemporaries: yet not without a sure hope that the love of truth, which men of saintly lives often seem to slight, is, nevertheless, accepted before God."

These brief extracts can only convey a very imperfect impression of an Essay extending over more than a hundred pages: they have been selected simply with a view of setting forth, in his own words, the author's leading idea, and indicating the general character and spirit of the treatise. In this way they may prove useful to some, as an introduction to the perusal of the Essay itself, by putting them at once in possession of the main scope and design of the author throughout. The importance of never losing sight of this is strikingly illustrated in the use made by opponents of subordinate passages which they have not hesitated to quote in a sense the very opposite of that intended by the author.

To correct this abuse the foregoing extracts from this and the preceding Essays, will, it is hoped, suffice, — at least in the judgment of the candid and impartial. They certainly show that the object of the writers of the "Essays and Reviews," so far as they have a common object at all, is the exact opposite of that which has been imputed to them,—that their object in putting forth this volume was not to create, but to remove difficulties in the way of the reception of "the truth as it is in Jesus;" to atone and reconcile the difficulties of reason with the high aspirations and demands of faith; to bring Christianity home as a living power to the heart; and so to rest our faith, "not in the wisdom of man, but in the power of God." "They have attempted, in short, mistakenly or not, to place Christianity beyond the reach of accidents, whether of science or criticism; to rest its claims on those moral and spiritual truths which, after all, are what have really won an entrance for it into the heart, not merely of the highly educated, but of the poor, the ignorant, the afflicted, in every age of the world. Not Anselm only, or Coleridge, but the humblest peasant who feels that the Gospel is an answer to all his needs; not Dr. Temple only, or Professor Jowett, but the Wesleyan missionary or preacher who appeals to the natural sense of sin and the natural need of a Saviour,—build alike not on any outward signs, but on the immutable relations between the moral law of God, and the moral conscience of man."* Even these extracts, brief and imperfect though they be, are sufficient to show that. I feel sure that, with Dr. Stanley, I may confidently appeal from the base and slanderous spirit of party warfare to the heart of the Christian reader, whether the spirit which breathes through them is likely to destroy or to confirm the faith of the rising generation; whether it is a spirit of an "enemy of Christ," or of those who are amongst His faithful followers; whether it is a spirit at variance or in unison with the Bible, the Catechism, and the Prayer-book—with the purest teaching and the highest interests of Christianity and of the Church of England. I would fain hope, too, that, apart from any mere temporary or controversial object, such a collection of passages from some of our most devout and deepest thinkers may (even with those who do not entirely agree with them) be generally useful for the purposes of Christian edification, as helps to a more careful and reverent study of the Bible, and as testimonies to its Divine inspiration and authority.†

* Ed. Rev. April, 1861.
† Cf. Preface to "Statements of Christian Doctrine and Practice, extracted from the Writings of Professor Jowett." Oxford: J. H. & Jas. Parker. See Appendix, Note E.

CHAPTER IV.

THE PERSECUTION—ITS ORIGIN IN THE MISAPPREHENSION OF THE PRINCIPLE OF AUTHORITY IN THE CHURCH—ITS IMMEDIATE OCCASION IN THE EXCITEMENT OF RELIGIOUS PARTIES CREATED BY THE APPEARANCE OF TWO ARTICLES IN THE "WESTMINSTER" AND "QUARTERLY" REVIEWS.

THE student of history, and more especially of ecclesiastical history, will always be careful to distinguish the often comparatively trivial *occasions* out of which great events appear to emerge from the true originating, but not unfrequently deeply hidden, *causes* of those events. The more, indeed, we study history intelligently, and learn to trace in it throughout the unfolding, through human agency, of a Divine plan, the more clearly shall we be able to distinguish between the immediate occasion and the originating cause of each event. The outcry, for instance, against the "Essays and Reviews" had for its immediate antecedents the articles in the *Westminster* and *Quarterly*, which excited the popular mind against the writers, and became the occasion of the persecution to which they have been since exposed. But he who should allege those articles as the true cause and origin of that persecution would show a very imperfect acquaintance with the great principles which determine the course of human events, and be taking a very inadequate and manifestly superficial view of the matter. The ground of the present controversy, and the cause of the outcry against the Essayists, must be sought rather in that conflict between reason and authority which is coeval with Christianity itself.

When Christianity first presented itself to the world it was as a new and divine life centering in those grand conceptions of sin, of righteousness, and of judgment to come; of salvation, of purity, and of heavenly love, which the Spirit of Christ had awakened in the minds of His immediate followers and Apostles. Such was Christianity to those, for instance, who embraced it on the day of Pentecost—a new spiritual life—an awakening of the soul to a consciousness of its life in God, and a consecration of that life with its powers to the service of God as revealed to man in Christ. But afterwards, as the ardour of their first love began to subside, came a time of calm contemplation and *reflection*, a time of inquiry and discussion, in which it was inevitable that the new truths of Christianity should be differently understood and expounded as they presented themselves as *questions* to the different understandings of those to whom they were addressed. The great questions of God's providence, Christ's redemption, and man's destiny, were discussed by the first Christians as by ourselves, and with a like reference to the teaching of Christ and His Apostles as a supreme *authority*. Hence the importance attached to the formation of the *canon* of the New Testament at the close of the second century.* This once fixed by general consent, all ground of dispute would, it was fondly hoped, be set at rest for ever. But a very short time sufficed to show that the questions at issue between the different parties in the Church were very far from being settled by the general determination of the canon of Scripture. In proportion as the human reason began to exercise itself upon the great questions involved in man's relation to the universe and to God, it became clearer and clearer that the Scriptures were not able, nor ever designed to answer every conceivable question of the understanding in its search after truth; that, however invaluable in other respects, they could not anticipate, by the sentence of authority, those conclusions which God had decreed to be the result of time and of labour, the hardly-gained answer to the questionings of ages of inquiry, of diligent, painstaking, unwearied research. Unfortunately, however, the Church undertook to supply the *authority* which the Scriptures themselves had proved unable to furnish. This she

* See Appendix, Note F.

endeavoured to do by summing up and embodying in her decisions the chief results of the Catholic thought of each age, and so far with success, that those ancient settlements of the faith do, indeed, appear to have furnished the only points of unity and agreement which were attainable by the theology of those times. "They were, in fact, expressions of dogma, which did act as comprehensions in their time. As, for instance, even the final expression of the doctrine of the consubstantiality of the Son with the Father comprehended as many as could possibly be comprehended within the terms of one and the same confession, considering the antagonistic theories between which that declaration placed itself. And we cannot rightly understand those ancient settlements of the creed without bearing in mind that there were great speculative struggles going on concurrently within and without the pale of the Church. The conflict between monotheism and polytheism coincided, as it were, or ran along a parallel line, with the conflict within the Church between the Sabellian and Arian hypotheses; which conflict within the Church was solved by the adoption of the orthodox creed. Again, the pantheistic and dualistic tendencies were represented among those who bore the Christian name, by the Eutychian and Nestorian parties respectively; and looked at merely as a solution of a speculative difficulty, there was no other besides the orthodox statement in which the opposite parties had any tendency or disposition to coalesce."* And hence doubtless their vitality and the degree of *authority* which they are still allowed to possess in the Church. The mistake was in representing their decisions as *final*, instead of advances towards the final; as themselves marking the " end of all controversy," instead of mere stepping-stones in the successful traversing of error; as degrees of ascent to the Temple itself of Truth. It was this mistake which during the middle ages led the Church on in the construction of a deductive scholastic theology, accumulating dogma upon dogma on the assumed foundation of a supernaturally communicated sacerdotal infallibility, stifling the reason and crushing the soul of humanity under a dead weight of Aristotelian forms and ecclesiastical domination.

The revival of science in the 16th century, and the rise of native literatures, accompanied by the invention of printing, in Italy and France, and Germany and England, ushered in a brighter and happier era — the era of the Protestant Reformation—restoring light and life and liberty to the Church. The Reformation was essentially a revolt of the reason against a gross misapplication and abuse of the principle of authority by the Papal hierarchy — an asser-

* Wilson's Bampton Lectures, p. 55.

tion of the natural and Christian freedom of churches and individuals against the assumption of Rome to impose dogma. Not, indeed, that we are to suppose the Reformers themselves to have fully comprehended the principle they asserted. Even while renouncing the claim of Rome to impose dogma they could not resist the temptation to set up a like claim for themselves. The appeal which they made to Scripture against the authority of the hierarchy and the infallibility of the Pope was evidently in effect an appeal to *Scripture as understood and interpreted by themselves*, to the authority of their own interpretation, and to the infallibility of their own judgment. They did not, in fact, at once perceive that their protest against Rome could only be maintained consistently on the principle of free inquiry and universal toleration. The real question between reason and authority they seem never to have looked fairly in the face; and they left it accordingly very much where they found it—a problem to be solved by the light of history, by the accumulated experience and maturer judgment of generations then unborn.

"With the Reformation," observes Dr. Temple, "commenced an entirely new lesson—the lesson of toleration. Unquestionably as bigoted a spirit has often been shown in defence of some doctrine or practice for which the sanction of the Bible has been claimed, as before the Reformation, in defence of the decrees of the Church. '*But no lesson is learned well all at once.*' To learn toleration well and really, to let it become, not a philosophical tenet but a practical principle, to join it with real religiousness of life and character, it is absolutely necessary that it should break in upon the mind by slow and steady degrees, and that at every point its right to go farther should be disputed, and so forced to logical proof. For it is only by virtue of the opposition which it has surmounted that any truth can stand in the human mind. The strongest argument in favour of tolerating all opinions is that our conviction of the truth of an opinion is worthless, unless it has established itself in spite of the most strenuous resistance, and is still prepared to overcome the same resistance, if necessary. Toleration itself is no exception to the universal law; and those who most regret the slow progress by which it wins its way, may remember that this slowness makes the final victory the more certain and complete. Nor is that all. The toleration thus obtained is different in kind from what it would otherwise have been. It is not only stronger, it is richer and fuller. For the slowness of its progress gives time to disentangle from dogmatism the really valuable principles and sentiments that have been mixed up and entwined in it, and to unite toleration, not with indifference and worldliness, but with spiritual truth and religiousness of life."

We have now gained an elevation from which we may regard the recent agitation against "Essays and Reviews" intelligently and dispassionately, with a just appreciation of its cause and well-assured confidence in the final issue. That agitation indicates simply the desire of the extreme sacerdotal and Biblical parties of our own day to erect their respective traditions and conceptions of truth into an absolute and immutable standard of orthodoxy. There is nothing new, nothing strange, nothing to surprise us in this. As it is the characteristic of all strong feeling to believe in the permanency of its own emotions, so is it the property of all strong conviction to believe in the infallibility of its own conclusions. As a man under the influence of love, hatred, sorrow, or any other strong and absorbing affection is prone to fancy that he will continue to feel always as he feels now, and that in exact proportion to the intensity of the feeling of the moment; so is he no less prone to believe his present convictions on any given subject to be the exact measure and standard of truth with respect to that subject. Not in the Church only, but in the family and in the State also this characteristic of human nature is very observable; it is evidently a tendency not peculiar to the individual, but common to all mankind. Time, however, experience, better information, and more extended inquiry dissipate these illusions in other matters, and prove to men the folly of trusting either to the permanence of their present feelings or to the infallibility and sufficiency of their present judgments. In the matter of religion only is it so difficult to persuade man of the altogether partial, uncertain, and illusory character of many of their deepest and most firmly cherished convictions. The reason of this is twofold: first, the substitution of doctrinal standards for moral ends as a basis of Church communion, thus making unity of opinion, instead of identity of principle, the test and bond of Christian fellowship; and secondly, the habit of confounding men's conceptions of things with the things themselves, and thus making human opinion the measure and standard of Divine truth. Incalculable, indeed, are the evils which have flowed to the Church from this twofold source of error and confusion introduced unawares, and perpetuated by men who, amidst all their professions of loyalty to Truth, have evidently no notion of Truth, except as what they themselves trow, nor any love of truth beyond that which urges them to force all other men to trow as they trow themselves, impiously seeking to narrow and confine within the space of their own puny intellects that eternal Truth which is indeed the very "Thought of God," the expression of that eternal " Reason which was in the beginning with God and is God."

But if this be so, it follows that, Truth being thus divine and infinite in itself, our knowledge of it must of necessity be partial and progressive. In our search after it, we may approach indeed indefinitely towards, but never actually reach it. He, therefore, who thinks to set a limit to this progress, and to say, So far shalt thou go and no farther, that man by this very opinion shows that he is yet very far short of Truth.

"Truth, indeed," remarks one who loved her with all his heart, "came once into the world with her divine Master, and was a perfect shape most glorious to look on: but when He ascended, and His Apostles after Him were laid asleep, then straight arose a wicked race of deceivers, who—as that story goes of the *Egyptian Typhon* with his conspirators, how they dealt with the good *Osiris*—took the virgin Truth, hewed her lovely form into a thousand pieces, and scattered them to the four winds. From that time ever since, the sad friends of Truth, imitating the careful search that *Isis* made for the mangled body of *Osiris*, went up and down, gathering up limb by limb, still as they could find them We have not yet found them all, nor ever shall do, till her Master's second coming; he shall bring together every joint and member, and shall mould them into an immortal feature of loveliness and perfection. Meanwhile the light which we have gained, was given us, not to be ever staring at, but by it to discover onward things more remote from our knowledge. . . . . . There be who perpetually complain of schisms and sects, and make it such a calamity that any man dissents from their maxims. 'Tis their own pride and ignorance which cause the disturbing, who neither will hear with meekness, nor can convince, yet all must be suppressed which is not found in their *Syntagma*. They are the troublers, they are the dividers of unity, who neglect and permit not others to unite those dissevered pieces, which are yet wanting to the body of Truth. To be still searching what we know not by what we know, still closing up truth to truth as we find it (for all her body is homogeneal and proportional), this is the golden rule in theology, and makes up the best harmony in a church; not the forced and outward union of cold, and neutral, and inwardly divided minds." *

It is plain, then, that according to this *golden rule* the standard of truth *to us* must be, like our knowledge of it, *progressive*. We must look to the past, not as an *authority*, but as an aid to interpret the present. Convinced that truth to

* Milton's Areopagitica.

man is progressive, we gaze with intense interest upon the course it has already run, not as though the realized truth of any past age could satisfy the present, but because we can the better understand by the light of history what is the most advanced thinking of our own time, and what is the true elevation to which we have ourselves attained. And this is exactly what Bacon means where he speaks of Truth as the offspring of Experience, "the daughter of Time, that author of all authors, and source of all *authority* to man." *Opinionum enim commenta delet dies; naturæ judicia confirmat.*

We protest, then, against the recent agitation and outcry against "Essays and Reviews" as a movement essentially retrograde and subversive of those great principles of free inquiry and mutual toleration on which the Church of England as a Protestant Establishment is founded; as an abandonment of the Protestant and a recurrence to the Catholic Theory of *authority* in the Church; and as such directly contrary and repugnant to the sixth, eighth, twentieth, and twenty-first Articles of Religion which maintain "the sufficiency of Holy Scripture" as a rule of faith, and refer us for the explanation of the creeds and formularies to the fountain-head of Scripture itself, interpreted, consistently with Protestant principles, according to the best lights and ability of those to whom in each successive age it comes.

But it is time to turn from the general causes to the particular circumstances and immediate occasions of this great religious excitement. The reader will remember that in the history already given of the theological movement, of which the volume before us is the result, we noticed Bishop Hampden's Bampton Lectures as indicating a change in the relations of theology to religion in the recognized application of the *inductive* method of inquiry to the grounds and origin of the historical records and dogmatic terminology of the Church. The Dogmatists were not slow to take the alarm, and raised a cry of heresy which, but for the firmness of the prime minister of the day, would have succeeded in excluding Dr. Hampden from the chair of Divinity at Oxford in 1836, and again from the see of Hereford in 1847. On this latter occasion the present Bishop of Oxford was conspicuous amongst the agitators, and actually went so far as to institute proceedings against Dr. Hampden on a charge of heresy in the Arches Court. This suit, however, he had the good sense very shortly to withdraw, on representations made to him from certain quarters, which speedily convinced him, however much against his will, of the inexpediency and iniquity of the whole proceeding. The rebuff which Dr. Wilberforce then met with, and the humiliating spectacle which he presented of a Bishop forced within a few weeks publicly to eat his own words, might surely have taught him a lesson of caution for the future.

There were not wanting besides other circumstances which might not unreasonably have been regarded by the Bishop as warnings to look at home and re-consider the consistency of some of his own opinions with his position in a Protestant Establishment. But not so reasoned Bishop Wilberforce. Alarmed at what he was pleased to denounce as the rationalistic and neological tendencies of the Critical school, he again came forward as the champion of the extremest dogmatism, only that in place of the Lectures of Dr. Hampden he selected the Commentaries of Professor Jowett for the object of his attack. Even into the University Pulpit the Bishop of the diocese did not hesitate to carry the acrimony of controversy,* and there in effect to accuse Mr. Jowett of denying everything he had endeavoured to explain. His Essay on the Atone-

---

* Since the institution of Select Preachers in the University, it is believed that no previous Bishop of Oxford has ever been nominated to that office. The governors of the University must, indeed, have been as forgetful of their duty to watch over its privileges as the Bishop himself was forgetful of good taste in the eagerness of controversy, when he was allowed to make that appointment the occasion of delivering theological fulminations from a pulpit which is not subject to his jurisdiction.

ment, in particular, was made the object of such vehement attack that the friends of justice and truth in the University felt they could keep silence no longer; and, much to his honour, the late Professor Hussey, in a remarkable ordination sermon on the "Atonement," preached in December, 1855, defended the doctrine of Mr. Jowett, and showed in guarded but decisive terms its substantial identity with that of the ancient Fathers.*

Having so far exhausted their violence on the Commentaries of Professor Jowett, the opponents of free inquiry in the Church found a new object of attack in his contribution to the "Essays and Reviews" of 1860, which they received with the significant cry, applied indiscriminately to all the Essayists,—"*They deny the Atonement.*" The Bishop of Oxford made the book and its authors the subject of a solemn warning and special peroration in his charge to his clergy in the autumn. Indeed, his Lordship may be said to have commenced the agitation on the side of the High-Church party, which was carried on *pari passu* by a number of clergymen of very opposite sentiments in the neighbourhood of Derby. Shortly afterwards appeared an article in the *Westminster*, which succeeded in creating a complete religious panic. The account of that

* See Stanley's Greek Church, Introduction, xliii.

article and its effect, in the *Edinburgh*, is drawn by a master's hand. I give it in the writer's own words:—

"In a well-known Review, advocating the extremest opinions, both theological and political, an article appeared, on which we do not hesitate to fasten the main responsibility of the whole subsequent agitation. It evidently proceeded from the hand of a writer who, whilst retaining a certain amount of religious sentiment, repudiated all belief in Christian Revelation, and who combined with a profound ignorance of nearly all that had been written on the questions at issue an almost fanatical desire to inveigle those who stood on more secure positions to the narrow ledge of the precipice on the midway of which he himself was standing. In an argument, not destitute of pathos or ability, but poisoned by a sinister intention too transparent to have escaped the notice of any but those who were willingly deceived, the Reviewer first parodied the book by exaggeration, by amplification, by suppression, by making every writer responsible for what every other writer had said or not said, either on the subjects discussed or not discussed, and then raised a cry of mingled exultation and remonstrance to the phantasm which he had conjured up—of exultation at the supposed novelty of what he was pleased to call a system of Neo-Christianity; of plaintive remonstrance at the reluctance of the writers to abandon all the truths which they most cherished, in order to adopt the mixture of Paganism and Catholicism, in which the followers of M. Comte have found a refuge. We know not what results the writer expected from this measure. Not by such arts, he may be well assured, not by such presumptuous ignorance, not by such unscrupulous misrepresentation, not by such malignant insinuations, will the wise or the noble-minded of any communion be tempted to surrender their belief in the justice and mercy of the Hebrew Prophets, the love and faith of the Christian Apostles.

"But, although the *Westminster* manifesto fell, as was to be expected, powerless on the ears of those to whom it was addressed, it found ready listeners elsewhere. Partly in genuine alarm, partly in greedy delight at finding such an unlooked-for confirmation of their own uneasy suspicions and dislikes, the partisans of the two chief theological schools in the country caught up and eagerly echoed the note of the infidel journal. They extolled the eloquence and ability of the article; they made its conclusions their own; they discerned, through its inquisitorial gaze, tendencies which up to that moment had escaped even their own keen scent for the track of heresy. Gradually the heterogeneous series began to assume that mystified form which it has worn ever since in the public eye. The

Essayists were discovered to be seven in number. They were the 'seven stars in a new constellation,'—or 'the seven extinguishers of the seven lamps of the Apocalypse,'—or 'the seven champions not of Christendom,'—or by the title which unhappily its blasphemous levity and its wicked uncharitableness has not excluded from journals professing to write in the name of religion, 'the *Septem contra Christum.*' Every part of the volume was now seen to have a close interdependence. In spite of the solemn disclaimer of joint responsibility and concert with which the volume was prefaced, every writer was assumed to have been acquainted with the production of every other. The first essay was supposed to contain in its successive pages the key-notes of the successive dissertations which followed, closing in the last, the climax and conclusion of the whole.

"It is believed that these scattered polemics gathered head at the meeting of a large number of clergy and laity which took place at Oxford for the election to the Sanscrit Chair. On that occasion, when the University lost the services of the most eminent scholar within her walls, there was arrayed against him a vast mass of the Conservative elements of the country, both theological and political. The well-known anathema issued on that occasion against the 'intellectuals,' —a fit precursor of the swarm of curses which have followed in its wake, admirably expressed the feeling of many who recorded their votes on the 7th of December (1860) against the illustrious German philologer. In the fermentation naturally engendered by the victorious combination of bodies of men for any common purpose arose, it is said, the first distinct conception of an organized attack on the volume with which Professor Müller's friends or country had been connected in the public mind. A meeting was held before the final dispersion of the electors, in one of the Oxford hotels; and there was breathed the earliest whisper of a demonstration against the book, which still remained in the modest obscurity of a small second edition.*

"The first decisive signal that the rising hostility had penetrated into a higher sphere was given by the principal organ of the Tory party, in an article which, passing beyond the region of indistinct inuendoes, or fantastic allusions, or profane jests, proceeded to challenge the several authors of the book to abandon their positions in the Church of England. From this moment it became apparent that a powerful ecclesiastical

---

* This statement requires some qualification. We are informed, that before the article appeared in the *Westminster* two editions of 1,000 each were exhausted, which was probably as large a circulation as was originally expected for the volume. A third edition of 750 was nearly run out at the beginning of December, to which extent the statement in the *Edinburgh* is incorrect.

influence was at work,* eager to seize the opportunity of crushing not merely the book, but the writers themselves, and all who, in any degree, shared their views. Like the article in the *Westminster* the article in the *Quarterly* displayed or affected the most astonishing ignorance of all that had passed in theological literature, in this and other countries, since the beginning of this century. It added to this a carelessness not equally surprising, but exceedingly curious, of the general facts of history and science. The doubtful if not exploded theory of absorption, as the doctrine of the Buddhists, was assumed as unquestionable; the Copernican system was described as having 'wholly passed away.' Everywhere the charges of inaccurate statement, of confusion in thought and expression, of want of faith in the Bible, return into its own bosom. But these and like imperfections were of little moment in an invective of which the object was the destruction of high reputations, stimulated

* The reader will hardly credit it, but it is not the less true, that simultaneously with the preparation of the Article in the *Quarterly* and the concoction of the episcopal manifesto, a pressure was actually put upon Mr. Parker, the original publisher of the volume, by influential clergymen, which induced him to request the authors that it might be transferred from his house elsewhere! If this altogether unprecedented and most improper interference with a publisher's business was intended to damage the circulation of the work, its failure was as signal as it was well deserved.

by the unreasoning dread lest inquiry into any single part of theological truth should overturn the whole of religion."

From this time the artillery of controversial warfare was brought fully into play. Meetings of the clergy were held, and a committee was formed under the auspices of the Rev. Drs. Irons and M'Caul,* who took upon themselves to solicit the signatures of the clergy throughout the

* These gentlemen appear to have been chosen to act as secretaries to the Clerical Committee, as representing respectively the High and Low Church parties. The position occupied by those parties with respect to the application of reason to the subject matter of theology is well explained by Professor Baden Powell. Of Dr. Irons, whom he cites as a type of the new, or Tractarian form, of the old High Church school, he remarks, that in his work on the Doctrine of Final Causes, he entirely rejects the whole argument from indications of design in nature as affording any real proof of a Deity from independent reasoning; *and this with the view of upholding more powerfully the authority of the Church as the sole source of religious truth.* "In these views of the *High* Orthodoxists," continues the Professor, "we cannot but notice a singular concurrence on the part of those earnest preachers of what is termed the *Low* or Evangelical school, who profess to discard all use of human wisdom in divine things as mere carnal blindness and sinful presumption, and who can find in all the guidance of intellect or nature nothing but still-deepening darkness, till they come to the simple acceptance of the literal declarations of Scripture, where alone they conceive they can discover to any purpose the slightest real indication of the will, the perfections, or even the existence of God." (Oxford Essays, 1857, p. 179.) When the extreme of such parties are seen combining to stifle free inquiry, it behoves all friends of truth and moderation to raise their voices in protest.

country to an address to the Archbishop of Canterbury condemnatory of the book and its authors. This address was accompanied by a series of garbled extracts from the volume, intended, as was naively confessed, "to *illustrate* the noxious character of the Essays." The Rev. Dr. Irons seems, indeed, to have a special taste for this style of *illustration*, for in a list of his published works we find the following :—" An Epitome of the Bampton Lectures of the Rev. Dr. Hampden, 1858." And, again, "Fifty-two Propositions: a Letter to the Rev. Dr. Hampden, submitting to him certain Assertions, Assumptions, and Implications in his Bampton Lectures, reduced to the form of Propositions, 1848." Whether these Propositions are identical with those on the strength of which a similar outcry was raised against Dr. Hampden in 1847, I know not, and care not to inquire. They are evidently of kindred origin, proceeding equally from the same spirit of calumny and detraction. But we are assured on high authority that the misrepresentations contained in those propositions are innocent compared to the calumnies on which the recent agitation against "Essays and Reviews" was founded. Yet so it was, on the strength of these garbled extracts, wrested from their context and so arranged as entirely to conceal the real purpose of the writers—often exactly inverting their meaning, often quoting passages of undoubted truth, as the Devil quoted Scripture, for the sake of giving them some wicked or heretical signification—on the strength, I say, of this precious list of garbled and disjointed extracts the clergy were called upon to sign an address to the Archbishop, and thereby constitute themselves the judges and accusers of their brethren. Of the value to be attached to signatures so obtained, the reader may judge from the following little anecdote, for the truth of which I can vouch. A friend of mine met two clergymen of his acquaintance, one of them a rural dean, and both men of some mark in their own neighbourhood—*inter suos nobiles*. The conversation turning on Essays and Reviews, they said *they had just signed the address against the authors.* On my friend asking how they came to do it, one of them replied, "*Oh, you know, I sign everything; but I have not read them.*" The other—the rural dean—shook his head, and said, "*It was an awful book;*" but, on being further pressed as to "*which of the Essays he thought the worst?*" he confessed "*that he had only read the extracts that had been sent round and—the article in the Quarterly.*"

From this little specimen the reader may judge how signatures to addresses of this kind are obtained by touting for them indiscriminately from the clergy through the country. The readiness with which such signatures can be obtained is, indeed, a burning shame and a disgrace to those who sign, and to their order generally. "Does it not," exclaimed Archdeacon Hare, when the same sort of demonstration was made against the present Bishop of Hereford— "does it not constrain us to hang down our heads in shame, when we hear of thousands, as it would seem, of our brethren rushing eagerly to protest, to remonstrate, to sign addresses, while there is scarcely any evidence that a single one among these thousands has thought it his duty to make out carefully and conscientiously how he ought to act, and while it is too plain that hardly one of them has studied Dr. Hampden's writings with a view of forming his decision? *In what other class of men could such a thing happen?* Would it happen among lawyers? among physicians? among soldiers or sailors? among merchants? *No!* it will probably be replied: *but then the matters they are concerned in are not of such deep, universal moment, and do not peril our eternal interests.* Yet surely this very consideration ought to make us more careful, more cautious, more scrupulous, ought to teach us that, though in other things we may allow ourselves to act on plausible presumptions, yet, in these matters of awful importance, it behoves us to use all our vigilance, to strain every eye of the mind, lest we deliver an unjust, and therefore an ungodly judgment.

Whereas our agitation, which is only the more tumultuous from the want of any reasonable grounds for it, has involved us in something like a November London fog, where there is no one, except the noisy link-boys of the religious newspapers, to show us the way. Darkness is the element of fanaticism; and they who walk in darkness are sure to stumble. It is only in the light that we can walk straight forward, calmly and steadily; and so, and so alone, can we have fellowship one with another."* At the very moment that this address to the Archbishop was being circulated through the country, and gradually assuming the form of a "*Monster Petition*" against the Essayists, the world was startled by the appearance, in the public papers, of the so-called "Episcopal Manifesto"—a letter of unknown authorship, sent by the Archbishop of Canterbury to a certain Mr. Fremantle, and to which were attached the names of all the English Bishops. The exact history of this document we may possibly never know; but of its effect on the minds of the more thoughtful and better-informed among the clergy and laity, there can be no doubt. In the literary and scientific world it was at once felt to be the heaviest blow that had been ever dealt at the prestige of the English Episcopate. In the

---

* Letter to the Dean of Chichester, p. 63.

Edinburgh it was well described as a " document without precedence in the history of the English Church—the counterpart of the Papal excommunication levelled against Italian freedom, filled with menaces borrowed from the ancient days of persecution, yet abstaining from all those distinct specifications of offence which alone could justify language so vehement. It demanded the removal from their position in the Church of five distinguished clergymen (and, by implication, of hundreds), yet brought no precise charges against any of them, and intimated that none could be brought. It was an unqualified censure of a book, of which the varied sentiments and unequal merits required the most discriminating judgment. It professed to be the solemn opinion of the united bench of Bishops, and yet found its way into print through the unauthorized hands of a private clergyman. The names of the Bishops were appended so carelessly, that one of them, that of ' H. EXETER,' is now known to have been added without his knowledge, and against his wish:* two, at least,

* The mode in which the signatures of the Bishops were obtained and attached yet remains to be explained. It was stated at the time that a delay in the action of the Bishops took place in consequence of the Archbishop being called from London by the death of a near relative. But from a statement made by the Archbishop himself, it appears that his signature was the last affixed, instead of the first—so that the question is, *Who affixed the signatures?* It is probable that the

of the most distinguished of the body had published opinions exactly coinciding with those which they condemned; and two others, on the first public occasion after the manifesto had been issued, had the good sense and feeling to avow that they excepted from their censure three at least of the five persons whose position and character 'the vague anathema' had been intended to blast. It is with sincere regret that we notice this singular collapse of the Episcopal order."

The following address to Dr. Temple appeared shortly afterwards in the public papers, and may be regarded as expressing the sense of the scientific world with respect to the attempt of the Bishops to stifle free inquiry, and persecute learned discussion in the Church :—

"To the Rev. Dr. Temple.

"We, the undersigned, have read with surprise and regret a letter, in which the Archbishop of Canterbury and the other Bishops have severely censured the volume of articles entitled 'Essays and Reviews.'

---

document is not, strictly speaking, authorized; but to avoid exposure, the particulars attending it have been allowed to remain in obscurity by those who might have cleared the matter up—οὐδὲ γὰρ ἀναβιβάσασθαι οἷόν τ' εστιν αὐτῶν οὐδ' ἐλέγξαι οὐδένα. ἀλλ' ἀνάγκη ἀτεχνῶς ὥσπερ σκιαμαχεῖν ἀπολογούμενόν χτε καὶ ἐλέγχειν μηδένος ἀποκρινομένου.

"Without committing ourselves to the conclusions arrived at in the various Essays, we wish to express our sense of the value which is to be attached to inquiries conducted in a spirit so earnest and reverential, and we believe that such inquiries must tend to elicit truth, and to foster a spirit of sound religion.

"Feeling, as we do, that the discoveries in science and the general progress in thought have necessitated some modification of the views generally held on theological matters, we welcome these attempts to establish religious teaching on a firmer and broader foundation.

"While admitting each writer in the 'Essays and Reviews' is responsible only for the opinions expressed by himself, we address to you, as author of the first article, this expression of our sympathy and thanks."

The following letters appeared in the *Times*, the first, February 18th, 1861; the second, March 2nd, 1861:—

"THE EPISCOPAL MANIFESTO.

"*To the Editor of the Times.*

"SIR,—The manifesto of the Bishops which appeared in the *Times* of Saturday is a remarkable document.

"It is one of a class, and must be viewed in connection with its predecessors. On three previous occasions we have had compositions of this kind. The first was the famous episcopal protest against the elevation of Dr. Hampden to the see of Hereford. It was subscribed by some of the most conspicuous of the present members of the Bench. It ended in the humiliating spectacle of the most eminent subscriber being forced within a few weeks publicly to eat his own words, and in the reception of the so-called heretic into the episcopal circle which now avails itself of his aid to persecute others. The second was a denunciation, issued in the panic of the 'Papal aggression,' and signed by all but two of the wisest of the Bench, to prevent the assumption of English titles by the Roman Catholic hierarchy. The results of this declaration are too well known to require description. The third was a censure pronounced by the four Primates of England and Ireland on a body of High Churchmen who had ventured to condemn the proselytizing practices of Bishop Gobat. Whatever may have been the effect of the document on Bishop Gobat, it has not affected in the least degree the opinions or the ecclesiastical position of the clergymen against whom it was levelled.

"The present Manifesto has peculiarities of its own. It is an unqualified condemnation of certain opinions, without any indication of what these opinions severally are, or how widely the condemnation is meant to extend. It attacks, or appears to attack, five living clergymen, of eminent learning but diverse sentiments, in language almost amounting to a libel, without drawing any distinction between the writers, without specifying either the precise charges against them or the formularies of the Church which they are supposed to contradict, although the highest ecclesiastical tribunal in the country has of late twice affirmed that without such specification charges of this nature cannot be entertained. It intimates that the gravest doubt exists as to the possibility of visiting the publication of those opinions in the ecclesiastical courts; and yet, notwithstanding this doubt, *it ventures, without a trial, to pronounce a condemnation which nothing but the clearest legal proof could justify.* It gives no indication of the opinions of any one of the subscribing Bishops on any one of the points at issue, although it is perfectly well known that on these points many of the Bishops are widely at variance with each other, and that some of them have published opinions coincident with those contained in the book which is condemned.

"And this document, so grave in its character and its results, if it means what it says, is suddenly published without any warning to the persons accused, although some of them have the strongest claims on the courtesy and the justice of those who thus accuse them; and it first finds its way into the public journals through the hands of a country clergyman, who does not even publish the address to which it is an answer, and which alone could render it intelligible.

"I am, Sir, yours, &c.,

"ANGLICANUS."

"ESSAYS AND REVIEWS.

"*To the Editor of the Times.*

"SIR,—When the Episcopal Manifesto appeared, ten days ago, I ventured to call attention to the fact that its predecessors in past years had been either wholly inoperative, or been disclaimed within a very short period by those who had put them forth.

"The declaration of the Bishops in the Upper House of Convocation, as reported in the *Times* of to-day, has effectually done this work for the protest of the present occasion within even a shorter period than that which witnessed the retractation of the anti-Hereford protest by the Bishop of Oxford in 1847.

"The remarkable features of the present document are that it condemned, as inconsistent with the Church of England and with the Christian religion, a whole volume of the most varied character; and that this condemnation was signed by all the Bishops, though holding the most varied sentiments on those very subjects.

"Both these peculiarities are now destroyed.

"That astounding unanimity of the Bench which so delighted the ardent spirits of the Lower House of Convocation has crumbled into a chaos of discord. Two, at least, of the Bishops have declared that they except from their censure two, if not three, of the five clergymen whom the Archbishop's letter called to renounce their position in the Church, the authors of those three Essays being the very three against whom the popular panic has, in the addresses which have been circulated so freely through the country, been most actively and pointedly directed.

"I rejoice that there are still to be found Bishops who, though tardily, prefer truth to clamour, and justice to prudence. It would have been well if they had attached to the document which bore their signatures the same disclaimer of partnership with their fellow-subscribers as that which is prefixed to the volume under their consideration, and which, in fact, completely fulfils all the requirements made of the Essayists by the Bishops themselves:—

"'*It will be readily understood that the authors are responsible for their respective articles only.*

They have written in entire independence of each other, and without concert or comparison.'

"I am, Sir, yours, &c.,

"ANGLICANUS.

"*Feb.* 28."

The above may be taken as presenting the scientific and theological aspects of the Bishops' Manifesto. Dr. Deane, in the course of his able defence of Dr. Williams, well expressed the more strictly legal view of the matter. "He said it openly and distinctly, *that he had not met in the whole of his reading, with a more unbecoming or a more cowardly act than the writing of that letter.* Those were strong words, but he would justify them. The writers of the letter were persons who, by their very office, were judges of the land in matters of this kind; and should this case unfortunately travel elsewhere (to the Privy Council), they would have some of them sitting on the bench to try the question. If a collision took place in the Channel, he could not conceive the learned Judge forthwith publishing a letter in which he expressed his opinion upon the case, and consequently upon the guilt of one or other of the parties. Or supposing a letter had appeared in a newspaper, containing he knew not what treason, blasphemy, or libel, could they imagine the fifteen judges meeting to condemn that treason, blasphemy, or libel, without once calling the writer before them? He wished again to use the words of Dr. Arnold, rather than his own; and with him he would say, 'If any one has preached heresy, let him be heard before the proper judge or judges. What was wanting to be done was merely Lynch law; and they might just as well run down any other man that was unpopular with the dominant party in Oxford, and pass a *privilegium* against him, without giving him a trial. But so always, in the course of human things, *the tail labours to sting the head.*'"

After such a demonstration on the part of the Bishops, the proceedings in Convocation need excite no surprise; they served simply to exhibit the *odium theologicum* in its most virulent and repulsive form, animated by a spirit at once factious and intolerant; combining with the turbulence and violence of a popular assembly all the narrowmindedness and exclusiveness of a particular caste.* When last they met for business, this spirit consumed itself in a series of attacks on Bishops Burnet and Hoadley, which ended in the celebrated " Bangorian controversy." The account given by our great constitutional historian of the character and issue of that controversy may well claim the attention of English Churchmen now-a-days.

* See Arnold's History of Rome, vol. ii. p. 155.

"The new Government at first permitted the Convocation to hold its sittings. But they soon excited a flame which consumed themselves by an attack on Hoadley, Bishop of Bangor, who had preached a sermon abounding with those principles concerning religious liberty, of which he had long been the courageous and powerful assertor. The Lower House of Convocation thought fit to denounce, through the report of a committee, the dangerous tenets of the discourse, and of a work not long before published by the Bishop. A long and celebrated war of pens instantly commenced, known by the name of the Bangorian Controversy, managed, perhaps, on both sides, with all the chicanery of polemical writers, and disgusting both from its tediousness and from the manifest unwillingness of the disputants to speak ingenuously what they meant. But as the principles of Hoadley and his advocates appeared, in the main, little else than those of Protestantism and toleration, the sentence of the laity, in the temper that was then gaining ground as to ecclesiastical subjects, was soon pronounced in their favour, *and the High Church party discredited themselves by an opposition to what now pass for the incontrovertible truisms of religious liberty.* In the ferment of that age, it was expedient for the State to scatter a little dust over the angry insects; the Convocation was accordingly prorogued in 1717, and has never again sat for business."* Since that time it has (till recently) been called for form only. "It is, however," remarks Burke, "a part of the Constitution, and may be called out into act and energy whenever there is occasion, and *whenever those who conjure up that spirit will choose to abide the consequences.* It is wise to permit its legal existence; it is *wiser to continue its legal existence only.* So truly has prudence the entire dominion over any exercise of power committed into its hands; and yet *I have lived to see prudence and conformity to circumstances wholly set at nought in our late controversies, and treated as if they were the most contemptible and irrational of all things.*" †

We have, indeed, all "lived to see prudence and conformity to circumstances set at nought" in the ill-advised proceedings of this Convocation of 1861, which then met for the first time under royal licence since 1717. This licence had been applied for and obtained by the Bishop of London in order to enable Convocation to alter the 29th Canon, and allow parents to become sponsors for their children at Baptism. But not content with this, the more ardent spirits proceeded at once, in defiance of all prudence, and in contravention of all law, to enter upon a business to which the

* Hallam's Constitutional History of England, vol. ii. p. 394.
† Letter to the Sheriffs of Bristol.

licence of the Crown did not extend. They carried a vote of thanks to the Bishops for their letter of condemnation directed against a book, whose contents they claimed the privilege of never having read, and which, having thus condemned, they subsequently undertook to examine through a committee, the chairman of which—the notorious Archdeacon of Taunton—had been himself convicted of heresy, and had barely saved his own clerical position by availing himself at the last moment of the merely technical objection that the proceedings against him had not been commenced within the time prescribed by the Clergy Discipline Act. Truly, many a wise and thoughtful Churchman, as he reflected on this mockery of common sense and English justice, must have sighed to witness the contempt which these turbulent and fanatical ecclesiastics were bringing upon themselves and their order by this ill-considered attempt to exercise a jurisdiction which did not belong to them, and to meddle in a business which was none of theirs.

Meanwhile, the effect of all this agitation and anathematizing on the part of the clergy, was simply to increase, as was natural, the interest of the laity in the book, which, from the publication of the Bishops' Manifesto, began to sell by thousands, each edition increasing in magnitude in exact proportion to the vehemence of the outcry. A friend writing from London, March

22nd, 1861, tells me—" The excitement increases momentarily, and throws the Revival movement and everything else into the shade. No novelist was ever so celebrated as are these Essayists— thanks to the endeavours of bigots to *crush* inquiry."

CHAPTER V.

THE PROSECUTION.

THE storm of denunciation which had burst upon the Essayists was beginning to subside, when the world was again startled by the appearance in the public papers of a letter from the Bishop of Salisbury, announcing his intention to institute legal proceedings against Dr. Rowland Williams in the Court of Arches. The letter was addressed to the Venerable Archdeacon Buckle, and dated Whit-Monday, 1861. At first people could hardly believe the Bishop to be in earnest. The volume had been already in circulation more than a twelvemonth, and had excited so much hostility in various quarters, that had it contained any real contradiction to the Articles and other formularies of the Church, it would certainly have been discovered and pointed out long before. The book does not profess to treat of dogmatic theology, and the questions raised in it are of a kind altogether beside and beyond the range of the Articles. The more thoughtful and better informed among the clergy had repeatedly pointed out this, and shown that there was in reality no opposition between the Articles and the doctrines of the book. Archdeacon Hale had warned the agitators in Convocation that the only result of their fanatical outcry would be "*the confirmation, by learned authorities, of the statements most complained of in the Essays.*" Indeed, to all sufficiently acquainted with the history of English theology, it was abundantly evident that there was no statement of doctrine or fact in this volume which had not been repeatedly set forth by Divines whose deep and sincere faith in the Christian religion cannot be denied without the very worst uncharitableness, and some of whom are actually regarded as among the chief luminaries of the Church. "If there be a conspiracy," observed the writer of the article on "Essays and Reviews" in the *Edinburgh* (April, 1861), "it is one far more formidable than that of the seven Essayists. For it is a conspiracy in which half the rising generation, one quarter of the bench of Bishops, the most leading spirits of our clergy, have been, and are, and will be, engaged, whatever be the results of the present controversy. Coleridge led the way. A whole generation arose under his Germanising influence. Even Dr. Pusey swelled the ranks for a time, and still retains in his teaching traces of his former associates. The translation of Niebuhr's 'History of Rome,' with its speculations on the origin of mankind by Hare and Thirlwall, called down the thunders of the *Quarterly Review* of that day, which were answered with burning indignation and withering scorn by the two divines who had undertaken that labour of love.*

"The Critical Essay of Schleiermacher on St. Luke's Gospel was ushered into the world by a Preface of the translator, which bears on every page the unmistakable stamp of the masterly hand of the Bishop of St. David's; essay and preface alike containing almost all the principles and many of the statements, which now—whilst he declares that no amount of orthodox statement can, without express disavowal, relieve a writer from the responsibility of his connivance at previous heterodoxy—that prelate denounces as incompatible with the profession of an English clergyman. Arnold's 'Life and Letters' has been allowed to pass through as many editions as the 'Essays and Reviews,' and yet contains not only all the fundamental principles of the present volume, which have been so much attacked, but particular passages almost verbally coincident with the language of Professor Jowett or Dr. Williams on the Book of Daniel, or even of Mr. Wilson on the early Jewish history. Dean Alford's edition of the Greek Testament abounds with passages on inspiration and on the Biblical discrepancies, exactly similar to those to which allusion is made in the second, fourth,

* Vindication of Niebuhr from the charges of the *Quarterly Reviw.* See especially pp. 62—64.

and seventh Essays.* Dean Milman's successive works, with all their weight of eloquence and learning, point in the same direction; and he, we are sure, will not think that his present high station exempts him from the duty and the privilege of sympathising with those who are now struggling with the obloquy which he has triumphantly surmounted. Mr. Westcott's cautious and valuable treatise on the Canon contains, it has been truly said, more startling (and, if we choose so to regard them, more dangerous) facts about the origin of the New Testament, than are to be found in the whole of the doomed volume."

So that, even assuming that there were statements in the book which could not well be reconciled with some of the formularies, they would be abundantly justified, both in law and in fact, by the authority of learned divines—the Court of Arches having ruled "*that if a doctrine had been held without offence by eminent divines of the Church, then, though, perhaps, difficult to be reconciled with the plain meaning of the Articles of Religion, still a judge ought not to impute blame to those who held it. That which had been allowed or tolerated in the Church,*

---

* See a collection of these and other like passages from living divines, in the seasonable " Defence of Essays and Reviews " by Dr. Wild.

ought not to be questioned by that Court.* But, in the present instance, no such justification was necessary. The questions raised by the Essayists are, for the most part, altogether *dehors* both the Articles of Religion and the Book of Common Prayer. "It would almost seem," observes the writer just cited, "as if, providentially, the confessions of most Protestant—indeed, we may say, of most Christian churches, had been drawn up at a time when, public and ecclesiastical attention being fixed on other matters, the doors had been left wide open to the questions which a later and critical age was sure to raise into high importance. *In spite of all the declamations on the subject, no passage has ever yet been pointed out in any of the five clerical Essayists which contradicts any of the formularies of the Church in a degree at all comparable to the direct collision which exists between the High Church party and the Articles, between the Low Church party and the Prayer-book.*† Dr. Pusey was, for three years, suspended from preaching, Archdeacon Denison was, for three years, pursued by the relentless Ditcher, as having broken faith, the one with the thirty-first,

---

* Burder *v.* Heath (Judgment).

† "We except from our consideration the lay and the deceased contributors; not that we wish to prejudge the question in either instance, but that we desire to simplify the case by reducing it to a practical result."

and the other with the twenty-ninth Article, respectively aimed against the Eucharistic Sacrifice and the Eucharistic Presence. The Baptismal Service and the Collects never could have been written by those who hold the ordinary Puritanical language on Baptism and on Justification. On these points the standards of the Church have given us its mind in express, if not in distinct, terms, and (in the case of the High Church party) with a special view to their particular case. *But, on the questions now debated, Articles and Prayer-book are alike silent.* There is no Article on Inspiration. The word occurs only once* throughout the formularies—namely,

---

* It occurs also, in the same sense, in the thirteenth Article, " Works done before the *Inspiration* of Christ's Spirit," and in the Collect for the Fifth Sunday after Easter—" O Lord, from whom all good things do come, grant to us Thy humble servants, that by Thy holy *inspiration* we may think those things that be good, and by Thy merciful guiding may perform the same, through our Lord Jesus Christ."

"It has been often remarked," observes Mr. Cretien, "that the word *inspiration* is employed in the Prayer-book only to express the action of the Holy Spirit on the mind and heart of the believer. It has not been so often observed, that even in these instances the word is of comparatively recent introduction. It occurs in the Ante-Communion Collect, and in the Collect for the Fifth Sunday after Easter. In the first of these places the Latin of the Sarum Liturgy has *infusio;* in the second, the Latin is, *Te inspirante.* The term occurs twice in our English Bibles. In one of these passages (Job xxxii. 8) its use is exactly the same as in the Prayer-book : '*There is a spirit in man, and the inspiration of the Almighty giveth them*

in the noble Collect which precedes the Communion Service, where it is used in the sense (in which alone it could be considered in a court of law) of the Divine influence on the hearts of all believers. *The technical use of the word, as equivalent to supernatural dictation, was not even known at the time when the English Formularies were composed. It first appears in this sense in the Helvetic Confession of* 1675. The one Article on the subject of the Bible (the sixth) excludes other authorities from a rank co-ordinate with Scripture ; *but of Scripture itself asserts no more than all the English Essayists and all the German Theologians have gladly—we will not say conceded to it, but—claimed for it.* The fact of the preservation of the ancient Jewish canon, which no modern scholar has ever doubted, is recognized, but without a word on the date, authority, or interpretation of any one of the books. On the question whether Job and Jonah be historical or allegorical, theologians may dispute as they have always disputed; but the Church of England has not spoken, any more than the Catholic Church of old spoke in the Four Councils, or (we

---

understanding.' The other place is the important text, 2 Tim. iii. 16, in which the word is introduced only by a partial mistranslation. There seems to be no Greek word answering to *inspiration;* in a theolgical sense, θεοπνευστία is, I believe, a mere barbarism."—*Sermons on Inspiration,* p. 179, Note xviii. See Appendix, Note B.

may add) any more than the Church of Rome has spoken in the Council of Trent. . . . . . On the New Testament the language of the Formularies is, if possible, even more open. Mr. Westcott,* whose learning and candour on the subject of the canon of Scripture give to his opinion unusual weight, well observes that the sixth Article distinctly recognizes books of whose authority there was, and others ' of whose authority there was never any doubt in the Church,' and promotes the latter alone to the full rank of ' Holy Scripture,' though in a later clause, and in a looser sense of the word, it concedes the title of canonical to all such ' as are commonly received and believed.' ' It seems impossible,' says Mr. Westcott, ' to avoid the conclusion that the framers of the Articles intended to leave a freedom of judgment on a point on which the greatest of the Continental Reformers and even of Romish scholars were divided. . . . . . Of this freedom,' he continues, ' the great writers of the Church of England have not availed themselves.' But it is a freedom which does not lapse by neglect. It is a freedom which, even according to the strictest letter of the law, justified Archbishop Howley in receiving Arnold, though he rejected the Epistle to the Hebrews,

---

* Dictionary of the Bible, p. 268. The interpretation of the Article is the only mode of escape from a grave historical error.

and which would have justified Archbishop Parker in receiving Calvin, though he doubted the authenticity of the Second Epistle of St. Peter."

"On the subject of external and internal evidence, the silence of the Formularies is still more impressive. There is no Article which bears, even remotely, on these most interesting topics. There is no definition of a miracle. There is no definition of a prophecy. Philosophical questions of the highest consequence may be raised concerning both. Paley and Coleridge, Elliott and Alford, may contradict each other and every one else. They are free to do so. *The Reformers of the sixteenth century were wiser in their generation than the Bishops of the nineteenth century have been in ours. They knew, or they were guided by a higher wisdom than their own to the concluclusion, that there are subjects which ecclesiastical decrees cannot control or touch; that what commends itself as proof to one age is repulsive to another; that the processes by which the human race holds communion with the infinite are too delicate, too complex, too subtle, to be comprised within the formula of any single age or any single school.*"

Indeed, it was admitted on all hands—tacitly and with reluctance by some, openly and thankfully by others—that there was nothing in the book which impugned the Articles of the Church, or which could by any ingenuity be distorted into an ecclesiastical offence. So far as the law was concerned, the Essayists were held to be quite unassailable. This point being established, it was conceived beyond all gainsaying, the Whitsuntide announcement of the Bishop of Salisbury, that he had determined to proceed against Dr. Williams in the Court of Arches, created no little surprise and astonishment. The first impression created by that announcement was, I say, a feeling of simple wonder and amazement, which, however, in the minds of the liberal party, soon gave place to feelings of the most lively indignation when they called to mind the *enormous* latitude which the Bishop had claimed for himself and his party in the interpretation of the twenty-ninth Article respecting the Real Presence in the Eucharist. The direct collision which exists between the High Church party and the Articles, between the Low Church party and the Prayer-book, we have already noticed. Once apply a rigid rule of construction, and the Articles on General Councils, on the Royal Supremacy, on the Sacraments, on Justification, must close the door as effectually against the Bishop of Salisbury and his admirers as the words of the Baptismal Thanksgiving would close it against the Low Church Bishops and the whole Evangelical party. Both these great parties owe in fact their very existence in the Church of England to that sort of mutual *compromise* which has been well described as the peculiar characteristic of our country, whose distinguishing excellence has always been a strong sense of practical unity amidst the utmost confusion of theoretical contradictions.* It is only, in fact, a *latitudinarian* principle of interpretation which enables the Church to receive the subscriptions and to tolerate the differences of both parties equally. These general considerations and the established practice of the Church, ought surely for very shame to have restrained any Bishop from saying or doing anything against the only principle of interpretation on which his own position could be for one moment defended. But in the case of the Bishop of Salisbury these general considerations derive a peculiar force and a personal application from an incident which occurred in 1856, on the decision of the Bath case. It appears that from the moment of his elevation to the episcopate his Lordship's connection with the new or Tractarian school of the old High Church party had excited in the minds of certain of his Evangelical clergy no small suspicion and mistrust, which feelings were greatly strengthened, and expressed in a very remarkable manner, on the decision of the Archbishop of Canterbury in the case of Arch-

* Edin. Rev. July, 1850.

deacon Denison. On that occasion the Archdeacon, it will be remembered, was convicted of having maintained, in direct contradiction to the twenty-ninth Article, these two propositions:—"*That to all who come to the Lord's table—to those who eat and drink worthily, and to those who eat and drink unworthily, the body and blood of Christ are given; and that by all who come to the Lord's table, by those who eat and drink worthily, and by those who eat and drink unworthily, the body and blood of Christ are received.*" A more direct contradiction than this to an Article which treats "*Of the wicked which eat not the body of Christ in the use of the Lord's Supper*," it is, indeed, impossible to imagine. But as the Archdeacon refused to acknowledge this and to revoke his error, he was convicted of heresy by the Court, and his deprivation was pronounced accordingly. Whereupon a body of ultra High Churchmen, and amongst them two of the Bishop's chaplains, put forth a declaration, in which they repeated, in fact, the offence condemned by the Court, protesting against its decision, and appealing from its jurisdiction in the following terms:—"We hereby protest earnestly against so much of the opinion of his Grace the Archbishop of Canterbury, in the case of 'Ditcher *v.* Denison,' as implies directly or indirectly, that such statements as we have cited above* are repugnant to the doctrine of the Thirty-nine Articles.

"And we appeal from the said opinion, decision, or sentence of his Grace, in the first instance, to a free and lawful synod of the Bishops of the province of Canterbury; and then, if need be, to a free and lawful synod of all the churches of our communion, when such by God's mercy may be had."

That declaration and protest gave, it appears, great offence to the Evangelical party in the diocese, who were celebrating a sort of triumph over the unfortunate Archdeacon, and rejoicing in the anticipation of future victories over his party in the Church. The names of the Bishop's two chaplains they naturally regarded as expressing indirectly his own opinion on the issue of the case, and they determined, accordingly, to seek some explanation from his Lordship on the subject. This they did by means of the following address, to which were attached the names of no less than forty-three of the clergy from the single archdeaconry of Dorset:—

"We, the undersigned clergymen of the archdeaconry of Dorset, beg most respectfully to

---

* The reference is to a list of extracts from divines of Archbishop Laud's school—a school whose own claims to toleration in the Church of England can only be consistently maintained on the broadest and most *latitudinarian* interpretation of our Articles.

represent to your Lordship the extreme pain with which we have seen the names of two of your Lordship's chaplains attached to a certain public protest against the recent decision of his Grace the Archbishop of Canterbury in the case of Archdeacon Denison. It would be a great relief to our minds if some step were taken to assure us that they have acted without your Lordship's sanction, in thus declaring themselves directly opposed to what has been solemnly, and, as we believe, most rightfully pronounced to be the doctrine of the Church of England."

To this address the Bishop replied in a letter, dated, "The Palace, Salisbury, Wednesday in Ember Week, 1856," remarkable chiefly for the enormous *latitude* of interpretation which, in face of the decision on the Bath case, his Lordship claims therein for himself and his party, and which reminds us very forcibly of the claim of Mr. Oakeley "*to hold all Romish doctrine*" consistently with his subscription to the Articles of the English Church. He declines to satisfy the memorialists directly as to his part in the protest referred to, "meeting their request with the mere expression of his regret that they should have allowed themselves to make it."

"*As long*" (says his Lordship) "*as my chaplains keep themselves within the limits fixed by our Church, I do not feel at liberty to impose upon their opinions more restraint than the Church has imposed upon you and the rest of the clergy.*" This must be acknowledged to be a somewhat extraordinary defence of the conduct of these gentlemen, who had just been parading, in a public declaration, their adhesion to a doctrine in direct contradiction to the Articles of the Church. His Lordship concludes with an exhortation to *charity*, which we would fain hope both he and his memorialists have not forgotten in the heat of later controversy. "*And now, in the earnest hope that all my clergy will endeavour to combine with a loyal jealousy for God's truth a spirit of forbearance and candour, and a desire, above all things, to do to others as they would be done by, I would entreat you, and through you all our brethren who minister in this diocese, to make the gracious purpose of our God, as declared by St. Paul, the life of your whole conversation—'Speaking the truth in love, let us grow up unto Him in all things.'*

"I remain your faithful brother and fellow-servant in the Lord,—

"W. K. SARUM."

After so large a claim for toleration in his own behalf and that of his party in the Church, and with so apparently just an appreciation of the spirit of Christian charity and forbearance, we cannot but regret to find the Bishop of Salisbury the first to seek to apply against an eminent clergyman in his diocese a rigid interpretation of the Formularies, such as, if only applied generally, would at once exclude both him and the whole High and Low Church parties from that toleration and consideration which they at present enjoy in what has been hitherto justly regarded as the most tolerant and Catholic of all communions—the National Church of England. Yet so it was, in an evil hour for himself and the peace of the Church, the Bishop announced, as we have seen, his ill-advised intention to institute legal proceedings against Dr. Williams for his review of Baron Bunsen's "Biblical Researches," thereby proclaiming between reason and faith an unholy and unnatural war, of which may God avert the dangers, and overrule to the establishment of the truth and the promotion of His glory the yet unknown consequences!

The example thus set by the Bishop of Salisbury was followed by a clergyman of the name of Fendall, who has obtained thereby an unenviable notoriety as the "voluntary promoter" of a similar suit against Mr. Wilson for his Essay on the National Church. That it should lie in the power of any private person in a diocese to put a clergyman, however eminent and distinguished for piety and learning, on his defence for heresy, seems monstrous enough. It is one of those anomalies of ecclesiastical law which it behoves the Legislature to put an end to. The good sense and good feeling of the clergy have hitherto prevented them from abusing this power; but its present odious and most offensive application abundantly proves the necessity for the intervention of the Legislature in order to prevent for the future the possibility of the recurrence of so truly scandalous and disgraceful a proceeding.

The case of Dr. Williams came on for hearing in the Arches Court, December 19th, 1861; that of Mr. Wilson, February 22nd, 1862. In both the admissibility of the articles of objection was opposed, and it was contended that no *primâ facie* ground had been, or could be, shown for the prosecution. In Dr. Williams's case, the pleadings were reported at considerable length in the *Guardian* and *Record;* and Mr. Fitzjames Stephen and Dr. Phillimore, the counsel respectively for the defence and prosecution,[*] have since published their speeches on the occasion. In Mr. Wilson's case the pleadings, though of equal importance, have not been as yet so fully reported. The reports of the *Guardian* and *Record* were very meagre, and altogether un-

---

[*] Dr. Phillimore (Q.C.), Mr. Coleridge (Q.C.), and Dr. Swabey appeared on behalf of the Bishop of Salisbury; Dr. Deane (Q.C.) and Mr. Fitzjames Stephen for Dr Williams. The counsel were the same in Mr. Wilson's case, with the exception of Mr. Coleridge, who was not retained again by the prosecution.

worthy of the occasion. To supply this defect here would be beyond the limits of the present sketch. Suffice it to say, that in both cases the object of the prosecution was the same—namely, *to narrow the range of theological speculation within the limits already prescribed to it by the Articles and other formularies of the Church.* This they sought to effect by a rigid application of the *letter* of the formularies altogether alien and opposed to their true spirit and intent.*

* " If ever there were characters who would naturally have been inclined to gather within the sweep of their institutions as large a mass of supporters as possible, they were the two first Protestant primates, Cranmer and Parker, and, above all, the great Protestant Queen, under whom the whole system was first compacted together. Without ascribing to them any remote prevision, or even any deliberate intention, they could hardly fail, by the very force of their nature, to accomplish the purpose which Fuller ascribes to their work, in language not inapposite to the circumstances of the present day : ' Some,' says that quaint and original writer, in speaking of the Thirty-nine Articles, ' have unjustly taxed the composers for too great favour extended in their large expressions clean 'through the contexture of these Articles, which should have tied men's consciences up closer, in stricter and more particularizing propositions ; which, indeed, proceeded from their commendable moderation : *children's clothes ought to be made of the biggest, because afterwards their bodies will grow up to their garments.* Thus, the Articles of the English Protestant Church, in the infancy thereof, they thought good to draw up in general terms, foreseeing that posterity would grow up to fill the same —I mean, these holy men did prudently prediscover that differences in judgment would unavoidably happen in the Church, and were loath to unchurch any and drive them off

Every word in them which could, by any ingenuity, be construed in opposition to some statement of the Essayists, was made the occasion of a charge of heresy; and where the *letter* of the Articles failed, an *inference* was never wanting which might be brought to bear, if not against what had been actually said, at least against the *interpretation* put by the prosecution on the author's words. By means of this artifice the very points on which, as we have remarked, the *silence* of our formularies is most significant and impressive, were made the grounds of the most serious charges in the indictment, and of the most violent attack in the pleadings.

On all the great questions of the day respecting the inspiration and interpretation of Scripture, the character of prophecy, the definition of miracles, the value of evidence, and the force of subscription,—questions all of them hitherto discussed with the greatest freedom by theologians, and which do not admit of any exact and formal determination—on all these the prosecution had a theory of their own, which they taxed their ingenuity to the utmost to foist upon the Church as the teaching of the Articles and Prayer-book. The

---

from an ecclesiastical communion for such petty differences; *which made them plan the Articles in comprehensive words, to take in all who, differing in the branches, meet in the root of the same religion.*' "—*Edinburgh Review*, July, 1850 (Article on the Gorham Controversy, p. 267).

utter sophistry of this proceeding was ably exposed by Dr. Deane and Mr. Stephen. The latter especially won great credit by the very learned, well reasoned, and eloquent speeches, which he delivered with the most telling effect on the occasion. " We stand," he said, " by the Articles of the Church of England, and by the Rubrics and Formularies. Show us that we have contradicted them, and that will put an end to the matter ; *but do not foist upon us a theory of your own, and try to give that theory the force of law.*" With respect to the question of inspiration, which we may regard as the cardinal question at issue, he observed, "The real gist and essence of the whole prosecution lies in this : *They want to draw a line between the influence which produced the Holy Scriptures and the other influences of the Holy Ghost.* Their wish is, I say, to draw a line between them, which the Prayer-Book does not draw, which the Articles do not draw, and which, in accordance with the Articles and Prayer-Book, Dr. Williams has not ventured to draw, and which I defy any living creature to draw upon any authorities laid down by the Church of England.* That is the real question in issue upon this case ; and I think I shall show you that, so far from its being heretical for any one to believe that the Holy Spirit

---

* See Appendix, Note B.

o

of God operates in the present day, and operates upon us who are now here, in our various situations and callings in life,—the continuance of that operation is a fundamental doctrine of the Church, which cannot be taken away without converting one-half of the services of the Church into something not at all unlike a blasphemous mockery."*

The contention for the prosecution, on the other hand, was " that the Church of England had held the doctrine of *Plenary Inspiration* always." " The necessary doctrine of the Church, for which we contend," said Dr. Phillimore, " is what is called *plenary inspiration;*" by which he appears to mean that the Bible does not *contain* merely, but *constitutes* and actually *is*, the very " Word of God," absolutely and in all its parts infallibly true, without any mixture of human error or infirmity. In denying this he contended that Dr. Williams had denied the doctrine of the Church, and virtually excluded himself from her ministry. But a few days elapse, and the learned counsel seems meanwhile not only to have changed his opinion, but to have entirely forgotten his former contention; for in reply to a question put to him by Dr. Lushington, in Mr. Wilson's case, as to *" whether he held that it was the doctrine of the Church of England that*

---

* Stephen's Defence of Dr. Williams, p. 206.

every word contained in the canonical books was true," he said, "*He had never contended for the doctrine of the plenary inspiration of the Scriptures.*"* He appears, in fact, to have been taken by surprise, and thrown completely off his guard by the question, and so to have fallen unawares into this glaring contradiction, disclosing thereby the true object of the prosecution, which was not in reality to maintain the authority of Scripture, but of the Church; to substitute the traditions of the hierarchy for the "pure Word of God" contained in Holy Scripture, and speaking to all good men of all ages in the still small voice of reason and of conscience. It is, indeed, not a little curious to

---

* It may not be out of place to observe here, that "Plenary Inspiration," with which the prosecution thus plays fast and loose, may be understood in two senses—" plenary " as equivalent to "literal," which is abandoned; and "plenary" as equivalent to "sufficient," which is not denied by Dr. Williams or Mr. Wilson. The *sufficiency* of inspiration is also twofold— 1. Sufficiency for the providential object of the Scriptures; 2. Sufficiency relative to the Church, in a Protestant sense, as affording a Divine rule of faith and practice in the Bible, exclusive of any supplementary or concurrent oral tradition, as supposed in the Romish Church. (*Cf.* Con. Trident. Sessio Quarta.) In this sense the "plenary inspiration" and "canonical authority" of the Scriptures are fully admitted by the Essayists. It is submitted that this admission quite satisfies the requirements of our Formularies, and ought, in all justice, to relieve Dr. Williams and Mr. Wilson from the imputation of any intention to disparage the Divine inspiration and authority of Holy Scripture.

notice how the sacerdotal party, who are now for their own purposes endeavouring to conciliate the Evangelicals by an affected reverence for the letter of Scripture, were, not many years ago, exaggerating the difficulties and questioning the *sufficiency* of Scripture, in order to recommend more plausibly the guidance of a traditionally received authoritative interpretation of it.

The manner in which this fallacy was exposed by Dr. Arnold is very suggestive, and specially significant with respect to the present controversy. "This argument (from the difficulties of Scripture) was pressed," he observes, "by Mr. Newman; and it was conducted, as may be supposed, with great ingenuity, but with a recklessness of consequences, or an ignorance of mankind, truly astonishing; for he brought forward all the difficulties and differences which can be found in the Scripture narratives, displayed them in their most glaring form, and merely observed, that as those with whom he was arguing could not solve these difficulties, but yet believed the Scriptures no less in spite of them, so the apparent unreasonableness of his doctrine about the priesthood was no ground why it should be rejected—a method of argument most blameable in any Christian to adopt towards his brethren; for what if their faith, being thus vehemently strained, were to give way under the experiment; and if, being convinced that the Scriptures were not more reasonable than Mr. Newman's system, they were to end with believing, not both, but neither?

"Therefore the question is one of no small anxiety and interest; *and it is not idly nor wantonly that we must speak the truth upon it, even if that may to some seem startling;* for by God's blessing, if we go boldly forward wherever truth shall lead us, our course need not be interrupted, neither shall a single hair of our faith perish.

"It is very true that our position with respect to the Scriptures is not in all points the same as our fathers'. For sixteen hundred years nearly, while physical science, and history, and chronology, and criticism, were all in a state of torpor, the questions which now present themselves to our minds could not from the nature of the case arise. When they did arise, they came forward into notice gradually: first, the discoveries in astronomy excited uneasiness; then, as men began to read more critically, differences in the several Scripture narratives of the same thing awakened attention; *more lately, the greater knowledge which has been gained of history, and of language, and in all respects the more careful inquiry to which all ancient records have been submitted, have brought other difficulties to light, and some sort of answer must be given to them.* Mr. Newman, as we have seen, has made use of these difficulties much as the Romanists have used the doctrine of the Trinity when arguing with Trinitarians in defence of transubstantiation. The Romanists said—'Here are all these inexplicable difficulties to the doctrine of the Trinity, yet you believe it.' So Mr. Newman argues with those who hold the plenary inspiration of Scripture, that if they believe that, in spite of all the difficulties which beset it, they may as well believe his doctrine of the priesthood; and many, if I mistake not, alarmed by his representations, have actually embraced his opinions.

"It has unfortunately happened that the difficulties of the Scriptures have been generally treated as objections to the truth of Christianity; as such they have been pressed by adversaries, and as such Christian writers have replied to them.

"But do we give to any narrative in the world, to any statement verbal or written, no other alternative than that it must be either infallible or unworthy of belief? Is not such an alternative so extravagant as to be a complete *reductio ad absurdum?* And yet such is the alternative which men seem generally to have admitted in considering the Scripture narratives: if a single error can be discovered, it is supposed to be fatal to the credibility of the whole.

"*This has arisen from an unwarranted interpretation of the word 'inspiration,' and by a still more unwarranted inference.* An inspired work is supposed to mean a work to which God has communicated his own perfections; so that the slightest error or defect of any kind in it is inconceivable, and that which is other than perfect in all points cannot be inspired. This is the unwarranted interpretation of the word 'inspiration.' But then follows the more unwarranted inference,—*If all the Scripture is not inspired, Christianity cannot be true*—an inference which is absolutely entitled to no other consideration than what it may seem to derive from the number of those who have either openly or tacitly maintained it.

" So much for the unwarranted inference, that if the Scripture histories are not inspired, the great facts of the Christian revelation cannot be maintained. But it is no less an unwarranted interpretation of the term 'inspiration,' to suppose that it is equivalent to a communication of the Divine perfections. Surely many of our words, and many of our actions, are spoken and done by the inspiration of God's Spirit, without whom we can do nothing acceptable to God. Yet, does the Holy Spirit so inspire us as to communicate to us His own perfections? Are our best words or works utterly free from error or from sin? *All inspiration does not then destroy the human and fallible part in the nature which it inspires; it does not change man into God.*

"In one man, indeed, it was otherwise; but He was both God and man. To Him the Spirit was given without measure; and as His life was without sin, so His words were without error. But to all others the Spirit has been given by measure—in almost infinitely different measure it is true; the difference between the inspiration of the common, and perhaps unworthy Christian, who merely said that 'Jesus was the Lord,' and that of Moses, or St. Paul and St. John, is almost to our eyes beyond measuring. Still the position remains, *that the highest degree of inspiration given to man has still suffered to exist along with it a portion of human fallibility and corruption.*" *

Such is Dr. Arnold's solution of the difficulty suggested by the sophistical objections to the sufficiency of Holy Scripture, urged by the very party who are now prosecuting Dr. Williams and Mr. Wilson for maintaining against them the same reasonable view of the sacred writings—for recognizing with Arnold a "human and fallible" element in the composition of the records of the earlier manifestations of God to man.

The authority of Arnold becomes too the more important in relation to the present controversy, from the use which the counsel for the prosecution have not hesitated to make of his name and writings. The feelings of burning indignation

---

* Sermons, vol. iv. pp. 480—488.

and sovereign contempt which would have filled the soul of that great man had he been spared to witness, or perchance to become himself the object of so shameless an attempt to stifle all free inquiry and fair discussion in the Church, may be imagined by those who knew him best. And is it to be endured, that now, within twenty years of his death, his name should be profaned, and his writings abused, to serve that very bigotry and intolerance of which he was through life the most determined and uncompromising opponent? It is true, indeed, that he was removed from among us before he had time to mature and develop his views on many of the great questions discussed in "Essays and Reviews;" but it is not the less true and the more remarkable, that his mind had notwithstanding already anticipated almost all the conclusions at which the Essayists have arrived; more particularly as regards the Inspiration of Scripture, the character of Prophecy, the authorship of the Book of Daniel, the figurative language of many parts of the Bible, the purely moral object and efficacy of the sacraments, the terms of communion and the force of subscription—on all these points the writings of Arnold furnish the clearest evidence that his views were substantially identical with those of the Essayists.

On the subject of "Inspiration," his most mature views may be gathered from the passage just cited. We shall find the same remarkable coincidence between him and the Essayists on the character of ancient Prophecy as a witness to the kingdom of God. With Dr. Williams, as we have seen, the prophetic gift consists in the power of seeing the ideal in the actual, or of tracing the Divine government in the movements of men, rather than in an actual foresight of the future, and anticipation of its events. Let us now turn to Arnold's Sermons on the Interpretation of Prophecy. "Now, first of all," he observes, "it is a very misleading notion of Prophecy, if we regard it as an anticipation of history," — a mere prognostication of future events. "History, in our common sense of the term, is busy with particular nations, times, places, actions, and even persons. If in this sense Prophecy were a history written beforehand, it would alter the very condition of humanity, by removing from us our uncertainty as to the future; it would make us acquainted with those times and seasons which the Father hath put in his own power. It is anticipated history, not in our common sense of the word, but in another and far higher sense:" *i. e.*, as he goes on to explain, "*as an enunciation of those eternal principles by which all history is determined.*"*

---

* Sermons, vol. i. p. 376. See also Stanley's Sermons and Essays on the Apostolic Age, p. 129; Sinai and Palestine, p. 272.

To the same effect remarks Mr. Wilson. "Prophecy, in the sense of an enunciation of a law, does not consist in prediction of particulars, while it implies insight and forthtelling. And yet the declaration of a universal law may be clothed in a description of particulars, and even be applicable to different sets of particulars. But it is unimportant to such forthtelling or enunciation, that this description should be perfectly accurate in all its traits, or fit equally in all its applications; it is also not essential to the enunciation of a law through a special instance, that it should be prophetic in the ordinary acceptation of that word, that is, have been set forth before the historical occurrence of the illustrative event. Hence it is obvious that Prophecy, in this which is conceived to be the higher sense of the word, is independent of chronological order, and the absence of evidence as to its date does not detract from its value as a vehicle of spiritual truth."*

So far respecting the character of Hebrew Prophecy generally. We next come to the question of the date and authorship of the Book of Daniel.

On this head, Dr. Williams observes, "The truth seems, that starting, like many a patriot

---

* Introduction to a Brief Examination of Prevalent Opinions on Inspiration, p. xxxvi. See Appendix, Note G.

bard of our own, from a name traditionally sacred, the writer used it with no deceptive intention, as a dramatic form which dignified his encouragement of his countrymen in their great struggle against Antiochus. The original place of the book, amongst the later Hagiographa of the Jewish canon, and the absence of any mention of it by the Son of Sirach, strikingly confirm this view of its origin; and, if some obscurity rests upon details, the general conclusion, that the book contains no predictions, except by analogy and type, can hardly be gainsaid."

To the same effect writes Dr. Arnold to Sir Thomas Pasley, Bart., January 25th, 1840:—
"I am very glad indeed that you like my Prophecy Sermons: the points in particular on which I did not wish to enter, if I could help it, but which very likely I shall be forced to touch on, relate to the latter chapters of Daniel, which, if genuine, would be a clear exception to my canon of interpretation, as there can be no reasonable spiritual meaning made out of the Kings of the North and South. But I have long thought that the greater part of the Book of Daniel is most certainly a very late work, of the time of Maccabeus; and the pretended prophecy about the Kings of Grecia and Persia, and of the North and South, is mere history, like the

poetical prophecies in Virgil and elsewhere. In fact, you can trace distinctly the date when it was written, because the events up to the date are given with historical minuteness, totally unlike the character of real prophecy, and beyond that date all is imaginary. It is curious, that when there was so allowed a proof of the existence of apocryphal writings, under the name of the Book of Daniel, as the stories of the apocryphal Esther, Susanna, and Bel and the Dragon—those should have been rejected, because they were only known in the Greek translation; and the rest, because it happened to be in Chaldee, was received at once in the lump, and defended as a matter of faith. But the self-same criticism which has established the authenticity of St. John's Gospel against all questionings, does, I think, equally prove the non-authenticity of great part of Daniel: that there may be genuine fragments in it, is very likely." *

We come now to the charges on the Sacraments, which are, perhaps, the most extraordinary of all those made against Dr. Williams. With respect to the subject of Baptism, the prosecution object to the statement—" The first Christians held that the heart was purified by faith; the accompanying symbol, water, became

* Stanley's Life, vol. ii. p. 194.

by degrees the instrument of purification." Herein they charge Dr. Williams with affirming "*that the element of water is not a divinely ordained means whereby we receive the spiritual grace in the Sacrament of Baptism.*" But what is this but a revival, and that, too, in an exaggerated and most repulsive form, of the old exploded *opus operatum* theory of the Church of Rome? This is, I believe, the first time that a Bishop of the Church of England, or, indeed, of any Church, reformed or unreformed, has been known seriously to maintain, "that the *element of water* is the divinely ordained means whereby we receive the spiritual grace in the Sacrament of Baptism." The theory of the Church of Rome, of which the theory of the prosecution is an exaggeration, makes the element of water not, indeed, the means, but *one* of the divinely ordained constituents of the rite whereby we receive the spiritual grace in the Sacrament of Baptism. It is founded on the dictum of St. Augustine, "*Accedit verbum ad elementum, et fit Sacramentum,*" which appears to be an adaptation of the then popular belief respecting the power of incantations and charms to the subject of religion.* The Church of England, on the contrary, makes the efficacy of the sacraments depend on the inward disposition and mind of

---

* See Bishop Hampden's Bampton Lectures, Lect. VII.

the recipient—"*In such only as worthily receive the same have they a wholesome effect or operation.*" "The virtue of the sacraments," observes Bishop Burnet, "being put in the *worthy receiving*, excludes the doctrine of *opus operatum*, as formally as if it had been expressly condemned." *

Let us now turn to Dr. Arnold, where he speaks of the views of the first Christians respecting the efficacy of Baptism. As an evidence of these he takes the Epistle of Barnabas, which, he remarks, "is directed mainly against the notions of the Judaizers. . . . . . It is true he speaks of Baptism under the name of 'water,' and applies to it several passages in the Old Testament, which speak of 'streams of water,' 'living springs,' &c. And from these expressions, it might be supposed that he was laying a stress on the outward act of baptism. For instance, the following words might be quoted as identifying baptism with regeneration:—'We go down to the water full of sins and filthiness, and we come up with our hearts bringing forth fruit; having fear and hope towards Jesus through the Spirit.' This, and other such passages, serve admirably well, when quoted separately, to make it appear that Barnabas held the Judaizing notions of the mystical virtue of the sacraments;

* Burnet on Article XXV.

but when we compare his strong language as to the utter worthlessness of the outward act of circumcision, and as to the circumcision of the heart being the only thing intended by the commandment, it is quite clear that, by parity of reasoning, the whole importance of baptism in his eyes must have consisted in the real change of heart which it implied, and the change of life of which it was the beginning; *and that the ceremony of baptizing with water was merely a symbol of the great and important change which a man underwent in passing from a state of heathenism to Christianity.* In this sense baptism, as synonymous with an admission to the benefits and promises of the Christian Church, could not be spoken of too highly; it was truly the turning point of a man's whole existence from evil to good. And in the time of Barnabas, when the real change involved in the act of baptism was so striking, and the superstitions connected with it had not as yet had full time to grow up, any one might speak of it as Barnabas has spoken, without suspecting that his words could be misinterpreted. St. Peter himself says,—'Baptism does now save us;' and it seems to me rather an instance of God's abundant goodness to hinder the Scriptures from giving any countenance to the Judaizing superstitions, than a necessary caution on the writer's part to save himself from misinterpretation, when he adds expressly, 'not the putting away the filth of the flesh, but the answer of a good conscience toward God.'

"It should be always remembered that the superstition of the Judaizers consists not in their reverence for the sacraments, which Christ appointed as great instruments of good to His Church; but in their having drawn off men's attention from the important part both of Baptism and the Lord's Supper to that which is external: to regard God's grace not as conveyed by them morally, because the joining Christ's Church in the first instance, and the constantly refreshing our communion with it afterwards, are actions highly beneficial to our moral nature; but as conveyed by them after the manner of a charm, the virtue being communicated by the water and the bread and wine, in consequence of a virtue first communicated to them by certain words of consecration pronounced by a priest. *It is the famous ' Accidit verbum ad elementum et fit sacramentum,' which contains the essence of the unchristian and most mischievous view of the sacraments entertained by the Romish and Anglican popery.* And, in order to show that the early Christian writers favour this notion, it is not enough to show that they speak strongly of the benefits of the sacraments; for in this the Scriptures and almost all true Christians would agree with them: but it must further be made evident that they lay the stress on the virtue communicated by the outward elements, after those elements have been first consecrated by certain formal words repeated by a priest. Unless they can be proved to hold this, we may interpret their language rather as agreeing with that of Christ and His Apostles, than as countenancing the superstition of the Judaizers." *

With respect to the heading in our English Bibles of the tenth chapter of the First Epistle to the Corinthians—"*The Jews' sacraments types of ours*"—Dr. Arnold observes: "Here is the self-same error, of making the outward rites or facts of the Jewish religion *subordinate* to the outward rites of ours, instead of regarding them both as *co-ordinate with one another*, and *subordinate* to some spiritual reality, of which both alike are but signs. In the passages referred to, St. Paul is showing that outward rites are no security for the existence of the real thing which they typify. Christians have been baptized with water, as an introduction into Christ's service; the Israelites passed through water also, as an introduction to their becoming God's people and receiving His law. Christians eat bread and drink wine, in token of their being united to their Lord and Saviour; and so the Israelites ate manna and drank of the rock, that manna and rock representing Christ their Lord, who

---

* Fragment on the Church, pp. 60—64.

was with them all their way, just as the bread and the wine of the Lord's Supper represent Him now. But Israel, notwithstanding these outward tokens of their belonging to God and depending on Him, sinned and fell; and, notwithstanding our outward tokens, the same may be our case if we are not watchful. It is altering the whole scope of the passage to say that it represents the Jews' sacraments as types of ours; as if our sacraments, any more than theirs, were necessarily or in themselves a reality. *The drift of the passage is not to magnify the sacraments, but to prevent us from superstitiously trusting to them.* The Jews had their sacraments, as we have ours, and both are types of the same thing; but the type in their case did not prevent them from forfeiting the substance, neither will it in ours.

"So again, when St. John records so earnestly his beholding the blood and water flowing out from Christ's side, and when in his Epistle, in manifest allusion to the same thing, he says,— 'This is he who came by water and blood, even Jesus Christ; not by water only, but by water and blood:' it makes the whole difference between Christianity and the great corruption of it, whether we understand these words as *co-ordinate with* Baptism and the Lord's Supper, or as *subordinate to* them; whether we say that they refer to the two sacraments, or that they refer to those great truths which the two sacraments were designed to image forth in emblematic action; that repentance towards God, and faith in the blood of our Lord Jesus Christ, are the sum and substance of Christianity.

"Finally, the memorable words of our Lord Himself to Nicodemus,—'Except a man be born of water and of the Spirit, he cannot enter into the kingdom of God,' contain, perhaps, the same figure in words that Baptism contains in action, although even this is not certain; but are not meant to refer to the outward rite of Baptism as the thing *indispensable*. They are co-ordinate with Baptism, it may be, but not subordinate to it. The same obvious reason which led the Jews, in common with many other people, to adopt the rite of washing the body as symbolical of the washing or cleansing of the soul from sin, led our Lord to express this cleansing of the soul by the term 'water.' A man must repent of his past evil life, and receive the grace of the Holy Spirit to enable him for the future to lead a new life, before he can enter into the kingdom of heaven. And if I am asked why I do not take the word 'water' literally, according to Hooker's canon of criticism, when he says that *in the interpretation of Holy Scripture that sense which is nearest the letter is commonly the safest*, I answer, *that such a canon, as applied to a collection of works, so different in point of style as those of the*

Scriptures, is at once ridiculous. In the simple narratives of the historical books, Hooker's rule will hold; in the prophetical and poetical books, it would be the very worst rule that we could follow. Now, our Lord's discourses, as recorded by St. John, are eminently parabolical; His language, both when speaking to the Jews and to His own disciples, is continually figurative. Hence the mingled surprise and pleasure of His disciples, when, towards the close of His last conversation with them, he dropped His usual style, and expressed Himself without any figure: 'Lo! now speakest thou plainly, and speakest no proverb.' He spoke of water to the woman of Samaria, and she, adopting Hooker's rule, understood Him literally: 'Lord, give me this water, that I thirst not, neither come hither to draw.' Was this, indeed, the true sense of His words; or was it so utterly mistaken as to lead to the extreme of folly and profaneness? And yet some think, that to interpret in a similar manner His words to Nicodemus is neither foolish nor profane, but rather that to interpret them otherwise is to explain away the words of Scripture! Explaining away the words of Scripture! when we make them refer to something spiritual and not bodily; to a reality, not to a symbol; to a moral act, not to a ceremony!" *

---

* Fragment on the Church, pp. 77—81.

With respect to the other sacrament, the passage objected to by the prosecution is one in which Dr. Williams comments on the corruptions introduced by the Church of Rome in substituting the sacrifice of the mass for the communion of the Lord's Supper. "When the priest," says Dr. Williams, "took the place of the congregation, when the sacramental signs were treated as the natural body, and the bodily sufferings of Christ enhanced above the self-sacrifice of His will, even to the death of the cross, the centre of Christian faith became inverted, though its form remained. Salvation from evil, through sharing the Saviour's spirit, was shifted into a notion of purchase from God through the price of His bodily pangs. The deep drama of heart and mind became externalized into a commercial transfer, and this effected by a form of ritual"— the form of the ritual of the mass. That, they say, is contrary to the thirty-second Article. The thirty-second Article uses these words about the ritual of which Dr. Williams speaks; it calls it a "dangerous fable and blasphemous deceit." "That is stronger language than Dr. Williams has used. He is giving an historical account of the growth of certain superstitions in the Church of Rome, and they have—I can only call it the impudence—to say he denies the doctrine of salvation according to the Church of England. Is the prosecutor prepared to say that this deep drama of heart and mind—the spiritual sacrifice of praise and thanksgiving offered by the whole congregation to God—is a commercial transfer and is effected by a form of ritual? If he is not, he is not at issue with Dr. Williams; and if he is, his proper place is not in the Church of England, but in the Church of Rome."*

The same process of corruption is traced by Dr. Arnold in a very similar manner: "When Christians met together and received the bread and wine of their common living as the body and blood of Christ, such an act had a real tendency to strengthen and confirm their souls, and the Holy Spirit made such a communion a constant means of grace to those who partook of it. But here there was no place for the priest; on the one side there was Christ's Church assembled, on the other there was Christ and His Spirit to bless them. The priest then steps in, diverts attention from the moral part of this communion, from its peculiar union of things divine and human, of social feelings and religious, from its hallowing of common life, by making us even eat and drink to God's glory and our own salvation, and fixes it upon a supposed mystical virtue conveyed to the bread and wine by the pronouncing of certain words over them by a certain person. The bread and wine became the sacrament of

---

* See Stephen's Defence of Dr. Williams, p. 309.

Christ's body and blood according to Christ's ordinance, by the assembled Church receiving them as such; by their converting an act of nature into an act of religion; by their agreeing to partake together as of their earthly food, so also of their spiritual, and thus being joined to one another in Christ. *The agreement, therefore, of those communicating, their common faith and love, constitute the real consecration of the bread and wine; it is this which, through Christ's spirit, changes the supper into the sacrament.*

"But the priest says, 'Not so: it is not your common faith and purpose to celebrate the communion; it is not the fact of Christ having died and risen again which can bring Him to you or you to Him: I must interpose, and pronounce certain words over the bread and over the cup, and then what neither your faith nor Christ's redemption of you had made other than common food, becomes now, through my mediation, a thing endowed with a divine virtue; nay, it is become Christ Himself. Whether there be any communion of yourselves or no, whether you are alone or with one another, whether you are concurring in spirit or no, still because I, the priest, have pronounced certain words over it, it has acquired a miraculous power, and unless you are partakers of this you cannot be saved.' So the communion of the Church, which morally was so essential, is thus made unessential; and the uttering certain words by a particular person, of which neither Christ nor His apostles had said anything, and which morally can have no virtue at all, is made essential. *And thus was the Church supplanted by the priest; and the communion, which is the very life of the Church, became the mass, with all its superstitions and idolatries."* *

We come now to the question of *Subscription*, a point on which the Essayists, and more especially Mr. Wilson, have been most clamorously assailed, and the authority of Arnold has been expressly invoked against them, with what justice, the reader may judge by comparing Mr. Wilson's Essay on the National Church with Dr. Arnold's pamphlet on Church Reform.

The point of view from which they both regard the Church in its relation to the State and the different theological and philosophical schools of the day, will be found to be substantially the same. The dominant idea, if I may so speak, of both is this—*That in a Christian nation the Church and the State ought to be co-extensive.* This they affirm to be the true principle of the Church of England—the ground-idea of our existing constitution in Church and State. The substitution of dogmatic standards for moral ends as forms of Christian union and communion, they

---

* Fragment on the Church, pp. 20—22.

both equally regard as the great impediment to its perfect realization.

"We all know," remarks Mr. Wilson, "how the inward moral life—or spiritual life on its moral side, if that term be preferred—is nourished into greater or less vigour by means of the conditions in which the moral subject is placed. Hence, if a nation is really worthy of the name, conscious of its own corporate life, it will develope itself on one side into a Church, wherein its citizens may grow up and be perfected in their spiritual nature. If there is within it a consciousness that as a nation it is fulfilling no unimportant office in the world, and is, under the order of Providence, an instrument in giving the victory to good over evil, and to happiness over misery, it will not content itself with the rough adjustments and rude lessons of law and police, but will throw its elements, or the best of them, into another mould, and constitute out of them a society which is in it, though in some sense not of it—which is another, yet the same.

"'That each one born into the nation is, together with his civil rights, born into a membership or privilege, as belonging to a spiritual society, places him at once in a relation which must tell powerfully upon his spiritual nature. For the sake of the reaction upon its own merely secular interests, the nation is entitled to provide from time to time, that the Church teaching and forms of one age do not traditionally harden, so as to become exclusive barriers in a subsequent one, and so the moral growth of those who are committed to the hands of the Church be checked, or its influences confined to a comparatively few. . . . . .

"*Speculative doctrines should be left to philosophical schools. A national Church must be concerned with the ethical development of its members.*" *

"Jesus Christ has not revealed His religion as a theology of the intellect, nor as an historical faith; and it is a stifling of the true Christian life, both in the individual and in the Church, to require of many men a unanimity in speculative doctrine, which is unattainable, and a uniformity of historical belief, which can never exist. The true Christian life is the consciousness of bearing a part in a great moral order, of which the highest agency upon earth has been committed to the Church. Let us not oppress this

---

* "That which has lately been made the ground of reproach against our Church, the scantiness of her dogmatical teaching, is rather one of her peculiar, Providential blessings. Our Reformers discerned that the business of a Church is not to lay down a system of dogmatical theology, but to bring her members to Christ, and to train them up in His knowledge and fellowship, merely setting her mark of exclusion on those errors of doctrine and practice which would draw them away from that spiritual communion."—*Archdeacon Hare's Letter to the Hon. Richard Cavendish*, p. 82.

work, nor complicate the difficulties with which it is surrounded; 'not making the heart of the righteous sad, whom the Lord hath not made sad, nor strengthening the hands of the wicked by promising him life.'"

So far Mr. Wilson. Let us now turn to Dr. Arnold.

"Our fathers," he observes, "rightly appreciated the value of Church unity; but they strangely mistook the means of preserving it. Their system consisted in drawing up a statement of what they deemed important truths, and in appointing a form of worship and a ceremonial which they believed to be at once dignified and edifying; and then they proposed to oblige every man, by the dread of legal penalties and disqualifications, to subscribe to their opinions, and to conform to their rites and practices. *But they forgot that, while requiring this agreement, they had themselves disclaimed what alone could justify them in enforcing it—the possession of infallibility.* They had parted with the weapon which would have served them most effectually, and strange were the expedients resorted to for supplying its place. At one time it was the Apostles' Creed; at another, the decrees of the four first General Councils; or, at another, the general consent of the Primitive Church, which formed an authoritative standard of such truths as might not be questioned without heresy. *But* *though the elephant might still rest upon the tortoise, and the tortoise on the stone, yet since the claim to infallibility was once abandoned, the stone itself rested on nothing.* The four first Councils were appealed to as sanctioning their interpretation of Scripture by men who yet confessed that the decisions of the Councils were only of force *because they were agreeable to the Scripture.* Turn whichever way they would, they sought in vain for an *authority* in religious controversies; infallibility being nowhere to be found, it was merely opinion against opinion; and however convinced either party might be of the truth of its own views, they had no right to judge their opponents. *

"It seems, indeed, to have been the boast hitherto of the several sects of Christians, to invent formulas both of worship and of creeds, which should serve as a test of any latent error; that is, in other words, which should force a man to differ from them, however gladly he would have remained in their communion. May God give us, for the time to come, a wiser and a better spirit; and may we think that the true problem to be solved in the composition of all articles and creeds and prayers for public use, is no other than this: how to frame them so as to provoke the least possible disagreement, without sacri-

---

* Miscellaneous Works, p. 273.

ficing, in our own practical worship, the expression of such feelings as are essential to our own edification.

"If it be said that this is contrary to the uniform example of the Christian world, it is unhappily too true that it is so; and let history answer how the cause of Christianity has prospered under the system actually adopted. Or, let those answer who, in attempting to acquaint themselves with ecclesiastical history, have groaned inwardly for very weariness at its dull and painful details. What ought to be more noble, or more beautiful, than the gradual progress of the spirit of light and love, dispelling the darkness of folly, and subduing into one divine harmony all the jarring elements of evil, which divided amongst them the chaos of this world's empire? Such should have been the history of the Christian Church: and what has it been actually? No steady and unwavering advance of heavenly spirits; but one continually interrupted, checked, diverted from its course—nay, driven backwards, as of men possessed by some bewildering spell—wasting their strength upon imaginary obstacles—fancying that the road lay to the right or left, when it led straight forward—hindering each other's progress and their own by stopping to analyse and dispute about the nature of the sun's light till all were blinded by it—instead of thankfully using its aid to show them the true path onward. In other words, *men overrated the evil of difference of opinion, and underrated that of difference of practice; and their efforts were thus diverted from a cause in which all good men would have striven together, to one where goodness and wickedness were mere accidental adjuncts, equally found on one side or on the other. . . . . . . In-fallibility or brute ignorance can alone prevent difference of opinion. Men, at once fallible and inquiring, have their choice either of following these differences up into endless schisms, or of allowing them to exist together unheeded, under the true bond of agreement of principle."* *

If we now turn again to Mr. Wilson's Essay, we shall find him lamenting in like manner the present alienation of so large a portion of our population from the National Church, and proposing in effect the same remedy for the evil as that suggested in 1833 by Dr. Arnold. This leads him, however, to examine, as a preliminary question, the extent of the legal obligation actually imposed by the act of subscription to the Thirty-nine Articles, and the declaration of assent and consent to all and everything contained in the Book of Common Prayer. In this case *the strictly legal obligation*, he reminds us, *is the exact measure of the moral one*.†

* Miscellaneous Works, pp. 285—287.
† The moral obligation of the minister of religion is to teach

In the absence of any formal declaration as to the meaning of subscription, the only authority on the subject is to be found, he observes, in the Canons of 1603, the fifth and the thirty-sixth. Of these, the fifth forbids the "*impugning*" of the Articles, which is further explained to be the affirming that any of the Thirty-nine Articles are in any part " superstitious or erroneous." Yet, an Article may be open to many reasonable objections which may be freely canvassed without pronouncing it to be either positively erroneous or necessarily superstitious.

The thirty-sixth Canon contains two clauses explanatory, to some extent, of the meaning of ministerial subscription, " That he *alloweth* the Book of Articles, etc.," and "that he *acknowledgeth* the same to be agreeable to the Word of God." But we all *allow** and *acknowledge* many

that which he shall be persuaded is the truth; and so far as this primary obligation is concerned, a legal enactment does not give a measure of the moral duty. But with respect to the forms established by our Acts of Uniformity, they have the nature of "*positive institutions;*" as such, and so far as they are limitations both of natural and Christian liberty, the legal obligation *is* the measure of the moral one.

* Mr. Wilson has met with a great deal of vituperation, in consequence of the meaning which he has given to the word "allow." Johnson, it is true, derives the word from *allaudare*. Even if that were its derivation, almost all his authorities as to the use of the word are inconsistent with the meaning of "approving." The real derivation, however, is very different, and the usual signification of the word is consistent with it.

things which we do not necessarily think to be wise or practically useful. We acquiesce in, submit to, and acknowledge them, it may be, as part of a constitution under which we live, and which we would on no account undermine, for the many blessings of which we are fully grateful.

"But after all, the important phrase is, that 'the Articles are agreeable to the Word of God.' This cannot mean that the Articles are precisely co-extensive with the Bible, much less of equal authority with it as a whole. Neither separately, nor altogether, do they embody all which is said in it, and inferences which they draw from it are only good relatively—and *secundum quid* and *quatenus concordant*—[according to what they really deduce from, and so far as they actually agree with it]. If their terms are Biblical terms, they must be presumed to have the same sense in the Articles which they have in the Scripture; and if they are not all Scriptural ones, they under-

---

It is from the French *allouer*, to pass an item in an account, as, *Je lui ai passé cette dépense*, &c. (See *Dict. Fleming and Tibbins; Dictionnaire de l'Institut*.) The French word comes from *allocare*, to set or place; *louer*, from *locare*, as *jouer* from *jocare*. *Allocatio*, in Latin forms of account, is the "allowance" side of the balance-sheet, opposed to *oneratio*, or the "charge." In the English version of the Bible, the word "allow" has certainly the sense of "approve"—"Ye *allow* the deeds of your fathers"—but generally in the older English, as well as the modern, "to allow" implies more or less of reluctance. In a well-known line "allowance" must be coupled even with "horror"—"The law *allows* it, and the court awards."

take in the pivot Article (the sixth) not to contradict the Scripture. The Articles do not make any assumption of being interpretations of Scripture or developments of it. The greater must include the less, and the Scripture is the greater."

The same principle is equally applicable to the declaration of "assent to all and everything contained in the Prayer-Book"—to all and everything, that is, understood and interpreted agreeably to the Scriptures, on which it professes to be founded, and consequently *in its Scriptural sense*.

Against a theory of subscription, at once so reasonable, so conciliatory, and so *orthodox*, the reader may well wonder what the counsel for the prosecution could possibly find in the writings of Dr. Arnold. They have lighted, however, on a passage which they fancied would serve their turn in his published correspondence, where he writes to an old pupil:—" I agree with you in thinking that subscriptions cannot be too carefully worded; but, after all, the real *honesty* of subscription appears to me to consist in a sympathy with the system to which you subscribe, in a preference of it, not negatively merely, as better than others, but positively, as in itself good and true in all its most characteristic points"—such a sympathy with, and hearty admiration for, the Church of England as is expressed by Mr. Wilson.* "Now, the most characteristic points of the English Church are two: that it maintains what is called the Catholic doctrine as opposed to the early heresies, and is also decidedly a reformed Church as opposed to the Papal and priestly system." And here the quotation of the prosecution stops, and that for very good reasons of their own; for, unfortunately for them, Dr. Arnold goes on to apply his principle in a manner rather embarrassing to those who have invoked his aid. "It seems to me," he says, "that here is the stumbling-block of"—whom? The Essayists? No; but "the *Newmanites*"—the name whereby, before the secession of Dr. Newman to the Church of Rome, the present followers of Dr. Pusey and of the Bishops of Oxford and Salisbury were known. "They" (the Puseyites), continues Dr. Arnold, "hate the Reformation, they hate the Reformers. It were scarce possible that they could subscribe honestly to the opinions of men whom they hate, even if we had never seen the process of their subscription in detail. Undoubtedly I think worse of Roman Catholicism in itself than I did some years ago. But my feelings towards [a Roman Catholic] are quite different from my feeling towards [a *Puseyite*, shall we say? The MS. is here imperfect: Dr. Arnold

* Essays and Reviews, p. 147.

probably wrote *Newmanite*], because I think the one a fair enemy, the other a treacherous one. The one is the Frenchman in his own uniform, and within his own præsidia; the other is the Frenchman disguised in a red coat, and holding a post within our præsidia, for the purpose of betraying it. *I should honour the first and hang the second."*

After this, the reader will, I think, allow that the counsel for the prosecution would have done well to have abstained from attempting to profane the name and abuse the authority of Arnold in support of the cause of bigotry, intolerance, Bibliolatry, and Puseyism. If they had thought proper to turn to his writings with a view of ascertaining his real sentiments, they would have found him constantly expressing the greatest *abhorrence* for the opinions they entertain, and the conduct they have adopted. "I would not," he writes to a friend, "willingly petition about the Canons, *except to procure their utter abolition*. I have an intense dislike of clerical legislation, most of all of such a clergy as was dominant in James I.'s reign. And if the Canons are touched ever so lightly, what is left untouched would acquire additional force—a greater evil to my mind than leaving them altogether alone. I think that I should

---

* Stanley's Life, vol. ii. p. 288.

myself prefer petitioning for a relaxation of the terms of subscription, and especially for the total repeal of the thirty-sixth Canon. *Historically, our Prayer-Book exhibits the opinions of two very different parties—King Edward's Reformers, and the High Churchmen of James I.'s time, and of 1661. There is a necessity, therefore, in fact, for a comprehensive subscription, unless the followers of one of these parties are to be driven out of the Church; for no man who heartily likes the one can approve of what has been done by the other."*

In short, it does not appear that Mr. Wilson claims for himself and others any greater latitude of opinion under the present terms of subscription beyond what is claimed generally† by

---

* Stanley's Life, vol. ii. p. 212.

† "As to the terms of subscription, it was of great importance that the public should not suppose them to be more rigid than they really were. His impression was, that a man who conscientiously believed the Church of England to be the Church in which he wished to live and die, and who was not more attached to any other form of Christianity than that which the Church of England presented, might fairly and safely make the subscriptions which were required of him by the present law. Those subscriptions were really not so strict as the noble lord (Ebury) seemed to imagine. They stated, that the person who subscribed accepted the Articles of the Church of England; that, if he took orders, he would act according to the Formularies of the Church; and that he upheld the royal supremacy."—*Extract from a speech of the Bishop of London in the House of Lords*, as reported in the *Times*, July 23rd' 1861.

"The truth is, as everybody knows, the terms of subscription

the liberal party in the Church. His peculiar merit consists in having suggested a *theory of subscription* consistent in itself, and obviously required to meet the admitted necessities of the case.

This theory of subscription, and the latitude of opinion which Mr. Wilson claims under it, must clearly be distinguished both from the claims of Mr. Whiston and the Arians, and from that of Mr. Oakeley and the Romanists. In those cases liberty was demanded for holding opinions against which certain of the Articles were expressly directed. The Arian opinions were distinctly opposed to parts of the five first Articles, as well as to clauses in the Nicene and Athanasian Creeds, known historically to have been directed against Arianism itself: no less than fifteen of the Articles of Religion are aimed more or less against Roman doctrines or practices, all of which doctrines Mr. Oakeley claimed to hold. On the other hand, Mr. Wilson has only claimed

are practically constituted by the understanding which accompanies them—an understanding of historical growth, thoroughly recognised and sanctioned, and, in fact, an essential part of the doctrinal fabric of the Church. Everybody knows what everybody is doing who signs the Articles,—all the Bishops know, all the Bishops' chaplains know, all University vice-chancellors know. It is as settled an understanding as that which accompanies the Queen's veto, or the champion's challenge, or the *congé d'élire.*"—*Times*, July 24th, 1861.

that the expression of opinion is free where the Articles have not expressly limited it—that, like all other limitations of natural rights, the restraint imposed by the Articles should be interpreted strictly on the side of the law—that is, liberally towards those who are affected by them. Thus, unless the words of an Article be contradicted in terms, in which case a judge would have no option, he would consider the doctrines of the Articles with reference to the history of their origin, and relatively to the particular errors they were intended to exclude, without extending their application by way of inference to controversies not contemplated when they were drawn up. " Even with respect to the Thirty-nine Articles," remarks a writer in the *Parthenon*, May 3rd, 1862, "many eminent Churchmen of various schools of divinity—Bramhall, Burnet, Paley, Stanley of Norwich — have expressly maintained that they are Articles of peace, and that the obligation contracted by subscription is satisfied if they are not contradicted—that is, if the error or opinions against which they were specifically directed are not held up in opposition to them; they are, almost all of them, controversial, and, as is well known, have reference chiefly to the Romish controversy. They contain relative declarations; and as the controversies to which they are relative die out, these relative statements should be considered as dying out too. At least, this is the common-sense view of the case."

It was simply childish on the part of one of the counsel for the prosecution to contend that Mr. Wilson's holding all *German* doctrine must be as contradictory to the Thirty-nine Articles as Mr. Oakeley's holding all Roman doctrine; for there is no scheme or system of doctrine known by the name of German, much less indicated in the Articles, nor had Mr. Wilson advanced any such foolish and unmeaning claim as was imputed to him. No doubt Mr. Wilson differs quite as much from some doctrines held by Germans as he agrees with others. This is so self-evident that we cannot but wonder the Court should have allowed its time to be occupied in listening to such nonsense.

The time, we believe, is not far distant when the wisdom of Mr. Wilson's suggestions on this matter of subscription will be recognized, and when the public will awake to a sense of the debt of gratitude they owe to him for the manner in which he has treated this very difficult and most important subject.

" It does not indeed," said the late excellent Bishop Stanley, of Norwich, " it does not become the Church of England—a Church founded on liberty of conscience and right of private judgment—to say that there shall be no latitude of opinion within certain limits; *and, therefore, I consider that, by in any way expanding the sense and meaning of subscription, a boon would be granted and a benefit conferred upon the scrupulous and tender consciences of many who are among, or may become, the brightest ornaments of the Establishment.* . . . . . If, indeed, the present subscription be universally understood with that latitude which the wide embrace of our Church renders not only desirable but absolutely necessary, this is precisely what I have felt it my duty to maintain, in conformity with what I have stated to be the principle and intention with which the Church of England drew up her terms of communion at the time of the Reformation. But, if every one who subscribes is supposed to subscribe his implicit and unreserved assent to every expression and proposition in the Articles and other formularies, in its full, obvious, and original sense, I confess myself unable to see how the Church and clergy of England would be able to extricate themselves from the difficulties into which such a course would throw them.

"If all those who belong to the so-called Low Church party are, for instance, to adopt, in their full and obvious sense, without any secondary explanation, all that was adopted from the ancient rituals to conciliate the Romanists; if all those who belong to the so-called High Church party are to adopt, in their full and obvious sense, all that was adopted by Cranmer or Jewel to conciliate the foreign Protestants; if all those whose studies, preparatory to ordination, have made them acquainted with historical criticism, are to adopt, in their full and obvious sense, those mistakes and oversights as to matters of fact which the state of knowledge rendered unavoidable in the sixteenth century, it is difficult to see how our whole system can be saved from dissolution. . . . . . I repeat that, if the subscription at ordination is understood to apply to every expression and every proposition, to every point, to every iota, in its full, obvious, literal, or original meaning, I never met (nor do I ever expect to meet) any persons who allowed that they thus agreed to it—*it is, indeed, morally impossible that they should.* . . . . . It is impossible that any men should agree in all details, for the simple reason that our Articles and Formularies involve contradictory points, which cannot both be held, and, consequently, an affirmation of the one must be a negative of the other. The whole subject-matter under discussion, in fact, is but a paraphrase of the following extract from Burnet:—

"'Some have thought that they are only *Articles of Union and Peace;* that the sons of the Church are only bound to acquiesce silently in them; and that the subscription binds only to a general compromise upon those Articles, so that there be no disputing nor wrangling about them. By these means they reckon that, *though a man should differ in his opinion from that which appears to be the clear sense of any of the Articles, yet he may, with a good conscience, subscribe them, if the Articles appear to him to be of such a nature that, though he thinks it wrong, yet it seems not to be of that consequence but that it may be borne with, and not contradicted;'* and that he had a leaning to this expansive character of subscription is clear from the conclusion he draws—viz., that a higher subscription would '*be a great hardship.*'"

Bishop Stanley then proceeds to quote from Bishop Bull and Archbishop Bramhall to the same effect—namely, that the intention of subscription is "*not to oblige any man to believe the Articles, but only not to contradict them;*" after which he continues:—

"Besides many of the more trifling discrepancies in our Rubric and services, which render literal acquiescence impossible, I would mention one or two of a more important character, in which Churchmen are neither unanimous in belief, nor universal in assent. Let me ask, deliberately and solemnly, whether there is a single clergymen living who believes that every individual not 'keeping whole and undefiled' the

Catholic faith, as it is minutely defined and analyzed in the Athanasian Creed, 'without doubt shall perish everlastingly'? Be it observed, the Creed, literally understood, makes no allowances, no distinctions, no contingencies, but unconditionally and unequivocally asserts that all who receive it not are doomed to irretrievable perdition. Granting (though the Creed makes no such concession), that 500,000,000 and upwards of pagans and heathens, out of the 800,000,000 inhabitants of our globe, are not meant to be included in this sweeping anathema, it should be remembered that the whole Greek Church, professed Christians as they are, must of necessity be included, as its members, after mature consideration, are at variance with other Christian churches respecting the procession of the Holy Ghost, a point especially referred to in this Creed—and yet every sincere and conscientious member of that Church, however firm in his belief and reliance on our common Saviour, must, in the estimation of every clergyman of the Church of England, who holds every point and iota of her Formularies in their literal sense, for ever be excluded from the merits of his Redeemer's death hereafter. *I repeat solemnly that I never met with a single clergyman who believed this in the literal sense of the words, and, for the honour of human nature and Christianity, I trust that not one lives in our enlightened age who would deliberately avow that such was his belief."* *

The reader will not, I think, find anything which goes beyond this in the whole of Mr. Wilson's Essay. And yet for this his invaluable contribution to the theological literature of his age, he has been persecuted, reviled, dragged before an ecclesiastical court, put on his defence, and actually threatened with expulsion from the ministry of a Church of which he is one of the greatest ornaments and supports. But "in like manner did their fathers unto the prophets."

Das ist das Loos des Schönen auf der Erde.

---

* See Speech in the House of Lords on Subscription, with Notes. Stanley's Memoir, pp. 87, 93, 101—107.

CHAPTER VI.

THE JUDGMENT OF THE ARCHES COURT.

Wednesday, the 25th of June, had been fixed as the day on which the Court was to deliver its judgment respecting the admissibility of the articles of charge against Dr. Williams and Mr. Wilson; as such it was anticipated by the Essayists and their friends with interest, but with no apprehension as to the character of the decision. The highest legal and ecclesiastical authorities had already decided that "the book contained no contradiction to the Articles," and the particular expressions articled and objected to by the prosecution were such that, to use the words of Professor Grote, "it is wonderful to think how legal criminality could ever have suggested itself in regard to them."* Under these circumstances, it seemed that the judge had a very clear and simple duty to perform—to dismiss the articles as failing on any single point to establish a contradiction between the statements of the Essayists and the Articles and Formularies of the Church, commenting, as he could hardly fail to do, on

* Examination of some Portions of Dr. Lushington's Judgment, p. 83.

the vexatious and litigious character of the prosecution. It was, therefore, with feelings of the utmost surprise that we listened to the learned judge, as he proceeded to assume to himself the office of a theological censor, putting on the Articles constructions of his own, new and hitherto unheard of in the Church of England, and drawing from these a variety of inferences and conclusions with which he declared certain portions of the Essays to stand in constructive opposition. The inability of the judge to point to a single expression in the Essays which amounted to a contradiction of any statement in the Formularies was apparent throughout, and ought surely to have secured to the defendants a prompt and honourable acquittal.* But

---

* This all-important distinction between a contradiction of the Articles, and a mere questioning of certain inferences popularly drawn from them, is well pointed out by the Bishop of St. David's. In reply to a memorial charging Dr. Williams with using language inconsistent with that of the Articles and the Prayer-Book, his lordship observes—"I am unable to gather, except by surmise, whether the discrepancy of which they (the memorialists) speak, amounts in their opinion to *an express and direct contradiction*, such as in the case of a beneficed clergyman would form a sufficient ground for legal proceedings which might issue in his deprivation, or only to *a virtual and implicit disagreement, which needs to be shown by a process of reasoning on which different minds may take opposite views;* in other words, *whether those statements* ' *clash* ' *with propositions formally laid down in the Articles and the Prayer-Book, or only with certain conclusions which may be argumentatively deduced*

this was not to be. Dr. Lushington had evidently assumed some standard of orthodoxy, which the Essayists had violated; that they were offenders was plain to his mind, and the only question was by what possible construction of the Church's Formularies they could legally be condemned. This question was practically solved by the selection in each case of three points on which the articles of charge were admitted. At the same time, notwithstanding the surprise and alarm created by certain portions of this judgment, we cannot doubt that the learned judge approached his duty with an earnest desire to adhere to the principles of strict law and justice. Of this we have the strongest proof in his determination to dismiss all charges of misinterpretation of Scripture as beyond his cognizance. "The Articles then," his Lordship ruled, "must be reformed by striking out all reference to extracts from the Bible found in the Prayer Book."

from their ' language.' And, in the absence of a more direct assertion, I should be the more loath to assume the former meaning, as the author of the work in question ('Rational Godliness') himself maintains, that his statements are consistent with the standards of our Church. *And the difference is one of the highest importance, being nothing less than the difference between the breach of a most solemn obligation contracted by every clergyman when he is admitted into holy orders, and the exercise of a right of private judgment which the Church allows to her ministers.*" (See also the Charge of the Bishop of St. David's, 1857, pp. 26, 27, 62, 63.)

Of the three points admitted in each case against the Essayists, the first is common to both—the statement of their views relating to Holy Scripture. The two others against Dr. Williams, relate to certain expressions in his Essay concerning Justification and Propitiation, derived, in fact, from Baron Bunsen, but with which the judge held Dr. Williams to have identified himself. The two charges remaining against Mr. Wilson refer to what he has said respecting the absence of any real distinction between what are commonly called "covenanted and uncovenanted mercies," and to his views on the final destiny of mankind.

That on any one of these points a charge of heresy can be sustained against the Essayists we do not believe. They will come under consideration again when argument is heard on the merits of the case, the original articles having been reformed by the prosecution in accordance with the decision of the judge.

The articles of charge so amended and admitted are as follows :—

Against Dr. Williams.

I. " We article and object to you, the Reverend Rowland Williams, that in the said Article, Essay, or Review are contained the following passages ; that is to say, at pages 60 and 61 :—

" ' As in his ' Egypt,' our author [Baron Bunsen] sifts the historical date of the Bible, so in his 'Gott in der Geschichte,' he expounds its directly religious element. Lamenting, like Pascal, the wretchedness of our feverish being when estranged from its eternal stay, he traces, as a countryman of Hegel, the Divine thought bringing order out of confusion. Unlike the despairing school, who forbid us to trust in God or in conscience, unless we kill our souls with literalism, he finds salvation for men and states only in becoming acquainted with the Author of our life, by whose reason the world stands fast, whose stamp we bear in our forethought, and whose voice our conscience echoes. In the Bible, as an expression of devout reason, and, therefore, to be read with reason in freedom, he finds record of the spiritual giants whose experience generated the religious atmosphere we breathe.'"

Then follows, in the article as originally exhibited, a passage from pages 82 and 83, which is excluded in the amended article as beyond the cognizance of the court.

"At pages 77 and 78:—

"'But if such a notion [Baron Bunsen's respecting the legendary character of the narrative in the Book of Jonah] alarms those who think that apart from omniscience belonging to the Jews the proper conclusion of reason is Atheism; it is not inconsistent with the idea that Almighty God has been pleased to educate men and nations, employing imagination no less than conscience, and suffering His lessons to play freely within the limits of humanity and its shortcomings. Nor will any fair reader rise from the prophetical disquisitions [of Baron Bunsen] without feeling that he has been under the guidance of a master's hand. The great result is to vindicate the work of the Eternal Spirit, that abiding influence which, as our Church teaches us in the Ordination Service, underlies all others, and in which converge all images of old time and means of grace now—temple, Scripture, finger, and hand of God; and again, preaching, sacraments, waters which comfort, and flame which burns. If such a Spirit did not dwell in the Church the Bible would not be inspired, for the Bible is, before all things, the written voice of the congregation. Bold as such a theory of inspiration may sound, it was the earliest creed of the Church, and it is the only one to which the facts of Scripture answer. The sacred writers acknowledge themselves men of like passions with ourselves, and we are promised illumination from the Spirit which dwelt in them. Hence, when we find our Prayer-Book constructed on the idea of the Church being an inspired society, instead of objecting that every one of us is fallible, we should define inspiration consistently with the facts of Scripture, and of human nature. This would neither exclude the idea of fallibility among Israelites of old, nor teach us to quench the Spirit in true hearts for ever. But if any one prefers thinking the sacred writers passionless machines, and calling Luther and Milton uninspired, let him co-operate in researches by which his theory, if true, will be triumphantly confirmed.'

"And we article and object to you, the said Reverend Rowland Williams, that in the passages hereinbefore recited, being portions of the said Article, Essay, or Review, you did advisedly maintain and affirm, that the Bible or Holy Scripture is an expression of devout reason, and the written voice of the congregation, not the Word of God, nor containing any special revelation of His truth, or of His dealings with mankind, nor the rule of our faith; or that you did therein advisedly maintain and affirm doctrines, positions, or opinions to that or the like purport and effect, and that the said doctrines, positions, or opinions are contrary to, or inconsistent with, the 6th, 7th, and 20th of the said Articles of Religion, and contrary to, and inconsistent with, that part of the Nicene Creed which declares in substance that the Holy Ghost spake by the Prophets."

II. "And we further article and object to you, the said Reverend Rowland Williams, that in the said Article, Essay, or Review, is contained the following passage, at page 81:—'Propitiation would be the recovery of that Peace, which cannot be, while Sin divides us from the Searcher of Hearts.'

"And we article and object to you, the said Reverend Rowland Williams, that in the passage hereinbefore recited, being a portion of the said Article, Essay, or Review, you did advisedly maintain and affirm, that the offering of Christ is not the propitiation for the sins of the whole world; or that you did therein advisedly maintain and affirm a doctrine, position, or opinion to that or the like purport and effect, and that such doctrine, position, or opinion is contrary to, or inconsistent with, the 31st of the said Articles of Religion."

III. "And we further article and object to you, the said Reverend Rowland Williams, that in the said Article, Essay, or Review, is contained the following passage, at pages 80, 81, in the words following, to wit:—'For though he [Baron Bunsen] embraces, with more than orthodox warmth, New Testament terms, he explains them in such a way that he may be charged with using evangelical language in a philosophical sense. But in reply, he would ask, what proof is there that the reasonable sense of St. Paul's words was not the one which the Apostle intended? Why may not justification by faith have meant the peace of mind, or sense of Divine approval, which comes of trust in a Righteous God, rather than a fiction of merit by transfer? St. Paul would then be teaching moral responsibility, as opposed to sacerdotalism; or, that to obey is better than sacrifice. Faith would be opposed, not to the good deeds which conscience requires, but to works of appeasement by ritual justification would be neither an arbitrary ground of confidence, nor a reward upon condition of our disclaiming merit, but rather a verdict of forgiveness upon our repentance, and of acceptance upon the offering of our hearts.'

"And we article and object to you, the said Reverend Rowland Williams, that in the passage hereinbefore recited, being portion of the said Article, Essay, or Review, you did advisedly maintain and affirm, that Justification by Faith means only the peace of mind, or sense of Divine approval, which comes of trust in a righteous God, and that justification is a verdict of forgiveness upon our repentance, and of acceptance upon the offering of our hearts; or, that you did therein advisedly maintain and affirm a doctrine, position, or opinion to that or the like purport or effect, and that such doctrine, position, or opinion is contrary to, or inconsistent with, the 11th of the said Articles of Religion. And this was and is true, and we article and object as before."

Such are the three articles of charge admitted against Dr. Williams. We turn now to those against Mr. Wilson. They are as follows:—

I. "We article and object to you, the Reverend Henry Bristow Wilson, that in the said Article, Essay, or Review is the following passage, at pages 175, 176:—'It has been matter of great boast within the Church of England, in common with other Protestant churches, that it is founded upon the 'Word of God;' a phrase which begs many a question, when applied collectively to the books of the Old and New Testaments; a phrase which is never so applied to them by any of the Scriptural authors, and which, according to Protestant principles, never could be applied to them by any sufficient authority from without. In that which may be considered the pivot Article of the Church, this expression does not occur, but only 'Holy Scripture,' 'Canonical Books,' 'Old and New Testaments.' It contains no declaration of the Bible being throughout supernaturally suggested, nor any intimation as to which portions of it were owing to a special Divine illumination, nor the slightest attempt at defining inspiration, whether mediate or immediate, whether through or beside, or overruling the natural faculties of the subject of it—not the least hint of the relation between the Divine and human elements in the composition of the Biblical books. Even if the Fathers have usually considered 'canonical' as synonymous with 'miraculously inspired,' there is nothing to show that their sense of the word must necessarily be applied to our own sixth Article. The word itself may mean either books ruled and determined by the Church or regulative books, and the employment of it in the Article hesitates between these two significations. For at one time 'Holy Scripture' and canonical books are those books 'of whose authority never was any doubt in the Church;' that is, they are 'determined' books; and then the other or uncanonical books are described as those which 'the Church doth not apply to establish any doctrine;' that is, they are not 'regulative' books. And if the other principal churches of the Reformation have gone farther in definition, in this respect, than our own, that is no reason we should force the silence of our Church into unison with their expressed declarations, but rather that we should rejoice in our comparative freedom. The Protestant feeling among us has satisfied itself in a blind way with the anti-Roman declaration, that 'Holy Scripture containeth all things necessary to salvation, so that whatsoever is not read therein, nor may be proved thereby, is not to be required of any man that it should be believed as an article of the faith,' &c., and without reflecting how very much is wisely left open in that Article. For this declaration itself is partly negative and partly positive: as to its negative part, it declares that nothing—no clause of creed, no decision of council, no tradition or exposition—is required to be believed on peril of salvation, unless it be Scriptural; but it does not lay down that everything which is contained in Scripture must be believed on the same peril. Or it may be expressed thus: 'The Word of God is contained in

Scripture, whence it does not follow that it is co-extensive with it. The Church to which we belong does not put that stumbling-block before the feet of her members; it is their own fault if they place it there for themselves, authors of their own offence.' '

"And we article and object to you, the said Henry Bristow Wilson, that in the passage hereinbefore recited, being portion of the said Article, Essay, or Review, you did advisedly declare and affirm in effect, that the Scriptures of the Old and New Testament were not written under the inspiration of the Holy Spirit, and that they were not necessarily at all, and certainly not in parts, the Word of God, or that you did therein advisedly declare and affirm a doctrine, position, or opinion to that or the like purport and effect. And that such doctrine, position, or opinion is contrary to, or inconsistent with, the sixth and twentieth of the Articles of Religion, and contrary to, or inconsistent with, the teaching of the Church as contained in that part of the Nicene Creed which declares, in substance, that the Holy Ghost spake by the Prophets; and as set forth in the Ordering of Priests in the Book of Common Prayer, to wit, in the words following: 'The Bishop shall deliver to every one of them the Bible into his hands, saying, Take thou authority to preach the word of God.' And we article and object as before."

II. "Also, we further article and object to you, the said Reverend Henry Bristow Wilson, that in the said Article, Essay, or Review, is the following passage, at pages 153, 154:—

"'And when we hear fine distinctions drawn between covenanted and uncovenanted mercies, it seems either to be a distinction without a difference, or to amount to a denial of the broad and equal justice of the Supreme Being. We cannot be content to wrap this question up and leave it for a mystery as to what shall become of those myriads upon myriads of non-christian races.'

"And we article and object to you, the said Henry Bristow Wilson, that in the passage hereinbefore recited, being a portion of the said Article, Essay, or Review, you did advisedly declare and affirm that the condition of men in a future state of existence will be determined by their moral conduct, according to the law or sect which they severally profess, exclusive of their religious belief; or, that you did therein advisedly declare and affirm a doctrine, position, or opinion to that or the like purport or effect; and that such doctrine, position or opinion is contradictory to, or inconsistent with, the eighteenth of the said Articles of Religion. And we article and object as before."

III. "And we further article and object to you, the said Reverend Henry Bristow Wilson, that in the said Article, Essay, or Review, is contained the following passage, at page 206:—

"'The Christian Church can only tend on those who are committed to its care, to the verge of that abyss which parts this world from the world unseen. Some few of those fostered by her are now ripe for entering on a higher career; the many are but rudimentary spirits— germinal souls. What shall become of them? If we look abroad in the world, and regard the neutral character of the multitude, we are at a loss to apply to them either the promises or the denunciations of Revelation. So, the wise heathens could anticipate a reunion with the great and good of all ages; they could represent to themselves, at least in a figurative manner, the punishment and the purgatory of the wicked; but they would not expect the reappearance in another world, for any purpose, of a Thersites or an Hyperbolos—social and poetical justice had been sufficiently done upon them. Yet there are such as these, and no better than these, under the Christian name, — babblers, busy-bodies, livers to get gain, and mere eaters and drinkers. The Roman Church has imagined a *limbus infantium*; we must rather entertain a hope that there shall be found, after the great adjudication, receptacles suitable for those who shall be infants, not as to years of terrestrial life, but as to spiritual development—nurseries, as it were, and seed-grounds, where the undeveloped may grow up under new conditions, the stunted may become strong, and the perverted be restored. And when the Christian Church in all its branches shall have fulfilled its sublunary office, and its Founder shall have surrendered the kingdom to the great Father, all, both small and great, shall find a refuge in the bosom of the Universal Parent, to repose, or be quickened into higher life, in the ages to come, according to His will.'

"And we article and object to you, the said Reverend Henry Bristow Wilson, that in the passage hereinbefore recited, being a portion of the said Article, Essay, or Review, you did advisedly declare and affirm in effect, that after this life and at the end of the existing order of things on this earth, there will be no judgment of God, awarding to those men whom He shall then approve, everlasting life or eternal happiness, and to those men whom He shall then condemn, everlasting death or eternal misery; or that you did therein advisedly declare and affirm a doctrine, position, or opinion to that or to the like purport and effect; and that the said doctrine, position, or opinion is contrary to, or inconsistent with, the teaching of the said Church, as contained in the Creeds commonly called the Apostles' Creed, the Nicene Creed, and St. Athanasius' Creed; and as contained in the Absolution or Remission of Sins, which forms part of the Morning Prayer in the said Book of Common Prayer, and in which the priest says : 'Wherefore let us beseech Him to grant us true repentance and His Holy Spirit, that those things may please Him which we do at this present; and that the rest of our life hereafter may be pure and holy; so that, at the last, we may come to His eternal joy, through Jesus Christ our Lord.' And as contained in the following part of the Catechism, which forms part of the said Book of Common Prayer: 'Question. What desirest thou of God in this prayer? Answer. I desire my Lord God our Heavenly Father, who is the Giver of all Goodness, to send His Grace unto me, and to all people. And I pray unto God that He will keep us from all sin and wickedness, and from our ghostly enemy, and from everlasting death.' And as contained in the following portions of the Order for the Burial of the Dead, which forms part of the said Book of Common Prayer: 'In sure and certain hope of the Resurrection to eternal life, through our Lord Jesus Christ, who shall change our vile body, that it may be like unto His glorious body, according to the mighty working whereby He is able to subdue all things unto Himself.' 'O Merciful God, the Father of our Lord Jesus Christ, who is the Resurrection and the Life, in whom whosoever believeth shall live though he die; and whosoever liveth and believeth in Him shall not die eternally; who also hath taught us by His holy Apostle, St. Paul, not to be sorry as men without hope, for them that sleep in Him; we meekly beseech Thee, O Father, to raise us from the Death of Sin unto the Life of Righteousness; that when we shall depart this life, we may rest in Him, as our hope is that our brother doth; and that at the general resurrection in the last day, we may be found acceptable in Thy sight, and receive that blessing which Thy well-beloved Son shall then pronounce to all that love and fear Thee, saying, *Come, ye blessed children of my Father, receive the kingdom prepared for you from the beginning of the world.*' And as contained in the following portions of the Commination Service, which forms part of the said Book of Common Prayer:—' The day of the Lord cometh as a thief in the night. Then shall it be too late to knock when the door shall be shut; and too late to cry for mercy when it is the time of justice. O terrible voice of most just judgment, which shall be pronounced upon them, when it shall be said unto them, *Go, ye cursed, into the fire everlasting, which is prepared for the Devil and his Angels.*' ' This, if we do, Christ will deliver us from the curse of the law, and from the extreme malediction which shall light upon them that be set upon the left hand, and he will set us on His right hand, and give us the gracious benediction of His Father, commanding us to take possession of His glorious kingdom.' And we article and object as before."

REVIEW OF JUDGMENT.

The above are the only articles of charge admitted, as amended, by the learned Judge. The first in each case is common to both, and amounts to nothing less than the *monstrous* proposition, that a recognition of the human implies a denial of the Divine element in Holy Scripture. "I hold," says Dr. Lushington, "that the sixth and seventh Articles of Religion impose the obligation of acknowledging that the Bible, in matters essential to salvation, is the written Word of God; that it was written by the interposition of the Almighty, supernaturally brought to operate. I hold that to declare the Bible to be *an expression of devout reason—* to be *the written voice of the congregation—*is a violation of the sixth and seventh Articles of Religion. I think such positions are substantially inconsistent with the all-important doctrine imposed by law, that the Bible is God's Word written. If it (the Bible) be God's Word written, as said in the twentieth Article, it is not the expression of devout reason. Devout reason belongs to the acts and doings of man, *and not to the works of the Almighty.*" To this extraordinary conclusion and apparent denial of any direct human agency in the production of the Bible, the learned Judge is led by what he holds to be implied in the epithets "HOLY" and "CANONICAL," as applied to the sacred volume in the sixth Article, and in the expression *God's Word written* in the twentieth Article.

The error into which the learned Judge has here fallen in this unfortunate attempt to *develope* and *define* the doctrine of the Church has been anticipated and corrected by the Bishop of St. David's. In express reference to this very controversy his Lordship remarks:—" The 'volume of Holy Scripture,' it is said in one passage, *'embodies the experience of the Church of old, the record of her Revelations, and the tradition of her spiritual life,—the transfusion, as it were, of her spirit into writing.'* In another it is granted—as an admission which may safely be made to the Romanist, as well as to many Anglicans—that *'the Church was before the Bible, as a speaker is before his voice ; and that Holy Scripture is not the foundation of the Christian faith so much as its creature, its expression, and its embodiment.'* It seems to have been thought," continues the Bishop, "that this language is at variance with the Divine origin of Scripture, and traces it to a human source. *But this appears to me a misapprehension.* There is certainly no contradiction between the statement that Scripture records the revelations of the Church, and the admission that those revelations proceeded from God. It is quite consistent to say that the Church was before the Bible, and that Revelation was before the Church; to say that Holy Scripture is not the foundation so much as the creature of the Christian faith; and yet, that Revelation is not the creature so much as the foundation of that faith. One who asserts that the sacred writers only 'expressed thoughts that were stirring in the breast of the Church,' need not be supposed to deny that what they made known was 'the mind of the Lord.' *No question is raised by such statements as to the origin of the Revelation, but only as to the mode of its transmission.* The truth that the Church was before the Bible, is not the less certain because it has been abused by the Romanist; and it is confirmed by the testimony of the Bible itself. *And then it follows that there must be a sense in which it is allowable and necessary to affirm, that Scripture embodies the experience, expresses the thoughts, makes known that which was the mind of the Church, no less than of the Lord."*

We might now, I venture to think, safely leave the charge of " depraving Scripture " as

---

* Charge delivered by the Bishop of St. David's, October, 1857, pp. 78, 79.

sufficiently disposed of and refuted by these wise and judicious and well-timed observations of the Bishop. But the charge as admitted against Mr. Wilson has peculiarities of its own, which we must not fail to notice.

The reader will observe, that the passage "articled and objected to" against Mr. Wilson is simply "a comment upon the sixth Article," on which Dr. Lushington observes, "It is true, as Mr. Wilson says, the sixth Article does not contain the expression 'Word of God.' It is true that it does not contain a declaration of the Bible having been *throughout* supernaturally suggested, nor any intimation as to which portions of it were owing to a special Divine illumination. Mr. Wilson then contends, that if the Fathers have usually considered 'canonical' as synonymous with 'miraculously inspired,' there is nothing to show that this sense of the word must necessarily be applied to the sixth Article.

"I cannot concur with this exposition of the meaning of the sixth Article. I think, as I have said before, that the averment that the Bible contains all things necessary for salvation, to that extent necessarily implies that it was written by the special interposition of the Almighty for that purpose. I think this construction strongly supported by the twentieth Article of Religion; the Bible is there called 'God's Word written.' I feel myself compelled to come to the conclusion that, in the passage quoted, Mr. Wilson, expressing the opinion which he himself holds, denies that the Bible was written by the special interposition of the Almighty power; and that such doctrine cannot be reconciled with the sixth and twentieth Articles."

Now, this is really very startling. The reader will observe, that Mr. Wilson *expresses no opinion of any kind whatever;* he simply remarks on the absence of any sufficient evidence to show that the word "canonical," as applied in the Article to Holy Scripture, is synonymous and convertible with *miraculously inspired.* If such evidence exists, where is it to be found? The very word *inspiration*, as we have already observed, only occurs thrice throughout the formularies,—in the collect which precedes the Communion Service, in the collect for the Fifth Sunday after Easter, and in the thirteenth Article, where it is used in the sense of the Divine influence on the hearts of all believers. The technical use of the term as equivalent to *miraculous dictation* belongs to a much later date, *and was not even known at the time when our Articles were first composed.** And as to the meaning of the word *canonical*, this, having never yet been precisely defined by the Church, has always hitherto been regarded as a legitimate subject of inquiry

* See Appendix, Note B.

and discussion by theologians. Wherein, then, consists Mr. Wilson's offence? Even assuming with Dr. Lushington that Mr. Wilson has misinterpreted the Article, to misinterpret is not to *contradict*. The former is simply a theological error, the latter an ecclesiastical offence. But, as Professor Grote very justly observes, we "cannot see why this comment of Mr. Wilson on the sixth Article should not have been written by the most orthodox prelate, if for any reason he should have occasion to explain to us what the Articles do not mean or contain, rather than what they do." *

What, however, we most object to in this portion of the judgment is, the *inquisitorial* character of the process by which the learned Judge allows himself to guess at the author's opinions, and to impose his own inferences on his words.

"It is no use," remarks the writer just quoted, "in Dr. Lushington to say (though I am rejoiced he does say it) 'There is no inquisitorial power'—'What the law takes notice of in a clergyman is not the opinions which he holds in private, but the opinions which he advisedly maintains and promulgates'—if a whole course of inference is permitted from what a clergyman says to what he must think, or he would not have spoken so. Extrajudicially, such a

* Examination of Judgment, p. 36.

course of proceeding must, to a certain extent, be considered allowable ; for we cannot, in reading a book, separate the author's published sentiments from an imagination, on our part, of a system of thought from which they flow. But even here not only charity, but the interests of theology, require that narrow limits should be set. Judicially, what an author *thinks*, we have nothing to do with: only what he distinctly says." *

We pass now to the second article admitted against Dr. Williams. Under this, Dr. Williams is charged with using language on the subject of *Propitiation*, inconsistent with and contrary to the thirty-first Article. " Propitiation," says Dr. Lushington, " is, by the thirty-first Article of Religion, the oblation of Christ finished upon the Cross for sin. Dr. Williams declares it to be ' the recovery of that peace which cannot be whilst sin divides us from the Searcher of hearts.' Such may be a consequence from propitiation or the oblation of Christ, but it is not propitiation itself. I think such declaration is inconsistent with and contradictory to the thirty-first Article."

But what this Article asserts is not, as Dr. Lushington puts it, " that propitiation is the oblation of Christ," etc., but that " the offering of Christ is *that* propitiation for all the sins of

---

* Examination of Judgment, pp. 36, 37.

the whole world," as St. John says, "He is the propitiation for our sins." Mr. Grote calls attention to the word *that* in the Article as a sort of emphatic demonstrative, equivalent to "which we all know about," or something to that effect. The object of the Article is to set forth the offering of Christ once made as the one perfect sacrifice for sin, and it is called *that propitiation* as being offered by Him who, in the words of the second Article, "truly suffered, was dead and buried, to *reconcile* His Father to us, and to be a sacrifice not only for original guilt, but also for actual sins of men." The one completed sacrifice of Christ is set forth, in opposition to the repeated sacrifices of the Mass, as the ground and source of the reconciliation and redemption of the world—"The offering of Christ once made, is that perfect redemption, *propitiation,* and satisfaction for all the sins of the whole world, both original and actual; and there is none other satisfaction but that alone." In short, the Article declares the sacrifice of Christ to be the source and ground of *that propitiation* which Dr. Williams supposes Baron Bunsen to describe *with reference to its effects on the heart and conscience of the believer* as "the recovery of that peace which cannot be while sin divides us from the Searcher of hearts."*

---

* And it should be distinctly remembered, that in this

There is nothing, surely, in such a statement inconsistent with the strictest orthodoxy or with the most rigid interpretation of the thirty-first Article.

We pass on to the third charge, which is, that Dr. Williams, in the extract pleaded, did maintain that justification by faith means only the peace of mind or sense of Divine approval which comes of trust in a righteous God; and that "justification is a verdict of forgiveness upon our repentance, and of acceptance upon the offering of our hearts." It is contended, on the part of the prosecution, that the doctrine is contrary to the eleventh Article of Religion,—on the justification of man. "We are accounted righteous before God only for the merit of our Lord and Saviour Jesus Christ by faith, and not for our own works or deservings." The passage objected to is as follows :—" Why may not justification by faith have meant the peace of mind, or sense of Divine approval, which comes of trust in a righteous God, rather than a fiction of merit by transfer ?"

"The words," observes Dr. Lushington, " are suggested by Dr. Williams as words which Baron Bunsen might speak in reply to a charge

---

passage Dr. Williams is simply giving the sense of "Propitiation" in Baron Bunsen's system—with a certain degree of sympathy, it is true, but by no means fully adopting it as his own.

of using evangelical language in a philosophical sense. But, looking to the whole context, I cannot doubt that Dr. Williams employs those words as a form of declaring his own sentiments. He is, therefore, responsible for them.

"Then as to the construction of the passage. I think the passage is repugnant to the eleventh Article; for in it justification is not represented to be justification for the merit of our Lord by faith, but is represented to be something distinct from it—namely, peace of mind, or a sense of Divine approval, which comes of trust in a righteous God. I think this is clear from the words which follow, '*rather than from a fiction of merit by transfer.*' These words seem to me to express an idea wholly inconsistent with the eleventh Article."

But here again the apparent contradiction seems to arise solely from the different aspects under which the justification of the sinner is regarded. The Article speaks of it *with reference to its efficient cause* as originating in the merit of Christ; whereas Dr. Williams supposes Baron Bunsen to be describing it *with reference to its subjective effect on the mind of the person so justified.* What Dr. Williams is here describing, is not simple justification, but justification *by faith*, with an emphasis on the expression *by faith*. He is, in fact, explaining the part of faith in justification, without implying any exclusion of the merit of Christ as its originating cause and the true object of that faith.*

"The miscarriage of justice in these points," observes Dr. Williams, "may be explained, with no great discourtesy, if we observe that the aspect under which Revelation presents itself to the legal mind is not as saving souls, but as material for framing Articles; and that a doctrinal contradiction thus technically elicited need not be a negative of any truth, but such a variation of tone or aspect as may admit of being harshly construed into a studied discrepancy. I must confess myself to have looked in vain through the judgment for any recognition of the manifold depth of theological truth, or of that function of the scholar which handles impartially all monuments of antiquity, without perverting in favour of any Church that by which all Churches profit in turn. Probably not one of the subjects is caught in the judgment at the point of view at which it must have presented itself to either one of the original disputants.

"I do not like the idea of calumniating myself, or of giving to persecutors the barren semblance of a triumph; but if I were technically to withdraw every expression reserved by the Court, in

---

* Cf. Professor Grote's Examination of Judgment, p. 51. See also Dr. Lushington's definition of Justification in Mr. Heath's case.

the sense which the Court has technically affixed to it, I should not thereby retract a particle of my meaning, or imply any modification of opinion. That sentence of the judgment which excluded Scripture from the indictment, decided in my favour every principle maintained by me. However technical its form, its result was the precise object of my aims. It restored to the Church that right of interpreting Scripture at large which our Articles preserve, while they limit it; and which, for the sake of sanctity and virtue, the wisest Christians must wish preserved. I do not mean that the theological principles of the Court, which I accept, appeared to me drawn out with the utmost felicity of discrimination of which they are capable; or that the doctrine of Divine Inspiration, which I have asserted, and not sinned against, derives from the judgment anything better than a novel and illogical authorisation of a truth which might be better grounded—perhaps, more wisely, limited. The first section of the Book of Homilies, in which the Word of God is said *not* to be identical with Scripture, but to be *contained in* it, might have suggested a happier discrimination."*

So far of the case against Dr. Williams. The second article admitted against Mr. Wilson charges him with a denial of the eighteenth

---

* Persecution for the Word. Postscript, p. 62.

Article of Religion, which is in these words:—
"They also are to be had accursed that presume to say, that every man shall be saved by the law or sect which he professeth, so that he be diligent to frame his life according to that law, and the light of Nature. For Holy Scripture doth set out unto us only the name of Jesus Christ, whereby men must be saved." The passage in which Mr. Wilson is held to have infringed this Article, is as follows: "When we hear fine distinctions drawn between covenanted and uncovenanted mercies, it seems either to be a distinction without a difference, or to amount to a denial of a broad and equal justice of the Supreme Being."

"I think," says Dr. Lushington, "the meaning of this passage is a denial of any distinction between covenanted and uncovenanted mercies. Now covenanted mercy is the mercy promised by our Saviour to those who believe in Him; uncovenanted mercy is that which God may be pleased to bestow, though no promise thereof has been made. Covenanted mercy is matter of absolute certainty, the fulfilment of the promise of the Almighty; uncovenanted mercy is speculation of what may happen upon a human idea of the Divine attributes. The two things appear to me clearly and essentially distinct. To deny any distinction appears to me to declare that a man may be saved by the law which he professeth. Whether this proposition be true or not, is not the question. I think the eighteenth Article prohibits it being declared; and therefore I must come to the conclusion that the Article has been infringed."

The reader will observe that this conclusion is arrived at through a series of supposed meanings and inferences, having only a remote and uncertain connection with the words of the Article and of Mr. Wilson. Dr. Lushington gives his own impression of what is popularly understood by *covenanted mercy*.* But is Mr. Wilson bound by this description? Is there anything in the Article which limits the covenanted mercy of God to "the mercy promised by our Saviour to those who believe in Him?" And if not, are there not other expressions in the formularies which suggest a wider and more comprehensive sense? What, *e.g.*, is the second thing which the Catechism teaches us to gather from the Creed? "Secondly, I learn to believe in God the Son, who hath redeemed me, *and all mankind*." And do not the second and thirty-first

---

* Dr. Lushington might feel himself bound to interpret terms occurring in the Articles; but he was certainly going beyond what any Judge of the Ecclesiastical Court had before attempted, when he undertook to lay down the only possible sense in which such words as *covenanted and uncovenanted mercy* can be understood—words occurring nowhere in the Articles, nor in any of the other formularies of the Church.

Articles speak of the sacrifice and offering of Christ, as "that perfect redemption, propitiation, and satisfaction *for the sins of the whole world?*" Does not the very word "*covenant*" remind us of the "mercy promised to our forefathers," and the "*Holy Covenant*" which God made with Abraham, *that in his seed should all the nations of the earth be blessed?*—to say nothing of those many passages of Scripture which speak the same language of infinite hope. "*The Lord is good to all, and His tender mercies are over all His works;*" and again, "*As in Adam all die, so in Christ shall all be made alive.*" Nay, does not this very eighteenth Article set forth the "name of Jesus Christ"—the revelation of God's love to us in Christ—as the ground and *covenanted pledge* of God's mercy to every human being, whether he be heathen, Jew, or Christian? Does it not re-affirm and enforce in the most emphatic manner the doctrine of St. Paul and of the eleventh Article—the doctrine of the Scripture and of the Church—that "there is no respect of persons with God," but that all who, according to the light and strength vouchsafed to them, are "doers of the law;" all who do what is right, and good, and true, as far as they know it—shall be made righteous, shall have God's righteousness freely given and imputed to them, shall be pronounced to be righteous, counted as righteous, dealt with as righteous,—

in one word, shall be regarded by God as His own dear children, not by virtue of any merit or claim which any one of them can derive from "the law or sect which he professeth," as if he could be saved from God's wrath by that, but by virtue of God's free grace alone, declared to us in His Son, Christ Jesus?*

It is true that from another point of view, and with that school which would represent the Sacrament of Baptism as absolutely necessary to salvation, the covenanted mercy of God is sometimes represented as extending only to the baptized. But that is, I humbly conceive, a truer view of the Sacrament of Baptism which regards it as the sign and seal and covenanted pledge to each one of us *individually* of what God has done for all mankind *collectively*. "Baptism," it has been well said, "is a visible witness to the world of that which the world is for ever forgetting—a common humanity united in God. Baptism authoritatively reveals and pledges to the individual that which is true of the race. Baptism takes the child and addresses it by name. Paul,—no longer Saul,—you are a child of God. Remember it henceforth. It is now revealed to you, and recognised by you, and to recognise God as the Father is to be regenerate. *You*, Paul, are

---

* Cf. Stanley's Canterbury Sermons, Sermon XIV.

now regenerate; you will have foes to fight—the world, the flesh, and the devil; but remember they only keep you out of an inheritance which is your own; not an inheritance which you have to win, by some new feeling or merit in yourself. It *is* yours; you *are* the child of God — you *are* a member of Christ—you *are* an inheritor of the kingdom of heaven. Baptism, then, does not *create* a child of God. It authoritatively declares him. It does not make the fact: it only reveals it. If baptism made it a fact, then and there for the first time, baptism would be magic. Nay, faith does not create a child of God any more than baptism, nor does it make a fact. *It only appropriates that which is a fact already.*"

Again, " Baptism proclaims a Church, humanity joined in Christ to God. Do not say that the separating work of baptism, drawing a distinction between the Church and the world, negatives this. Do not say, that because the Church is separated from the world, therefore the world are not God's children. Rather that very separation proves it. You baptize a separate body in order to realize that which is true of the collective race, as in the text—' There is neither Jew nor Greek.' In all things it is the same. If you would sanctify all time, you set apart a Sabbath—not to show that other days are not intended to be sacred, but for the very purpose of making them sacred. If you would have a nation of priests you set apart a priesthood; not as if the priestly functions of instruction and assisting to approach God were exclusively in that body, but in order, by consecration, to bring out to greater perfection the priestly character which is shared by the whole, and then thereby make the whole more truly 'priests to God to offer spiritual sacrifices.' In the same way, if God would baptize humanity, He baptizes a separate Church, in order that that Church may baptize the race. The Church is God's ideal of humanity realized."*

The third article admitted against Mr. Wilson relates to the expression of a hope, in the concluding passage of his Essay, of a merciful dealing on the part of the Almighty with those whom it is hard to call either good or evil—of a spiritual training in another life—and even of a possible final salvation for all.

The question of ecclesiastical law here raised depends entirely on the meaning to be attached to the words *eternal* and *everlasting* in the formularies as representing the αἰώνιος of the Scriptures and original creeds. Dr. Lushington takes them without hesitation, in what he calls "their plain, literal, and grammatical sense;" meaning, apparently, thereby, their common,

---

* Robertson's Sermons, Second Series, pp. 63, 66.

popular, and colloquial signification—as equivalent to *endless*.

"The Creed of St. Athanasius," he observes, "contains the following words : ' And they that have done good shall go into life everlasting; and they that have done evil, into everlasting fire.' "

On these he remarks—" I am of course aware of the controversies which have arisen upon the meaning to be attributed to these words, but I must construe them in their plain, literal, and grammatical sense, and that is clearly to assert that eternal life shall be the portion of the good, and everlasting fire the destiny of the bad." (The learned judge seems to forget that, until the meaning of the words in question is determined, this simple reiteration of them in the judgment decides nothing.) " To the same effect is the passage from the Catechism : ' That God will keep us from all sin and wickedness, and from our ghostly enemy, and from everlasting death.' Similar expressions are found in the Commination."

I turn now to what Mr. Wilson has written. The substance of the passage extracted is, that such is the neutral character of the multitude, that neither the promises nor denunciations of Revelation are applicable to them; that a hope must be entertained that, after the great adjudication, receptacles may be found for those who shall be infants as to spiritual development, when the stunted may become strong, and the perverted may be restored; and "when the Christian Church in all its branches shall have fulfilled its sublunary office, and its Founder shall have surrendered His kingdom to the Great Father, all, both small and great, shall find a refuge in the bosom of the Universal Parent, to repose or to be quickened into higher life in the ages to come, according to His will."

"I believe I put the true construction upon this passage, when I say it declares that a hope must be entertained of an intermediate state, and that finally all, both small and great, will escape everlasting condemnation. I cannot reconcile the opinions thus declared with the passages cited of the Creeds and Formularies, and I must admit the article."

Now, on this we remark first, that Mr. Wilson declares no opinion. His words throughout are only the expression of a hope, and are so described by Dr. Lushington. But we may well ask with Professor Grote—" Is such an expression of hope to be considered 'advisedly teaching?' And are the clergy of the Church of England prepared to accept this, that not only everything which they teach as doctrine, but everything which their hope and imagination may suggest to them, and lead them to suggest to others, as what may *possibly* be, is to be matter (and that without any charge against them of *mala fides,* or of intending to convey an impression different from what their words bear) for courts and trials like this? Is it condemnable in the Court of Arches to breathe the thought that the Divine mercy and wisdom may find a way (and what will then seem the natural way) out of difficulties which to us are insoluble, and make it appear that though there is justice for all, there is love for all as well?"

But for whom does Mr. Wilson venture to express this hope? For those primarily—"rudimentary spirits, germinal souls"—to whom "we are at a loss to apply either the promises or the denunciations of revelation," and with whom accordingly the words of the Creed, referring respectively to the good and the bad, have nothing to do. "If we compare with the words of the Athanasian Creed, on the one side, what Mr. Wilson says on the other, we find that what he says, saving for the present the last paragraph, has to do with a class the existence of which the Athanasian Creed in no way negatives, and of whose future lot, if they exist, it says nothing— neutral souls, seeming alike unfit for reward or punishment—germinal souls, in whom good and evil are alike undeveloped. If Mr. Wilson chooses to supplement the Athanasian Creed, in his imagination, with a speculation on the probable lot of these, there is nothing in that Creed to hinder him. In regard of them, whatever there may be in Mr. Wilson *besides* the Creed, there is nothing, for there can be nothing, in contradiction of it." *

But beyond this, does Mr. Wilson suppose the possibility of a final salvation for all, even the confessedly wicked? If so, it is in the concluding passage of his Essay, which is merely a paraphrase of the words of St. Paul—"Then cometh the end, when He shall have delivered up the kingdom to God, even the Father; when He shall have put down all rule, and all authority, and power. For He must reign, till He hath put all enemies under his feet. And when all things shall be subdued unto Him, then shall the Son also Himself be subject unto Him, that put all things under Him, *that God may be all in all.*" † The object of this passage is evidently to set forth the end of Christ's mediatorial kingdom as the consummation and triumph of His work of Redemption. "It is, indeed," observes Dr. Stanley, "a most remarkable passage. As expressing what the Apostle looked to as the consummation of the world, it must be regarded as in one sense the consummation of his teaching. *In almost all later systems of religion and philosophy, there has been an element corresponding to this Apostolic aspiration, a belief that God is, or is to be, everywhere, and in all things.* The Apostle's

---

* Grote's Examination of Judgment, pp. 64, 65.
† 1 Cor. xv. 24, 25, 28.

words (ὁ θεὸς πάντα ἐν πᾶσιν) may almost seem to have given birth to the name literally based on them, though now always used in reproach—*pan-theism*. . . . . . In some later systems of theology it has been customary to represent God as the object of fear, Christ as the object of love; God as the source of justice, Christ as the source of mercy. The Apostle's object here is, if we may so say, directly the reverse: Christ is spoken of as the representative of power, of authority, of control; *God is spoken of as the Infinite rest and repose*, after the close of that long struggle for which alone power and authority are needed—"*When all, both small and great, shall find a refuge in the bosom of the Universal Parent, to repose or to be quickened into higher life in the ages to come, according to His Will.*"— The pagan views of the divinity never shrunk from multiplying the agencies, the persons, the powers of God; wherever an operation of nature or of man was discernible, there a new deity was imagined, on which the minds of the worshippers might rest without ascending higher. It is this feeling which the Apostle combats. Even if in this present world a distinction must be allowed between God, the Invisible Eternal Father, and Christ, the Lord and Ruler of man, the representative to our dull senses of Him who is above and beyond all, he points our thoughts to a time when this distinction will cease, when the reign of all intermediate objects, even of Christ Himself, shall cease, and God will fill all the universe (πάντα), AND BE HIMSELF PRESENT IN THE HEARTS AND MINDS OF ALL (ἐν πᾶσιν)." *

Such, remarks Neander, is the magnificent prospect of the final triumph of the work of Redemption, which was first opened to the mind of the great Apostle, by means of that love which impelled Him to sacrifice Himself for the salvation of mankind. Nor is there, he adds, anything in this prospect of a universal restitution inconsistent with the doctrine of *eternal punishment,* as it appears in the gospels and creeds of the Church; "for although those who are hardened in wickedness, left to the consequences of their conduct, their merited fate, have to expect endless unhappiness, yet a secret decree of the Divine compassion is not necessarily excluded, by virtue of which, through the wisdom of God, *revealing itself in the discipline of free agents,* they will be led to a free appropriation of redemption."†

From this point of view we must interpret the words *eternal, everlasting,* according to a well-known principle of Scripture language,‡ as ex-

* Stanley's Commentary on the Corinthians, vol. i. p. 370.
† History of the Planting of Christianity, *ad finem.*
‡ "At, inquies, si Christus traditurus est regnum Deo ac Patri, quo pacto erunt vera illa, Heb. i. 8, *ad Filium autem,*

pressing "*a relative eternity, an unbroken per-perpetuity for a given time, holding on through a period or system of things to which a reference is understood to be made.*"* Such a period would be the duration of Christ's mediatorial kingdom, which would thus be regarded as occupying, so to speak, the narrower field of positive Revelation, without excluding the possibility of a wider sphere beyond, where "God shall be all in all," and even the reign of Christ Himself, which holds together the churches which walk "in the fear of the Lord," shall cease in that intimate, all-embracing communion of man with God,

thronus tuus, Deus, in sæculum sæculi. Dan. vii. 14: *Cujus dominatus, dominatus est perpetuus qui non præterit; et regnum ejus regnum quod non corrumpitur.* Luc. i. 33: *Regni ejus non erit finis.* Respondeo, regni ejus non fore finem in sæculum sæculi, id est, dum mundi sæcula durabunt, donec *tempus non erit amplius.* Apoc. x. 6: Donec omnia implebuntur quorum causâ regnum accepit: non itaque præteribit regnum illud quasi irritum, non corrumpetur; neque erit finis ille dissolutionis, sed perfectionis potius et impletionis, ut finis ille legis, Matt. v. 18. Quo sensu alia quoque multa dicuntur nunquam præteritura, sed perpetua atque æterna fore; ut circumcisio, Gen. xvii. 13, et lex ipsa cæremonialis, Lev. iii. 17, et xxiv. 8; et terra Canaan, Gen. xiii. 15, Jer. vii. 7, et xxv. 5; et sabbathum, Exod. xxxi. 16; et sacerdotium Aaronis, Num. xviii. 8; et monumentum illud lapideum ad Jordenem, Jos. iv. 7; et signa cœlestia, Psal. cxlviii. 6; et terra, Eccles. i. 4; haec tamen omnia finem aut habuerunt aut habitura sunt."—*Milton's Doctrina Christiana*, p. 382.

* See Davison on Prophecy, pp. 204, 205.

which is the last and highest hope to which we can look forward.*

It is also of importance to observe, that this hope is in no way inconsistent with the doctrine of the Scripture and of our Church respecting " the judgment of God, awarding to those men whom He shall then approve everlasting life, and to those men whom he shall then condemn everlasting death." Such a judgment of God is, indeed, expressly presupposed, and all that is suggested is a hope that the punishment *then* awarded may prove to be *remedial* in its design and in its effect. That there is nothing in the description of that punishment as *eternal* inconsistent with that hope, we have already shown; and, as a matter of fact, it is notorious that such a hope has been held and openly expressed in every period of the Church's history. It has been held without disguise and without blame by numbers of our own most eminent and learned divines.

And as this hope is not inconsistent with, but presupposes a previous judgment of God, so is it clearly to be distinguished from the doctrine of *Purgatory* as taught in the Roman Church. The Purgatory of the Church of Rome is an *intermediate* state interjected, so to speak, parenthetically within the field of revealed re-

---

* See Stanley on Corinthians, vol. i. p. 371.

ligion, *between death and the judgment*, without any warrant from Scripture. The hope expressed by Mr. Wilson has certainly nothing to do with this, and refers to what may be supposed to take place not *before*, but " *after* the great adjudication."

I have hitherto spoken of the words eternal and everlasting in what would, I suppose, be commonly regarded as their " plain literal sense," as referring to *duration*. But it may well be questioned whether those words as found in the New Testament and the Creeds have any regard at all to duration. The views of Mr. Maurice on this subject are well known, and there are not a few among the clergy who think with him.

"Those," remarks Mr. Maurice, "who would not own Christ in His brethren, who did not visit Him when they were sick and in prison, *go away*, He said, *into eternal* or *everlasting punishment*. Are we affixing a new meaning to these words, or the very meaning which the context demands, the only meaning which is consistent with the force that is given to the adjective by our Lord and His apostles elsewhere, if we say that the eternal punishment is the punishment of being without the knowledge of God, who is love, and of Jesus Christ who has manifested it, even as eternal life is declared to be the knowledge of God and of Jesus Christ? (*Cf.* John

xvii. 3.) *If it is right, if it is a duty, to say that eternity in relation to God has nothing to do with time or duration, are we not bound to say that also in reference to life or to punishment, it has nothing to do with time or duration?"* *

To the same effect observes Canon Stanley:—

"The distinction drawn between 'this life' and 'eternal life,' has no foundation in Scripture. 'Eternal life' is not a period of time, but a gift of God given to man, either now or hereafter (such, *e. g.*, is the sense of 1 Tim. iv. 8, 'The promise of life both now and in the next world' τῆς νῦν καὶ τῆς μελλούσης). The use of ζωή in any way for a period of existence is very rare in the New Testament, and occurs only in Luke xvi. 25." †

So wrote Dr. Stanley in 1854; and is it to be endured that in 1863 the Dean of the Court of Arches should be summoned *quasi Deus ex machinâ* to declare that *eternal* means, and can only mean, "endless," and that it is *criminal* in a clergyman to indulge in the remotest hope of deliverance for myriads upon myriads of our fellow men from eternal, everlasting, irremediable, unspeakable woe?

The spirit of ecclesiastical intolerance has done its worst, and this is the result. We congratulate it heartily on the success of its efforts.

---

* Maurice's Theological Essays, pp. 449, 450.
† Stanley on the Corinthians, vol. i. pp. 366, 367.

In reply to these charges the defendants put in what is technically called an "allegation," formally repudiating the inferences sought to be drawn from their writings, and declaring that they have not, in any of the passages recited by the prosecution, "advisedly or at all maintained or affirmed any strange or heretical doctrines, positions, or opinions contrary to the doctrine and teaching of the United Church of England and Ireland as by law established, or to the Statutes, Constitutions, or Canons Ecclesiastical of the Realm, or against the peace or amity of the Church."

On December the 15th, 1862, the cases came on for further hearing on the articles admitted in the previous judgment; but the proceedings were chiefly formal, the learned Judge declaring his determination to abide by his former judgment, "that he had nothing to retract, nothing to alter, nothing to explain." He considered the articles proved, and he proceeded accordingly to pass sentence against the defendants, which was, "that they should be suspended *ab officio et beneficio* for one year, and that they should pay the costs."

Thereupon Mr. Dubois, the defendants' proctor, immediately lodged an appeal to the Privy Council, and the proceedings terminated in the Arches Court.

As to the ultimate result of this appeal, we

cannot for one moment allow ourselves to doubt. The condemnation of the Court of Arches is clearly founded not on any contradiction of the Articles or other formularies of the Church, but on certain *inferences* which Dr. Lushington has drawn from those documents on the one hand, and the writings of the Essayists on the other. Whether these inferences are correctly drawn or not is, we submit, a question of theology and literary criticism quite beyond the cognizance of a court of criminal law. A court of law has certainly no warrant for demanding from a clergyman assent to any particular explanation of an Article, or to any particular consequence deduced from it, except so far as the Church has herself explained and defined her meaning on the point at issue. "Inferences," remarks the late Archdeacon Hare, "which may appear to us essential and irrefragable, may not be seen in the same light by minds differently constituted and trained. The rule both of justice and equity, a deviation from which would open a gate to all manner of arbitrary injustice, is that laid down by the Court of Appeal for its own guidance in this (the Gorham) case, in the words of that great judge, Sir William Scott, that '*if any Article is really a subject of dubious interpretation, it would be highly improper that the court should fix on one meaning, and prosecute all those who hold a contrary opinion regarding its interpretation.'* " *

"On the one hand," observes the Bishop of St. David's, " I hold myself bound to resist the introduction of all error contrary to the teaching of the Church; on the other hand, I regard it as a no less sacred and important part of my duty, to respect, and, so far as lies in me, to protect, that freedom of thought, word, and action, which the Church has hitherto granted to her ministers and members, and neither to make nor to sanction an attempt to place it under any new restriction which she has not thought fit to impose. *I also consider it as a plain rule of equity, that no man shall be held responsible for opinions which he disavows, and that every one shall be allowed to interpret his language in his own sense, and shall not be convicted of heresy—above all, when the conviction is to involve penal consequences—on a construction of his words which he does not himself admit. To sustain a charge of unsound doctrine, involving penal consequences, nothing, as it appears to me, ought to suffice, but the most direct unequivocal statements, asserting that which the Church denies, or denying that which she asserts.*" †

---

* Letter to the Hon. Richard Cavendish. Miscellaneous Works, p. 10.

† Charge, 1857, pp. 27, 62, 63.

To the above lucid expositions of the only principle which ought to guide any English court of justice, I need add nothing. The reader will see at once the equity of the principle as well as the great danger and extreme impolicy of forsaking it for any mere theological investigation. In the words of Dr. Lushington we may, indeed, well exclaim, "*How unsatisfactory would such an investigation be to the clergy and people of this realm! What confusion would be introduced by the diverse opinions of Ecclesiastical Judges! What mistakes would necessarily arise! Into what a state of uncertainty would the clergy of our Church be plunged!*"

* Dr. Lushington's Judgment, p. 13.

APPENDIX.

(A.)

"TO THE ARCHBISHOP OF DUBLIN.

"I HAVE been thinking of what you say as to a book on the Origin of Civilization, and considering whether I could furnish anything towards it. But history, I think, can furnish little to the purpose, because all history properly so called belongs to an age of at least partial civilization; and the poetical or mythical traditions which refer to the origin of this civilization cannot be made use of to prove anything, till their character has undergone a more complete analysis. I believe with you that *savages* could never civilize themselves, but *barbarians*, I think, might; and there are some races, *e.g.*, the Keltic, the Teutonic, and the Hellenic, that we cannot trace back to a savage state, nor does it appear that they ever were savages. With regard to such races as have been found in a savage state, if it be admitted that all mankind are originally one race, then I should say that they must have degenerated; but, if the physiological question be not settled yet, and there is any reason to suppose that the New Hollander and the Greek never had one common ancestor, then you would have the races of mankind divided into those improveable by themselves, and those improveable only by others; the first created originally with such means in their possession, that out of these they could work indefinitely their own improvement, the ποῦ στῶ being in a manner given them; the second without the ποῦ στῶ, and intended to receive it in time, through the instrumentality of their fellow-creatures. And this would be sufficiently analogous to the course of Providence in other known cases, *e. g.*, the communicating all religious knowledge to mankind through the Jewish people, and all intellectual civilization through the Greeks; no people having ever yet possessed that activity of mind, and that power of reflection and questioning of things, which are the marks of intellectual advancement, without having derived them, mediately or immediately, from Greece. I had occasion in the winter to observe this in a Jew, of whom I took a few lessons in Hebrew, and who was learned in the writings of the Rabbis, but totally ignorant of all the literature of the West, ancient and modern. He was consequently just like a child—his mind being entirely without the habit of criticism or analysis, whether as applied to words or to things; wholly ignorant, for instance, of the analysis of language, whether grammatical or logical; or of the analysis of a narrative of facts, according to any rules of probability external or internal. I never so felt the debt which the human race owes to Pythagoras, or whoever it was that was the first founder of Greek Philosophy.

. . . . . "The interest of present questions, involving as they do great and eternal principles, hinders me from fixing contentedly upon a work of past history; while the hopelessness of persuading men, and the inevitable odium which attends anything written on the topics of the day, hinder me on the other hand from writing much about the present. How great this odium is, I really could have hardly conceived, even with all my former experience." *

(B.)

" Some years ago," writes Dr. Stanley, "this noble passage was† invested to me with an additional interest by an accident which befel me in Russia. I was on my way to the country residence of the venerable Archbishop and Metropolitan of Moscow, Philaret, in company with a Russian general, who had undertaken to act as interpreter. During our drive we discussed the topics of conversation suitable to the interview ; and I suggested some question relating to the Old Testament, as a subject to which, it was understood, the Metropolitan had paid special attention. The general himself started the difficulty, which, he said, had often occurred to him, of the apparent vindictiveness and cruelty of the precepts in the Old Testament, compared with the milder spirit of the New. We discussed this difficulty as we went; and I ventured, among other solutions, to suggest the words of the text, which, as well as the Epistle from which it is taken, was wholly new to him. In the interview with the archbishop which followed, the topic of the difference between the Old and the New Dispensations was the one which he introduced to the aged Primate. The Metropolitan immediately broke into an animated argument, in the course of which the general turned round with unfeigned

* Extract from a Letter addressed by Dr. Arnold to the Archbishop of Dublin, March 22, 1835, (Stanley's Life, vol. I., p. 417).
† Hebrew I., 1, 2.

astonishment and delight, and said, ' He has quoted the very same passage to which you referred, in our conversation, and has pointed out how in the expression *sundry times and divers manners* there is a complete acknowledgment of the gradual and successive modes of imperfect Revelation before the full light of Christianity.'

" It is, indeed, an obvious statement and answer of the whole difficulty. I mention this simple incident; first, because it shows how naturally it occurs to serious students of the Old Testament, under circumstances the most widely different; and secondly, because it shows how a doctrine which in our own country is often regarded at the present day with extreme hostility and suspicion, was familiar and congenial to the mind of the most venerable authority of the most orthodox of European Churches.

"But it may be well to say a few words in answer to an objection. It may be said that the doctrine contained in the Sacred Text is inconsistent with that theory of a uniform and equal inspiration of every word and letter of the Bible, which is at present regarded almost as an article of faith by many religious persons in this country. That such a divergence exists, I freely admit. The doctrine of the author of this great Epistle, and the facts of the Bible generally, are alike irreconcilable with this modern hypothesis.* *Neither is the theory to which I allude contained in any of the formularies of the Church of England.* In

---

* " I have called it 'modern' as regards the history of Christendom. No doubt such a theory prevailed in regard to the Old Testament amongst the Rabbinical schools. In Christian Theology it appears to have been first systematized in the *Formula Consensus Helvetica*, 1675."

the only instances* in which the word Inspiration and its cognate verb are used in the Liturgy and in the Articles, the sense is invariably that of the Divine influence suggesting all good thoughts and wise counsels to the hearts and minds of all men. *To deny this wide signification of the word, and to restrict its meaning to any single exercise of the Divine operations, would be an offence against the letter, if not the spirit, of the Formularies, which ought not to be needlessly incurred."* †

"If we refer," observes Bishop Thirlwall, "as we are bound to do, to the Church's standards of doctrine, we find that she has pronounced no decision—has laid down no definition on the subject [of inspiration]. It was hardly possible that she should have done so. For the whole question as to the nature and extent of the inspiration of Scripture, is one of modern and, among ourselves, of very recent origin. And there was nothing in any of the controversies in which she was engaged to call for or suggest a formal exposition of her views on these points. . . . . . She could have had no inducement to frame an article for avoiding diversities of opinions on these subjects, unless she had been able to foresee the speculations

---

* "The Collect in the Communion Service, 'Cleanse the thoughts of our hearts by the *inspiration* of Thy Holy Spirit.' The Collect for the fifth Sunday after Easter, 'That by Thy holy *inspiration* we may think those things that be good;' the prayer for the Church Militant, '*Inspire* continually the universal church;' the *Veni Creator*, 'Come, Holy Ghost, our souls *inspire*;' Article xiii., 'Works done before the *inspiration* of Christ's Spirit.'"

† The Bible, its Form and its Substance. Three Sermons preached before the University of Oxford, by the Rev. A. P. Stanley, D.D. Preface, pp. iii.—vi.

and controversies which were to spring up in later times with respect to them. Some may wish that she had been endued with such prescience; others may think that it was wisely and graciously withheld. *But the fact remains, that she has not bound her ministers by any authoritative statement on these questions, but has left them at liberty to inquire for themselves, and to arrive at such conclusions as best satisfy their own judgments.* . . . . . . This freedom has been used by men of whom it is impossible to doubt that they heartily accepted and reverenced the Scriptures as the Divine rule of Faith and Practice, and yet conceived their infallibility to be not absolute, but relative. *And when the principle is conceded, its application must be left to the discretion of each individual, which cannot be rightfully limited by any authority lower than that of the Church."**

"As to the question of Inspiration," remarks the writer of the article on *Essays and Reviews* in the *Edinburgh*, "there is nothing in the present volume which ought to excite surprise beyond what has been said a hundred times before. The Essayists require no precise theory of Inspiration. It is only their opponents who demand this from them, or calumniously assert this of them. Most certainly must we maintain with Professor Jowett, that our only idea of Inspiration is that which we form from our knowledge of the Bible itself. It is a question to be solved, not by speculating what the Bible ought to be, but by seeing what it actually is. The Bible might have been uniform—perfect, without varieties of text or statement, without faults of grammar or diction, without difference

* Bishop Thirlwall's Charge, 1857, pp. 67, 69.

of style or progress of doctrine. The Bible is nothing of the kind. It is full of the inequalities, variations, pauses, silences, lights, and shades which indicate the hand of God in Creation, and which indicate it no less in the multiform diversity of His own express Revelation. In this lies its inexhaustible strength, its boundless versatility, its unbroken hold on the hearts and consciences of men—the true signs of a Book wherein resides the voice of Him whose voice is as the voice of many waters: the language in which we all of us hear, 'every man,' as it were, 'in the tongue wherein we were born, the wonderful works of God.' And, if in this Book the Divine and human be necessarily intermingled, is it (we do not say rational, but is it) pious—is it reverential—to deny the human in order to exalt the Divine? The same microscope of criticism that reveals to us the depths of the inner meaning of the Divine message in all its manifold fulness—reveals to us also the imperfections, the contradictions of the human messenger. We cannot have the one without the other. It is because we so prize the kernel that we are content to break the shell, and yet even in the shell to recognize and to value the roughness of the flaws which prove it to be a genuine and not an artificial product. *To that recognition we are persuaded that every student of the sacred text and history must sooner or later be brought."*

* Edin. Rev., April, 1861, p. 482.

(C.)

THE SACRIFICE OF ISAAC.

" The history of the world and of the Church requires us to notice the act of faith which takes us back into the innermost life of Abraham himself, and marks at least one critical stage in the progress of the True Religion. There have been in almost all ancient forms of religion —in most modern forms also—strong tendencies, each in itself springing from the best and purest feelings of humanity, yet each, if carried into the extreme suggested by passion or by logic, incompatible with the other, and with its own highest purpose. One is the craving to please, or to propitiate, or to communicate with the Powers above us by surrendering some object near and dear to ourselves. This is the Source of all Sacrifice. The other is the profound moral instinct that the Creator of the world cannot be pleased, or propitiated, or approached by another means than a pure life and good deeds. On the exaggeration, on the contact, on the collision of these two tendencies have turned some of the chief corruptions, and some of the chief difficulties, of Ecclesiastical History. The earliest of these we are about to witness in the life of Abraham. There came, we are told, the Divine intimation, 'Take now thy son, thy only son Isaac, whom thou lovest, and offer him for a burnt offering on one of the mountains which I will tell thee of.' It was in its spirit the exact expression of the feeling of self-devotion without which religion cannot exist, and of which the whole life of the Patriarch had been the great example. But the form taken by the Divine trial or temptation* was that which a stern logical consequence of the ancient view of sacrifice did actually assume—if not then, yet certainly in after ages—among the surrounding tribes, and which cannot therefore be left out of sight in considering the whole historical aspect of the narrative. Deep in the heart of the Canaanitish nations was laid the practice of human sacrifice—the very offering here described, of 'children passing through the fire,' 'of their sons and of their daughters,' 'of the first-born for their transgressions,'—the fruit of their body for the sin of their souls. On the altars of Moab, and of Phœnicia, and of the distant Canaanite settlements in Carthage and in Spain; nay, even at times in the confines of the Chosen People itself, in the wild vow of Jephthah, in the sacrifice of Saul's sons at Gibeah, in the dark sacrifices of the Valley of Hinnom, under the very walls of Jerusalem—this almost irrepressible tendency of the burning zeal of a primitive race found its terrible expression. Such was the trial which presented itself to Abraham. From the tents of Beersheba he set forth at the rising of the sun, and went unto the place of which God had told him. It was not the place which Jewish tradition has selected on Mount Moriah at Jerusalem, still less that which Christian

---

"That this temptation, or trial, through whatever means it was suggested, should in the sacred narrative be ascribed to the overruling voice of God, is in exact accordance with the general tenor of the Hebrew Scriptures. A still more striking instance is contained in the history of David, where the same temptation, which in one book is ascribed to God, is in another ascribed to Satan. '*The Lord* moved David to say, Go, number Israel' (2 Sam. xxiv. 1). '*Satan* provoked David to number Israel' (1 Chron. xxi. 1)."

tradition shows, even to the thicket in which the ram was caught, hard by the Church of the Holy Sepulchre; still less that which Mussulman tradition indicates on Mount Arafat, at Mecca. Rather we must look to that ancient sanctuary, the natural altar on the summit of Mount Gerizim. On that spot, at that time the holiest in Palestine, the crisis was to take place. One, two, three days' journey from Beersheba—in the distance the high crest of the mountain appears. And 'Abraham lifted up his eyes, and saw the place afar off.'

"The sacrifice, the resignation of the will, in the father and the son, was accepted—the literal sacrifice of the act was repelled. On the one hand, the great principle was proclaimed that mercy is better than sacrifice—*that the sacrifice of self is the highest and holiest offering that God can receive.* On the other hand, the inhuman superstitions, towards which the ancient ceremonial of sacrifice was perpetually tending, were condemned and cast out of the true worship of the Church for ever.*

"There are doubtless many difficulties which may be raised on the offering of Isaac; but there are few, if any, which will not vanish away before the simple pathos and lofty spirit of the narrative itself, provided that we take it, as in fairness it must be taken, as a whole—its close not parted from its commencement, nor its commence-

---

* "According to the Phœnician tradition, 'Israel, king of the country, having by a nymph called Anobret [the Hebrew fountain] an only son, whom they called Icoud, the Phœnician word for only son [so applied to Isaac, Gen. xxii. 2], on occasion of a great national calamity adorned him with royal attire, and sacrificed him on an altar which he had prepared.'—*Sanchoniathon.* See Kenrick's 'Phœnicia,' 288."

ment from its close; the subordinate parts of the transaction not raised above its essential primary intention. And there is no difficulty which will not be amply compensated by reflecting on the near approach, and yet the complete repulse, of the danger which might have threatened the early Church. Nothing is so remarkable a proof of a Divine and watchful interposition, as the deliverance from the infirmity, the exaggeration, the excess, whatever it is, to which the noblest minds and the noblest forms of religion are subject. We have a proverb which tells us that '*man's extremity is God's opportunity*.' St. Jerome tells us that the corresponding proverb among the Jews was '*In the Mount of the Lord it shall be seen*,' or '*In the mountain the Lord will provide*;'—that is, '*As He had pity on Abraham, so He will have pity on us*.'

". A few words remain to be added on the relation of this crowning scene of the beginning of sacred history to the crowning scene of its close. The thoughts of Christian readers almost inevitably wander from one to the other; and without entering into details of controversy or doctrine, which would be here out of place, there is a common ground which no one need fear to recognize. The doctrine of the types of the ancient dispensation has often been pushed to excess. But there is a sense in which the connection indicated thereby admits of no dispute, and which may be illustrated even by that of other history than that with which we are now concerned. Not only in sacred, but even in Grecian and Roman history, do the earliest records sometimes foreshadow and represent to us the latest fortunes of the nation or power then coming into existence. Whoever is (if we may thus combine the older and the more modern use of the word) the *type* of the nation or race at any marked period of its course is also the type of its final consummation. Abraham and Abraham's son, in obedience, in resignation, in the sacrifice of whatever could be sacrificed short of sin, form an anticipation, which cannot be mistaken, of that last and greatest event which closes the history of the chosen people. We leap, as by a natural instinct, from the sacrifice in the land of Moriah to the sacrifice of Calvary. There are many differences—there is a danger of exaggerating the resemblance, or of confounding in either case what is subordinate with what is essential. But the general feeling of Christendom has in this respect not gone far astray. Each event, if we look at it well and understand it rightly, will serve to explain the other. In the very point of view in which I have just been speaking of it, the likeness is most remarkable. Human sacrifice, it has been well said, which in outward form most nearly resembled the death on the cross, is in spirit the farthest removed from it. Human sacrifice, as we have seen, which was in outward form nearest to the offering of Isaac, was in fact and in spirit most entirely condemned and repudiated by it. The union of parental love with the total denial of self is held up in both cases as the highest model of human, and, therefore, as the shadow of Divine love. '*Sacrifice*' is rejected, but '*to do Thy will, O God*,' is accepted."*

* Stanley's Lectures on the Jewish Church, pp. 47—51.

(D.)

The following letter appeared in the *Daily News*, August 21st, 1861.

TO THE EDITOR OF THE "DAILY NEWS."

"Sir,—Your contemporary the *Times* has at last broken silence on the great topic of the day, and has recently put forth two articles, in which the position of the Essayists as ministers of the Church of England is represented as practically indefensible. Now, as a lover of justice, you will, I think, agree with me, that in thus assailing the position of the Essayists, the writer of these articles was bound by every moral and social obligation to state that position accurately. Had he done so, it would have become at once apparent that the alleged discrepancy between the belief of these clergymen and the popular faith is nothing more nor less than the inevitable difference between the intelligent belief of the scholar and the loose traditional ideas of the less educated classes. The chief ground of complaint against them as public teachers appears to be the introduction of the ideological method of interpretation in the exposition of Holy Scripture. But, I need not remind you, sir, that there is nothing, in fact, strange or peculiar to the Essayists in the application of this method of interpretation to certain parts of Scripture. It is adopted repeatedly by the writers of the New Testament in reference to the Old, and notably by St. Paul, Gal. iv. 21—31. Mr. Wilson, against whom the remarks of your contemporary appear to be most pointedly directed, has not informed us to what extent he is prepared to carry the principle. He simply introduces his remarks on the subject as suggestive of a principle of comprehension in the national church, and in doing so is careful to guard his readers against the danger of misapplying and carrying the principle to excess. As an instance of such a misapplication, he mentions the writings of Strauss, 'which resolve into an ideal the whole of the historical and doctrinal person of Jesus.' And so again he adds, 'much of the allegorising of Philo and Origen is an exegetical ideology, exaggerated and wild.' The question he proposes to consider seems, he says, to narrow itself to this—' How can those who differ from each other intellectually in such variety of degrees, as our more educated and our less educated classes, be comprised under the same formularies of one national church —be supposed to follow them, assent to them, appropriate them, in one spirit?' Now, as this difference was not created by the Essayists, so can they be in no respect responsible for its existence, whilst the reconciliation of it suggested by Mr. Wilson, is, I submit, one of the most valuable portions of his Essay—itself, perhaps, the most valuable and highly suggestive contribution to this now celebrated volume.

" No sufficiently well-instructed Christian in these days would hesitate surely to admit that the chief importance of the Scripture records depends on their spiritual significance; and, consequently, that whatever change may be needful in our mode of conceiving certain events is of comparatively little moment, so long as their moral and spiritual lessons remain unaltered. And yet, sir, this is all that Mr. Wilson's theory of ideology appears to involve.

"Nothing, indeed, can be more false and injurious to the Essayists than to represent them as desirous to explain away and reject the real and historical element in Holy Scripture. They simply evince as scholars a wish to ascertain the facts as they are, and to present these freely, fairly, fully, without colouring or distortion of any kind to the public. 'If a clergyman,' says Dr. Williams, 'is led to investigate important facts, he is not responsible for what they may turn out, but only for faithfulness in stating them as they are. He has no jurisdiction over languages, sciences, or the reasonings of ancient fathers; and to brand him for their results (as if they were opinions contingent on his volition) is an outrage, at which, if it were attempted in regions where common sense and fairness are brought to bear, the world would ring first with laughter, and then with indignation. Only the indifference of men of the world suffers theologians, falsely so called, to attempt anything so iniquitous. Yet I know not that, even in theology, so flagrant a wrong has been attempted in England, since Bishop Standish denounced Erasmus for printing the Greek Testament as the MSS. gave it, instead of forging a more orthodox text.' (See letter to the Bishop of Llandaff.) 'You shall have your tithes a little longer, but preach short sermons, and do not trouble us with disputes,' is, I fear, still, in more senses than one, the oracle of the *Times*. But, as the writer just quoted most truly observes, 'Woe to the people which traverses sea and land, with glance seldom raised to the guidance of the stars and of Him who upholds them all. If any Bishop desired to root the fear of God out of the world, he could adopt no course more likely to do so than by forging fetters for the immortal spirit when it questions of things to come, and strives even dimly to give a reason for its faith.'

"It may, indeed, well happen that, as many years since Dr. Arnold clearly foresaw, we shall be called upon to correct, in some respects, our notions as to the Scriptures, and so far to hold views different from those of our fathers; but in doing so we need not in any way disparage them. For, in the words of that great writer, 'we should consider that our fathers did not, and could not, stand in our circumstances; that the knowledge which may call upon us to relinquish some of their opinions was a knowledge which they had not. Till this knowledge comes to us, let us hold our fathers' opinions, as they held them; but when it does come, it will come by God's will, and to do His work; and that work will assuredly not be our separation from our fathers' faith; but if we follow God's guidance humbly and cheerfully, clinging to God the while in personal devotion and obedience, we may be made aware of what to them would have been an inexplicable difficulty, and which was, therefore, hidden from their knowledge; and yet, "through the grace of our Lord Jesus Christ, we believe that we shall be saved even as they."'*

"I am, Sir, yours, etc.,
"R. B. KENNARD, *Rector of Marnhull.*
"MARNHULL RECTORY, *August* 17, 1861."

* Sermons, vol. iv., p. 492.

(E.)

The following extract from a letter addressed, in 1862, by a dear friend to the author is an instance of the real support and comfort which many earnest, truth-loving minds, dissatisfied with the various conflicting religious dogmas and parties of the day, have derived from the study of "Essays and Reviews":—

The attention of the writer (who is not a clergyman) was first called to the book by the *Record* newspaper in which, he says: "I read a violent article against a book entitled 'Essays and Reviews,' and, though I was not disposed to attach much value to the opinions expressed in that paper, yet, as the writers of the book in question were decidedly spoken of as disseminators of infidel opinions, I thought no more of the subject. A short time afterwards I saw a circular, a copy of which was sent to all the clergy, and in which they were exhorted to sign a memorial against this same book of 'Essays and Reviews.' The circular was accompanied by several short extracts from the work—specimens of its most objectionable parts. I read these extracts—I was startled by some sentences, but I felt it was impossible to judge fairly of them, taken as they were, away from their context; but I found in other sentences such indications of thoughts coincident with my own, that I could not rest till I had provided myself with the proscribed volume. In reading it, such feelings of delight and thankfulness passed through my mind as no pen can describe! That men, good, wise, and 'devoutly brave,' critics and scholars, should have thought some of the same thoughts, and come to many of the same conclusions, that I, an obscure individual, in my retirement had come to, without human aid, and against human sympathy, seemed incredible! Yet, the more I read the more I was convinced that it was indeed so. I could only account for it from the fact that my study of God's laws, and observation of His works, had given me an utter distaste for any artificial system of religion, and that I, like the Essayists, had been convinced that 'the liberty wherewith Christ has made us free' was intended to be made use of; and I could no longer be satisfied with any system of religion, or any religious ideas that were not based upon laws that would bear the strictest scrutiny. I could no longer feel that duty requires us to lay aside our reasoning powers in order to accept the good news of salvation, nor could I feel that God would have us 'know nothing but Christ, and Him crucified,' in the sense which would exclude all interest in 'those laws of Nature, those Divine laws' by which the Creator of the Universe has built all things, and by which he carries on, with the grandest simplicity, the ever-moving machinery of His own Creation. It would seem, then, that the recognizing of these laws, and the desire to bear them in mind in the interpretation of Scripture, was the ground on which I met the authors of 'Essays and Reviews.' . . . . .

"I had been much struck in the year 1855 by the perusal of a speech delivered at Birmingham by his Royal Highness the deeply-lamented Prince Consort.* The more I learned of God's laws and their connection with and dependence upon one another the more did I see to

* See The Prince Consort's Principal Speeches and Addresses, pp. 165—171.

admire in that masterly speech. I perceived that that noble mind recognized distinctly the connection between true religion and real science, and that, swayed by no party spirit, he was the friend and the champion of both, and in his life evidenced that both were *practical*."

(F.)

Mr. Chretien calls attention to the First Epistle of St. Paul to the Thessalonians, as containing, at its close, a very remarkable indication of the manner in which the New Testament canon was formed. "I charge you by the Lord," thus wrote St. Paul at the close of the Epistle, "that this Epistle be read unto all the holy brethren." "The detached portions of the New Testament gradually gathered round the infant Church. Book after book, with or without definite authority, was read in the congregation. By no technical law, it would seem, but in obedience to a deep and hidden instinct, the writings of apostles and holy men were brought together, and joined into a volume.

"The time came ere long when a new process was to begin. The Church began to examine more closely the contents of the sacred volume which she had collected. So far as we can judge, the New Scriptures were no longer the exponents of a Divine Life burning brightly and freshly in the Church. *They* spoke the same language, and breathed the same thoughts as ever; but men heard them not with the same feelings: the first spirit of the Apostolic times was gone. The second stage had arrived, when men, from simply feeling with those early writings, and sending their hearts spontaneously with them, looked at them, in some measure, from without, were anxious to see what they contained and proved, and therefore, of necessity, criticised them. It became a question of importance, what books should, and what should not, be admitted into the Canon. The Churches left no means at their disposal unemployed for ascertaining the truth in this matter. They pondered long and inquired widely. They used both external and internal evidence; but they seemed to have placed their chief reliance on definite historical testimony. About several books they long doubted, and, even when they received them at last, left some points doubtful about them. Thus was the Canon constructed in different parts of Christendom, with a wonderful agreement in all its general features, though with differences, to the last, about some particular books.

"Individuals, it is universally allowed, did not precisely agree about the Canon in the fourth and fifth centuries. The case is much the same with Councils. The Canon, as we accept it, was practically formed in the latter part of the fourth century. But the Council of Laodicea (*circ.* A.D. 365) does not include the Revelation in its list, if, indeed, that list be genuine; while the third Council of Carthage, which met some thirty years later, completes, indeed, the Canon of the New Testament, as we receive it, but also reckons the Wisdom of Solomon, Tobit, Judith, and two Books of Maccabees, as Canonical Scriptures. These were, of course, provincial councils; the Church universal of that day made no decree on the subject.

"Mr. Westcott, in his able and learned work on the

canon of the *New Testament,* calls attention in the following passage to the remarkable fact, that the Church of England has not defined beyond reach of dispute the canon of the Sacred Volume:—

" 'The authoritative teaching of the Church of England on the Canon of the New Testament is not removed beyond all question. In the Articles of 1552 it was affirmed, that *Holy Scripture containeth all things necessary to salvation,* but nothing was said of the books included under that title. In the Elizabethan Articles of 1562 (and 1571) a definition was added: '*In the name of Holy Scripture, we do understand those canonical books of the Old and New Testament of whose authority was never any doubt in the Church.*' Then follows a statement *Of the names and number of the canonical books,* in which the books of the Old Testament are enumerated at length. A list of the Old Testament Apocrypha is given next, imperfect in the Latin, but complete in the English; and at the end it is said: '*All the books of the New Testament, as they are commonly received, we do receive and account them for canonical;*' but no list is given. A strict interpretation of the language of the Article thus leaves a difference between *canonical books and such canonical books as have never been doubted in the Church.*' " *

* Six Sermons on the Inspiration of Holy Scripture, pp. 8, 9, 10, and Note.

(G.)

"What, then, is the essence of the prophetic teaching? It may be divided into three parts, according to the three famous words of St. Bernard—*Respice, Aspice, Prospice. The interpretation of the Divine will respecting the past, the present, and the future.*

"It is well known that in the popular and modern use of the word since the seventeenth century, by a 'Prophet,' is meant almost exclusively one who predicts or foretells; and to have asserted the contrary has even been thought heretical. It is evident that this assumption is itself a grave error.* It is wholly unauthorized, either by the Bible or by our own Church. It has drawn off the attention of the fundamental idea of the prophetical office to a subordinate part. It has caused us to seek the evidence of Prophecy in those portions of it which are least convincing—in those parts which it has most in common with other systems, rather than in those parts which distinguish it from all other systems. . . . .

"The predictions of the Hebrew Prophets are almost always founded on the denunciations of moral evil, or the exaltation of moral good, not on the mere localities or cities concerned. *The nations whose doom is pronounced*

---

* "It is simply a mistake to regard prediction as synonymous with prophecy, or even as the chief portion of a prophet's duties. Whether the language be Hebrew, Greek, or Latin, the ancient words for prophecy all refer to a state of mind, an emotion, an influence, and not to prescience."—*Mr. Payne Smith's Messianic Interpretation of Isaiah*, Introd., p. xxx.

thus become representatives of moral principles and examples to all ages alike. Israel, Jerusalem, Egypt, Babylon, Tyre, are personifications of States or principles still existing, and thus the predictions concerning them have, as Lord Bacon says, constantly germinant fulfilments. The secular events which are thus predicted, are (with a few possible exceptions*) within the horizon of the Prophet's own age and country. As in the vision of Pisgah, the background is suggested by the foreground. No object is introduced which a contemporary could fail to appreciate and understand in outline, although its remoter and fuller meaning might be reserved for a far distant future. These predictions are also, in several striking instances, made dependent on the moral condition of those to whom they are addressed, and are thus divested of the appearance of blind caprice or arbitrary fate, in which the literal predictions of both ancient and modern divinations so much delight. 'Yet forty days and Nineveh shall be overthrown.' No denunciation is more absolute in its terms than this, and of none is the frustration more complete. The true prophetic lesson of the Book of Jonah is, that there was a principle in the moral government of God more sacred and more peremptory even than the accomplishment of the most cherished prediction. 'God saw their works, that they turned from their evil way, and God repented of the evil that He had said that He would do unto them, and He did it not.'

---

* "The cases referred to are such as need not be here discussed They are either confessedly exceptional, or else admit (on quite independent grounds) of another explanation; and they can only be treated justly by being considered in detail."

(Jonah iii. 10.) What here appears in a single case is laid down as a universal rule by the Prophet Jeremiah. 'At what instant I shall speak concerning a nation . . . . to destroy it; if that nation . . . . turn from their evil, I will repent of the evil that I thought to do unto them. And at what instant I shall speak concerning a nation . . . . to build and to plant it; if it do evil in My sight, that it obey not my voice, then I will repent of the good wherewith I said I would benefit them.' (Jer. xviii. 7—9.)

"With these limitations, it is acknowledged by all students of the subject, that the Hebrew Prophets made predictions concerning the fortunes of their own and other countries which were, unquestionably, fulfilled. There can be no reasonable doubt, for example, that Amos foretold the captivity and return of Israel; and Micah, the fall of Samaria; and Ezekiel, the fall of Jerusalem; and Isaiah, the fall of Tyre; and Jeremiah, the limits of the captivity. But, even if no such special cases could be proved, the grandeur of the position which the Prophets occupy in this respect, is one which it needs no attestation of any particular prediction to enhance, and which no failure of any particular prediction can impair. From those lofty watch-towers of Divine speculation, from that moral and spiritual height which raised them far above the rest of the ancient world, they saw the rise and fall of other nations long before it was visible to those nations themselves. 'They were the first in all antiquity,' it has been well said, 'to perceive that the old East was dead; they celebrated its obsequies in advance of the dissolution

which they saw to be inevitable.' * 'They were,' as Dean Milman has finely expressed it, 'the great tragic chorus of the awful drama that was unfolding itself in the Eastern world. As each independent tribe or monarchy was swallowed up in the universal empire of Assyria, the seers of Judah watched the progress of the invader, and uttered their sublime funeral anthems over the greatness and prosperity of Moab and Ammon, Damascus and Tyre.' †
And in those funeral laments and wide-reaching predictions we trace a foretaste of that universal sympathy with nations outside the chosen circle—of that belief in an all-embracing Providence—which has now become part of the belief of the highest intelligence of the world. There may be many innocent questions about the date or about the interpretation of the Book of Daniel and of the Apocalypse. But there can be no doubt that they contain the first germs of the great idea of the succession of ages, of the continuous growth of empires and races under a law of Divine Providence, the first sketch of the Education of the World, and the first outline of the Philosophy of History.

"Again, it was the distinguishing mark of the Jewish people that their golden age was not in the past, but in the future; that their greatest hero (as they deemed Him to be) was not their founder, but their founder's latest descendant. Their traditions, their fancies, their glories, gathered round the head not of a chief, or warrior, or sage that had been, but of a King, a Deliverer, a Prophet who

* Quinet, Génie des Religions, p. 372.
† History of the Jews, i. 298.

was to come. Of this singular expectation the Prophets were, if not the chief authors, at least the chief exponents. Sometimes He is named, sometimes He is unnamed; sometimes He is almost identified with some actual Prince of the coming or the present generation; sometimes He recedes into the distant ages. But again and again, at least in the later prophetic writings, the vista is closed by His person, His character, His reign. And almost everywhere the prophetic spirit, in the delineation of His coming, remains true to itself. He is to be a King, a Conqueror, yet not by the common weapons of earthly warfare, but by those only weapons which the prophetic order recognized—by justice, mercy, truth, and goodness—by suffering, by endurance, by identification of Himself with the joys, the sufferings of His nation, by opening a wider sympathy to the whole human race than had ever been opened before.

"That this expectation, however explained, existed in a greater or less degree amongst the Prophets, is not doubted by any theologians of any school whatever. It is no matter of controversy. It is a simple and universally recognized fact,—that, filled with these prophetic images, the whole Jewish nation, nay, at last, the whole Eastern world, did look forward with longing expectation to the coming of the future Conqueror. Was this unparalleled expectation realized? And here, again, I speak only of facts which are acknowledged by Germans and Frenchmen, no less than by Englishmen; by critics and by sceptics, even more fully than by theologians and ecclesiastics. There did arise out of this nation a character by universal consent as unparalleled as the expectation which had preceded Him. Jesus of Nazareth was, on the most superficial no less than on the deepest view we take of His coming, the greatest name, the most extraordinary power, that has ever crossed the stage of history. And this greatness consisted not in outward power, but precisely in those qualities on which, from first to last, the prophetic order had laid the utmost stress—justice and love, goodness and truth."*

* See Stanley's Three Sermons preached before the University of Oxford, pp. 55—87; and Lectures on the Jewish Church, Lect. XX.

www.ingramcontent.com/pod-product-compliance
Lightning Source LLC
Chambersburg PA
CBHW030009240426
43672CB00007B/884